# VENTURES IN POLITICAL SCIENCE

# VENTURES IN POLITICAL SCIENCE

## Narratives and Reflections

### GABRIEL A. ALMOND

LYNNE
RIENNER
PUBLISHERS

BOULDER
LONDON

Published in the United States of America in 2002 by
Lynne Rienner Publishers, Inc.
1800 30th Street, Boulder, Colorado 80301
www.rienner.com

and in the United Kingdom by
Lynne Rienner Publishers, Inc.
3 Henrietta Street, Covent Garden, London WC2E 8LU

**Library of Congress Cataloging-in-Publication Data**
Almond, Gabriel Abraham, 1911–
    Ventures in political science : narratives and reflections / Gabriel A. Almond.
      p. cm.
    Includes bibliographical references and index.
    ISBN 1-58826-055-0 (alk. paper)—ISBN 1-58826-080-1 (pb : alk. paper)
    1. Political science.   2. Comparative government.   3. Political culture.   I. Title.
JA71.A476   2002
320—dc21

                                        2002017810

**British Cataloging in Publication Data**
A Cataloguing in Publication record for this book
is available from the British Library.

# Contents

*Contents*

# 1

# Introduction

MOST OF THE CHAPTERS IN THIS BOOK were written in the 1990s, the decade of my eighties. The book treats topics appropriate for an octogenarian—historical narrative about the political science discipline, and reflections about democracy and democratization. But in this first part of this introduction I write about my *lehrjahre,* my education and early career, which gave me the tastes and distastes that I express in this and other publications.

I had a long apprenticeship. I wasn't really on my way, so to speak, until 1946, after World War II, when I was in my mid-thirties. It was then that my European and German experience combined with my University of Chicago training to give me access to research opportunities in comparative politics and international relations. How this came about is told in Chapter 5, "A Voice from the Chicago School," where I place my beginnings in the setting of the University of Chicago in the great days of Charles Merriam and Harold Lasswell. The University of Chicago thread takes me from the Midway in the 1930s to Yale in the 1940s.

It was the Yale Institute of International Studies under the leadership of Frederick S. Dunn and William T. R. Fox that I was to join after World War II. Fox, trained under Quincy Wright, Merriam, and Lasswell at the University of Chicago, had been brought in by Dunn to help develop the institute along the lines of the new political science. Fox in turn had brought in Bernard Brodie and Klaus Knorr—also Chicago Ph.D.'s, the former specialized in military and security affairs, the latter in international economic affairs. Bringing me in furthered the Dunn-Fox strategy of basing postwar international relations research and teaching on the social sciences, in addition to its traditional legal and institutional components.

1

I had returned from the wars no longer a fit with my Brooklyn College job, where I was limited to the teaching of U.S. government. I was bursting with the latest information on the politics of post–World War II Europe. And I had a set of methodological tools, primarily from Harold Lasswell, waiting impatiently to be put to use on challenging problems. I needed an academic setting where I could pursue my studies of the new world of politics that was taking shape at the end of World War II. Yale had pioneered in the development of international and comparative studies, establishing a research institute in international affairs and offering graduate degrees in international relations already in the 1930s. With the University of Chicago additions, Yale was very strong, clearly the strongest center in the country.

Within a few short years it had published the book that defined the structure of the postwar system of international relations (Fox, 1944), the book capturing the essence of the new postnuclear international security system (Brodie, 1946), and the first book treating U.S. foreign policy from a sociocultural perspective (Almond, 1950). However, this very prominence and visibility, and its research support by foundations, made the institute vulnerable to the envy of parts of Yale not so favored, and to the anger of disappointed colleagues.

My shift from Yale to Princeton might be explained by wounded vanity, that of a Yale president whose tenure had been delayed, who was said to have been "born with a silver foot in his mouth" by a Princeton president who described these events in classic Ivy League terms: "Yale fumbled and Princeton recovered the ball." For all of its pointlessness, the Ivy League battle spread Yale's treasure of innovating scholarship in international studies to Princeton, Columbia, MIT, and the Rand Corporation. It provided me a career with foundation support and limited teaching obligations from 1946 to 1963. The privileges and resources made available to me during these years made it possible for me to produce my U.S. foreign policy book (1950), *The Appeals of Communism* (1954), *The Politics of the Developing Areas* (with James Coleman and others, 1960), and *The Civic Culture* (with Sidney Verba, 1963).

To explain this productivity I would have to go back a bit in time, and away from the coasts where I spent my mature career, to the Middle West and the University of Chicago during the time of the Great Depression, which coincided with my graduate years. I did my first serious research while directly experiencing the depression, and then later in World War II in Washington, D.C., and Germany. From these beginnings I have always thought of political science as dealing with very urgent and palpable evils, such as civil conflict, economic breakdown and poverty, and war, and hence being strongly impelled toward the applied rather than the pure side. Its subject matter is rather more like the "clouds" of meteorology than the "clocks" of physics.

Chance brought me to the University of Chicago at a time when great innovators in the social sciences were at work in the improbable setting of the Chicago Midway in the 1920s and 1930s. I believe we are still living off the solid yield of Chicago's Merriams, Lasswells, Gosnells, V. O. Keys, and Trumans, while some of the recent "innovations" in political science may turn out to be affectations.

I received a notice from the university in the spring of 1932 of my admission to graduate study in political science, with a "service" scholarship. It seemed the logical thing to do after receiving the admission notice to go to the bookstore and buy a copy of Aristotle's *Politics*. It is interesting that I did not buy Plato's *Republic*. Aristotle was empirical and quantitative, a political sociologist, attaching significance to the same variables that had been emphasized in the social sciences in my undergraduate years at the University of Chicago. Whatever my motive in reading Aristotle, it left me with a respect for the tradition of political theory, and with a healthy regard for classification and typology.

The value of a graduate "service" scholarship then was $300, just enough to cover tuition for three quarters, and one had to do a certain amount of departmental work (like grading papers) to "earn" the scholarship. In order to save a bit of money, and help relieve financial pressure at home, I got a job as a casework aide in the Stockyards district of the Unemployment Relief Service. Since the rate of saving was slow on a monthly salary of $87.50, I delayed my entry into graduate school until February of 1933. But my early employment at the relief service had a great influence on my future, as did my entrance into the University of Chicago at this creative time.

My job at the Stockyards unemployment office was to interview newly unemployed applicants for relief, and relief clients who had complaints. They were mostly foreign-born—Poles, Russians, Ukrainians, Bohemians, Slovaks, Lithuanians, as well as Greeks and Italians, Mexicans, and African Americans. It was my job to hear their stories, and decide whether they should be seen by a caseworker, a great responsibility for a twenty-one-year-old fresh out of college. The caseworker would have to decide how needy they were, whether they had other sources of income or support, and the like. I sat at a front desk with two other complaint aides, taking down pleas, demands, even threats as these men made their cases (they were all men, mostly fathers; it didn't strike me as odd at the time). As I sat there day after day writing complaints on three-by-five slips of paper, it occurred to me that I was witnessing human behavior, and that perhaps it was interesting and researchable. I had taken a course in "Nonrational Factors in Political Behavior" with Harold Lasswell in my senior year at the University of Chicago, in which Lasswell had invited us to consider all human interaction and behavior as relevant to politics.

I remember, as though it were yesterday, telephoning him from a phone booth near my place of work and telling him with great excitement what I was doing, where I was working, and that it looked like a great research opportunity. He agreed with me, and we set up a project under which I would have the complaint aides in that office record on each slip of paper how the client acted—whether he made aggressive demands, was submissive and ready to go away at the least show of administrative impatience, or wheedled and smiled his way to a favorable outcome. Over a period of six months we would have several thousand complaint slips, each marked to indicate how the client made his complaint. Over the six-month period most clients would have appeared several times, before more than one complaint aide, satisfying the need for control. We then could classify our cases according to their behavioral propensity, and look into their case histories to explore the association between behavioral patterns and demographic, occupational, educational, even police backgrounds.

The article that Harold Lasswell and I wrote, reporting these data, appeared in a 1934 issue of *American Political Science Review,* under the title "Aggressive Behavior by Clients on Public Relief." Lasswell supplied the theory, which argued that protest and revolutionary politics would emerge out of the anger of the resentful unemployed, and that the aggressive types among the unemployed were the potential protest elite. In other words, this apparently innocent research enterprise at the Chicago Stockyards was giving us some hints on what the revolutionary American elites might be like, if there were an American revolution. And in 1932 in the Chicago Stockyards district, riot and revolution didn't seem so farfetched. In this enterprise I supplied the data and basic analysis. This early published evidence of my commitment to research convinced Lasswell, Harold Gosnell, and most important, Charles Merriam, that I might be worth carrying through to a Ph.D.

To do that I had not only to pass examinations in all of the major fields of political science, but to write a dissertation. At the time, these two hurdles seemed like insurmountable heights. I remember sitting next to V. O. Key Jr. at one of our departmental teas. He had passed his prelims the year before, and I asked him, naively, whether he thought that someone like me could pass the prelims. In his slow, Texas way, V. O. said he did not put it beyond the realm of possibility. Those of us who passed their prelims that spring of 1935 went to the Edgewater Beach Hotel (which no longer exists) and danced by the then sparkling waters of Lake Michigan.

As for my dissertation, Lasswell was developing "elite" theory at around this time, arguing that politics could be boiled down to "a struggle of elites over who gets income, power, and safety." The book he was writing then was called *Politics: Who Gets What, When, and How* (1936). The student milieu in which I lived in the 1930s was alive with left-wing politics. There was a sit-down strike at the Republic Steel plant, which drew students into sympathetic participation. The Young Communist League, the Young Socialist League, and the Trotskyites were actively recruiting on the campus. Socialism, Marxism, and Communism were all in the air, and Fascism was the threatening enemy. I was moved by all these events and trends, but part of me was detached, wanting to get into the causes and consequences of it all.

I was granted a predoctoral field fellowship by the Social Science Research Council in 1934, enabling me to spend the academic year 1935–1936 in travel, research, and writing. I decided to do a dissertation on the political power and influence of the economic elites in the United States, doing nothing less than an empirical test of Marxist theory that bourgeois democracy was dominated by capitalism.

I decided to do the dissertation in New York City, since its colonial origins gave me some historical background to compare with the present, while Chicago, where I had begun my research on elite politics, had a shallow past, no more than a century. This was a fateful choice, for in New York City I sought out Hans Speier, who was then engaged in recruiting for the "University in Exile" of the New School for Social Research. I sought him out for what he could tell me of Max Weber, who had become my scholarly hero. He and Lisa Speier conspired to bring me together with Dorothea Kaufmann, my future wife and life companion, the mother of my children, and a steadfast advocate of the welfare of the child.

The unifying philosophy of *Ventures in Political Science* is that the politics we study in political science is an objective reality and probabilistic in its unfolding. The aggressive unemployment behavior that I recorded, numerated, and interpreted in my first political science research encounter in the summer, fall, and winter of 1932–1933 gave me an empirical grounding that lasted the rest of my academic life. That winter was a hard winter, made brutal by hunger and hopelessness. The desperation and anger of the unemployed was an "objective reality," not a "constructivist" one as some of our contemporary methodologists might assert, nor something that could be captured in mathematical equations.

I spent the academic year of 1935–1936 in the New York Room of the New York Public Library, poring over biographies, memoirs, reports of social clubs, old almanacs, and records of philanthropic activities. I called my dissertation *Plutocracy and Politics in New York City.* What I was able to demonstrate in this study of the relation of the economic elites to politics over the course of the three centuries of New York's history was a transition from an economic oligarchy to what I called an open plutocracy. This was an ambiguous kind of power structure in which the business elites were influential but not all-powerful, and not in direct control. They had access to political organizations and elites who defended their interests in return for financial support. When the corruption of the politicians got out of hand, part of the business elite entered directly into politics through reform movements, reestablishing some equilibrium between the political "machines" and the public service. Similarly in the crises of depression and war, the business elites would be drawn into more direct involvement in politics and public service.

For my dissertation, I in effect had done a case study of New York City's politico-economic development, in a test of the Marxist proposition regarding the control of the polity, despite appearances, by the economic elite. Marxism was a hypothesis at this point in my thinking about politics, and my dissertation research left me with a sense of the interrelation between economics and politics more subtly modulated than was prescribed by Marxist theory. It took a bit of chutzpah to do that kind of dissertation, and not all of the departmental faculty viewed it as an appropriate topic. But Harold Lasswell, Harold Gosnell, and Charles Merriam were the members of my dissertation committee. And these blessed scholarly innovators combined to give me my doctoral imprimatur.

Some explanation is necessary for the fact that my doctoral dissertation was not published until 1998, sixty years after it had been accepted by the department. In 1938 it was a quasi-requirement, not enforced, that doctoral dissertations had to be published in order to complete the requirements for the Ph.D. degree. It was my intention in 1938 to revise my dissertation for publication, and I did indeed work on it for several years. One of the principal conclusions of the manuscript I submitted in 1938 was that while the democratization of the suffrage in the nineteenth century had broken the political monopoly of the economic elites, they nevertheless were enabled to exercise control and protect their interests through indirect means (e.g., pressure groups, control of media, and the like) and through occasional direct involvement in politics, as in times of depression and war. I had nagging doubts over the adequacy of these observations about the relation of wealth to politics in American democracy, in view of the spread of psychoanalytic ideas and theories into the social sciences in the 1930s and 1940s.

Two of the great European powers seem to have gone berserk in the 1920s and 1930s. They were mobilized and in lockstep following violently nationalist, charismatic leaders and resolved to overturn the balance of power if necessary by resort to war. These perturbations could not be accounted for by simple economic interest or rational motivations. As the world moved toward war in the 1930s, social scientists sought an explanation for this militarism and hyper-nationalism in Freudian instinct theory, in psycho-anthropological theories of childhood socialization and national character. What came to be known as the psychocultural approach was spreading among social scientists, and in the course offerings of the universities. My doctoral dissertation became increasingly obsolete in my thinking, insofar as it seemed to make the assumption that political attitudes were unambiguously derivable from economic self-interest, and that the holding of public office, or the participation in policymaking, by a business elite necessarily meant that this power would be exercised in a conservative direction. The new psychocultural approach assumed that there was an intervening psychological variable that would make the relation between economic self-interest and political policy consequences more complex than posited by the theory of economic interest.

So I spent my leisure hours in Brooklyn and in Washington, D.C., in the next several years researching and writing a new part to my dissertation, one that I called "The Political Attitudes of Wealth." This new part, its theory based primarily on versions of Freudianism emphasized in the writings of Karen Horney, Erich Fromm, Ruth Benedict, Margaret Mead, Erik Erikson, and Harold Lasswell, presented three chapters containing case histories of wealthy conservatives, liberals, and reactionaries, claiming to show how parent/child/family relations affected the political development and attitudes of such figures as Chauncey Depew, Dwight Morrow, Elihu Root, Jay Gould, John D. Rockefeller, Abram Hewitt, Andrew Carnegie, and the like.

In retrospect this revision of my dissertation reflected much hubris, adding an additional venturesome component to what was already a venturesome dissertation. In 1944, when I submitted my revised dissertation to the University of Chicago Press, the department was in a shambles. Scorned by Robert Hutchins, the humanist president of the university,

Lasswell and Gosnell had departed. Merriam had retired; there was no effective department chair. When I talked to Merriam about the submission of the dissertation in its revised form, he seemed to be in a deep depression. He only said one thing—that I should remove the new part on the political attitudes of wealth. The press soon informed me that they were not prepared to publish the book. Since I had invested a substantial amount of pride in this addition to my dissertation, I went away from this experience in a mood of anger and defiance. The war was going a bit badly at the time, and I had an invitation to go overseas as a civilian employee of the U.S. Air Force. So I sent the disputed part of my dissertation to the *Journal of Politics* and went off to the war. Thus it turned out that the only part of my doctoral dissertation that got published was the disputed part—"The Political Attitudes of Wealth"—in the August 1945 issue of that journal.

The dissertation sat in manuscript in Harper Memorial Library from 1938 on, where it was occasionally examined by curious students, who spread the notion that failure to publish *Plutocracy and Politics in New York City* demonstrated how capitalism suppressed scholarship. Charles Merriam—the leading funder of social science scholarship at the University of Chicago—was accused of suppressing a major study on the power of economic interests in the United States in order to protect the Rockefeller family, who were major benefactors of the social sciences and of political science.

The difficulty with this explanation of the fate of my doctoral dissertation is that it flies in the face of the evidence. The part of the dissertation that Merriam wanted to have removed was the psychological part, the part that was least Marxist, or most critical of Marxist materialism. The original dissertation of 1938 only considered the material–political power case. Other motivations were not considered. I have been convinced for some time that Merriam acted on grounds of quality control. The new chapters that I submitted were based upon a pretty thin collection of biographical data, perhaps justifying an article in a journal, but not a serious work of scholarship put out by a university press.

To return to the earlier narrative, I got my first teaching job as an instructor at Brooklyn College, and in my first three years in that junior rank I taught American government in its legal-institutional version some thirty times, five times a semester for six semesters. Coming on top of my University of Chicago social science training, this gave me a balance of institutional and behavioral sensitivity early in my career, such that I could never understand the "institutions old and new, lost and regained" polemic of the 1980s and 1990s. What had the "new institutionalists" really added to the lively Merriam "institution-behavior" discussion in his presidential address of 1925, "Progress in Political Research" (1970)?

As I went from class to class teaching American government at Brooklyn College from 1939 to 1941, the sounds of the Asian and European battlefields kept coming nearer and nearer, until they finally broke through on December 7, 1941, with FDR's "Day of Infamy." The United States declared war on December 8. I was in Washington employed by the Office of Facts and Figures, later to be renamed the Office of War Information, in February 1942. I was put in charge of a small unit assigned to gather information about the enemy—Germany, Italy, and Occupied Europe. I had a small but distinguished staff including Herbert Marcuse, who then was a relatively harmless Hegelian Marxist; Henry Ehrmann, who later became a leading authority on French politics; and a couple other European specialists. Beginning with a knowledge of German, I began to think of myself as a European specialist, and as a comparativist, during these middle years of the war.

This opportunity to experience World War II as a form of postdoctoral training was greatly enhanced when I was hired by the air force to participate in the work of the U.S. Strategic Bombing Survey (USSBS), an agency established by the air force to study the effects of strategic bombing on the German war effort. The idea was to learn from our European experience and apply it to the strategic bombing plan for Japan. The Morale Division of the USSBS, led by social psychologists Rensis Likert and Angus Campbell (of later University of Michigan fame), was then experimenting with survey research. For the first time, they were using probability sampling technique. Their task was to do a survey of a probability sample of the German population in the immediate aftermath of the war, to ascertain what effect strategic bombing had had on German attitudes and behavior. Supplementing the survey of German attitudes, I was given the special assignment of hunting up documents dealing with the air war, and of interrogating police and Gestapo officials regarding problems of internal order in the last years of the war as the air bombardment intensified. My team spent fifteen weeks "in the field"—from April until July 1945—interviewing former Gestapo, SS, and police officials in British and U.S. internment camps, and searching in SS, police, and party headquarters for documents that might have relevant information.

My team did indeed turn up a remarkable German document with details of the impact of British and U.S. air raids from their beginning until mid-1944, in the form of half a dozen large notebooks containing the day-by-day telegraphic ticker tape record sent from the regional offices of the Nazi Propaganda Ministry to the Berlin headquarters. As recounted in Chapter 5, this document had been evacuated along with the contents of the ministry library (including the librarian and his family) as the fall of Berlin became imminent, to a rural inn not far from the Elbe-Mulde river crossing, which demarcated the U.S.-USSR military boundary. The inn bore the sign "Gasthaus zum Goldenen Fass" (Inn of the Golden Barrel).

My team was located in Leipzig, not far from the U.S.-USSR temporary boundary, where we spent the first two weeks after VE (Victory in Europe) Day digging in smoldering heaps of documentary records and interrogating police officials and individuals who identified themselves as members of anti-Nazi movements. Something like a German "underground" surfaced in the last months, weeks, and days of the war, and in a number of cases contributed to peaceful surrender of such towns as Halle, where we did some investigating from our Leipzig headquarters.

In these early post-VE days there was a stream of refugees coming out of the Soviet zone, mostly "slave laborers" freed by the Russians and walking homeward, living off the countryside and the handouts of friendly mess sergeants. One of these, a Belgian, learning that our team was "air force intelligence," stopped by our quarters and told us the strange tale of an evacuated Goebbels ministry library, whose librarian, together with his family, had taken shelter at the Inn of the Golden Barrel. The Belgian had spent the night there and the librarian had confided in him and shown him some of the library's treasures. The librarian was hoping to escape Soviet capture. At the moment, this area where the U.S. and USSR troops had made their Elbe meeting had lost its military quality. Americans and Soviets were fraternizing, exchanging drinks and toasts, visiting each other's barracks, and sightseeing on both sides of the boundary. The Saxon fields through which we passed in our jeep and weapons carrier on our way to the Inn of the Golden Barrel the next morning were littered with the prone bodies of Soviet troops sleeping off hangovers.

The Belgian had told us of the Propaganda Ministry's air war intelligence cache, and we had quickly organized a visit and inspection. The Soviet commander, intrigued by the sightseeing Americans and proud of being able to offer us Lucky Strikes in exchange for the Camels we offered him, waved us across the river, and we soon found the Golden Barrel on the outskirts of Torgau. The contents of the Goebbels library consisted of a variety of files and records, cameras and photocopying equipment, a graphic art collection, and other art objects. We decided to take only the air war record, on the theory that if the Soviets discovered what we were up to we could justify the records as mission-related, while anything else would look like espionage compounded by looting.

As we sat there in the inn with our fabulous intelligence document, and surrounded by valuable art and hardware, fantasies of prison cells and firing squads passed through our imaginations. Actually we got safely home through a simple ruse. Still playing innocent tourists when we got back to the river, we begged the Soviet officer in charge to give us some Soviet boundary flags for souvenirs. He waved us through in embarrassed haste, and did not take the trouble to look into the weapons carrier, where the notebooks were lying hidden under a tarpaulin.

We lost no time in getting the Propaganda Ministry's air raid record to our local G2 headquarters, where we sat down and laboriously made a copy of the record, using a blueprint machine, if I remember correctly. It took several hours to copy the several-hundred-page document. We wanted the copy for our own analysis; the original we felt bound to send to central air force intelligence at Supreme Headquarters Allied Expeditionary Forces (SHAEF) in Frankfurt. We had a tight schedule of cities to cover, so we left our copy at our own headquarters, where we expected to retrieve it and analyze it on our return from the field.

In fact, when we returned to our headquarters at Bad Nauheim in mid-July, expecting to find our documentary materials, including the air raid record, available for analysis, we were told that the document had been cut up for content analysis and simply didn't exist anymore. For our social psychologists, who were making the survey study of the recollections of the German population about how the air raids had impacted morale and working effectiveness, the Propaganda Ministry's air raid log and local reports over the four-year period were simply examined for any references to morale in the aftermath of bombing. These were coded and treated like the responses of the later interviewees.

I reacted to this with shock. It was my first experience with the "mechanization" of social science research. Though I had an appreciation of survey research and later directed a major cross-national survey of political attitudes myself, I retained great respect for the historical perspective, for in-depth "case studies," and for "clinical" studies as means of formulating hypotheses. What we had in the Propaganda Ministry's record of air raids, day by day, night by night, city by city over four years of the war—from 1940 to 1944—with descriptions of types of bomb, areas of destruction, extents of destruction, popular reactions, and so forth, was a detailed account of the impact of the air war as it occurred and where it occurred. This should have been used in the analysis of the later survey; and should have made possible a more subtle analysis, comparing the responses and experiences in different areas, and at different times, of differing degrees and kinds of bombing. Instead this detailed record was assimilated and lost among the several thousand German respondents who were interviewed in July and August 1945 about their reactions to air raids during the war.

I cite this experience as illustrative of a kind of fanaticism and reductionism endemic in the social science enterprise. The survey research methodology used by the Morale Division of the USSBS came out of the psychology discipline, which emphasized experiment and statistics as the essence of science. The documents, interrogations, and interviews that my team was picking up did not fit into their methodology. They had just developed cross-section interview and sampling technique, and they were not prepared to examine German intelligence materials for contemporary, in-depth data. The Propaganda Ministry's full log of reports on air raids had no place in their analysis and report, and I had to conclude that the risk that my team and I had taken in crossing into and operating within the Soviet zone was quite futile.

This experience should have prepared me for the kind of scientific zealotry that was to occur frequently in my later professional life in the rapidly growing field of area and comparative studies. The Committee on Comparative Politics of the Social Science Research Council, on which I served from the 1950s until the 1970s, encouraged area specialists to enhance their understanding of their own countries' institutions and processes by comparing them with those of other countries within and across cultural areas. These studies stimulated a literature on cross-national institutions and processes, such as public opinion and political culture (Almond and Verba, 1963; Inglehart, 1977), bureaucracy (LaPalombara, 1963), political parties and pressure groups (LaPalombara and Weiner, 1970; Ehrmann, 1958), political oppositions (Dahl, 1966, 1973), legislatures (Loewenberg, 1979), and courts (Ehrmann, 1976), and a bit later a sophisticated literature on methodology began to flourish. These methodological studies avoided exclusive emphasis on statistics and large numbers, showing how case studies might be used as an explanatory strategy (Eckstein, 1975), how they could be used in combination with statistical studies in a complementary strategy (George and Bennett, 1997), and generally speaking, how explanation in political science could be adapted to situations of both large and small numbers (King, Keohane, and Verba, 1993; Collier, 1993).

Despite these developments in comparative politics from the 1960s to the 1990s, there were those who argued that every country was a unique case and hence "incomparable." And at the other extreme were those who argued that the aim of comparative analysis was to convert individual countries into sets of variables, and to eliminate the names and uniquenesses of individual countries (Przeworski and Teune, 1970). A similar extremism was expressed during the leadership of Kenneth Prewitt and Robert Bates of the Social Science Research Council in the mid-1990s when they "decommissioned its area study committees," replacing them with "collaborative research networks" (Bates, 1996). These area committees had been the glory of the council since its founding, bringing support for social science research to parts of the world then little known, and sustaining that research at some level, regardless of the particular issues and themes then dominating international politics. While the council had been running on the same tracks for almost half a century, and could have used some shaking to advantage, a strong move toward topical and analytical studies might have been made by Prewitt and Bates without abolishing these committees, without reducing the visibility of culture within the ambit of the council.

Another USSBS experience that had an influence on my later interests and publications came out of a trade I was able to negotiate with the Office of Strategic Services (OSS), providing them with copies of my interviews with opposition leaders in the various German cities in which my team had operated, in exchange for the April–June 1944 Gestapo arrest statistics taken from the "Meldungen aus dem Reich," the "morale" report published by the Sicherheitsdienst (Security Service) of the SS. The OSS had somehow gotten some of these reports and was prepared to share them with me in exchange for my interviews. The trade was arranged by Alexander George, then working for the OSS, who had been sent to track me in the field. We negotiated "jeep to jeep," so to speak—my interviews for his copy of the "Meldungen aus dem Reich." It is, of course, a remarkable and treasured coincidence that we later became close colleagues and lifetime friends.

My report to the USSBS was recently unearthed from the National Archives by a German scholar, and has been reprinted in *PS: Political Science and Politics* (Almond with Krauss, 1999). It contains material from the SS reports, as well as my own interviews with opposition leaders. Dated and biased though the material in this report is, because of the sources—Nazi bureaucrats in the one case, and self-described resistance leaders in the other—it is nearly contemporary to the events of the Holocaust. The report deserves a cautioned hearing.

We know from the media reports of the time that as the Allied armies entered German towns in 1945, they were frequently met by small contingents of people waving white flags and identifying themselves as anti-Fascists or anti-Nazis. They later came to be described generically in the Allied media as "Antifas." They were ordered to disband by SHAEF, since in many cases they had begun to remove the Nazi street signs and elsewise exercise authority independently of the Allied forces. At the same time, many of these people evidenced having been in concentration camps, or could prove their bona fides in other ways. We encountered these groups attached loosely to the local military-government organization and providing more or less acceptable advice on "de-Nazification" of the governmental services and the media. These Antifas were the survivors of whatever resistance to the Nazis there had been in the area. And we interviewed them more broadly about their experiences under the Nazis, as well as about their estimates of the effects of bombing on morale.

The evidence that we gathered in these first months after VE Day supports a statistical view of the Holocaust rather than the essentialist view that has been argued by Daniel Goldhagen (1995) in his book on "ordinary Germans and the Holocaust." The evidence offered by the SS statistics that I received from the OSS in the summer of 1945 gave a reported political arrest figure for April–June 1944—for all kinds of resistance and oppositional activity for the German population of "the Greater German Reich, the Protectorate, and parts of Poland"—of 8,588. Even assuming an overcount, the number of arrests does not appear to have been negligible. Around half of these were for individual treasonous acts, such as listening to the BBC, telling an anti-Nazi joke, scribbling anti-Nazi graffiti on a wall, making subversive remarks, and the like. The number arrested for "Communism-Marxism" (presumably for membership in such a group) during the three-month period was 1,724. One would have to assume that if political arrest figures approximated 10,000 during this period, then the total number of Germans carrying on activities of this kind must have been larger. Indeed the numbers in the various categories increased from April to May to June. Since Nazi repressive activity increased even more after the July 20, 1944, attempt on Hitler's life, one must assume that the number of more or less active anti-Nazis in 1944 ran into the tens of thousands.

In addition to these Gestapo statistics, I had my team's own interviews and interrogations—several dozen of them—in Leipzig, Halle, Hamburg, Bremen, Lubeck, Hanover, Cologne, Frankfurt, Munich, and other cities. These involved details of time and place of oppositional activities, for example, the size of left-wing cells on the wharves in Hamburg and Bremen, in munitions plants in the Ruhr; how communications were maintained, slogans circulated; and in the last months, how efforts were made to preempt the last-ditch resistance of the Volksturm, the desperate militia made up of levies of untrained boys and old men. Our findings, later published in the *New Republic* (1946) and in *The Struggle for Democracy in Germany* (1949), a book I edited containing a report on the German resistance by myself and Wolfgang Krauss, contrast with those of Daniel Goldhagen and suggest that there were some anti-Nazi Germans who paid heavy prices for their resistance. It serves no useful purpose to deny to Germany this small credit on its ledger.

The exchanges between Abraham and Yahweh in the book of Genesis 18:23 regarding punishment for the wicked citizens of Sodom capture the essence of this difference between Goldhagen and myself. When Yahweh tells Abraham of his intention to destroy the Sodomites—man, woman, and child—Abraham sorrowfully asks Yahweh, "Will the judge of the whole earth not administer justice? . . . Perhaps there are fifty just men in the town . . . will you not spare the place for the fifty just men in it?" Yahweh replies, "If at Sodom I find fifty just men in the town, I will spare the whole place because of them."

There then follows the negotiation between Abraham and Yahweh in which Abraham seeks the most forgiving equilibrium he can get, forty-five just men, forty, thirty, twenty, ten, with Yahweh finally answering, "I will not destroy it for the sake of the ten." Sodom, in other words, had zero virtue, and only this degree of wickedness would justify Yahweh's rule for total condemnation and destruction.

In the logic of the biblical parable, Goldhagen found Germany totally lacking in just men and hence justifying total condemnation. The evidence I presented, on the other hand, which has been confirmed in other sources (Benz, 1994), would seem to argue for halting somewhere between the fifty and the ten, on the Abrahamic side of the negotiation, with a little wickedness left over for the non-German partners to the crime of the Holocaust.

\* \* \*

The combination of my University of Chicago training, my World War II experience with the German and European resistance and emerging European party systems, my membership in international research centers at Yale and Princeton universities, and my tenure as first chair of the Social Science Research Council's Committee on Comparative Politics, put me in the center of what contemporary scholars speak of as the political "development" movement as this took form in the 1950s and 1960s.

In the late 1950s as the group who wrote *The Politics of the Developing Areas* (Almond and Coleman, 1960) sat at Princeton debating a suitable title for their book, they had in front of them a telegram from Dankwart Rustow, the author of the book's chapter on the Middle East, threatening to withdraw from the project if one proposed title, "The Politics of the Underdeveloped Areas," were selected. No one opposed Rustow's protest. The subordinate world opened up by World War II could not be labeled "underdeveloped." But already there was an available alternative— "the developing areas"—that had been put forward not long before by "Engine Charley" Wilson, CEO of General Motors, in a widely circulated speech on economic policy. Without hesitation, the Princeton group adopted the title *The Politics of the Developing Areas,* thereby ensuring the diffusion of that euphemism throughout the academic community.

In its first formulation, the term *development* referred to the prospects foreseen by the post–World War II scholarly generation as they confronted the now "emancipated" world divided à la "area studies" into East, Southeast, and South Asia; the Middle East and North Africa; sub-Saharan Africa; and Latin America. These scholars (Talcott Parsons and Edward Shils, Daniel Lerner, Lucian Pye, Seymour M. Lipset, and Karl Deutsch), heirs to nineteenth-century industrialization and modernization theory— as formulated by Auguste Comte, Henry Maine, Karl Marx, Max Weber, and others—viewed the prospects of these formerly colonial, and "non-Western" areas as probably repeating with variations the trends and patterns made familiar in the nineteenth- and early-twentieth-century history of Europe and North America. *Development,* used interchangeably with *modernization,* came to be specified as involving the subprocesses of industrialization and urbanization, the spread of the mass media of communication and education, and the spread of literacy. These socioeconomic processes were viewed as synergistic, and as setting in motion a political mobilization involving democratization, and/or populistic forms of authoritarianism.

As the World War II alliance chilled into the Cold War, the dual world structure that the Princeton group had in mind of developed and developing worlds became a threefold world—the first world capitalist, the second world socialist, and the third world dependent and in need of development aid in the eyes of the first world, dependent and ruthlessly exploited in the eyes of the second world. And as the Vietnam War in the 1960s and 1970s divided the academic community, the university intellectuals in the United States and Western Europe began to share these views, that the third world was held in chains of dependency by the exploitative first world, which could only be broken by revolution and some form of socialism. The scholarship of the 1950s, 1960s, and early 1970s was discredited in part by the scholarship of the late 1970s and 1980s. The literature of modernization, the work described above, backed up by more than a century of empirical and theoretical scholarship, was discredited as ideological cover for what was described as the shameless exploitation of the dependent colonial world.

In the last decade, with the collapse of the Soviet Union and the termination of the Cold War, the polemic against "modernization" and "development theory" has substantially abated. With modifications, modernization theory is being revisited, and has been found to have significant explanatory power (Lipset, 1981; Marks and Diamond, 1992). It is a privilege to have lived through this polemic, and to have survived into a less contentious scholarly era.

\*   \*   \*

Part 1 of this book, "Historical Perspectives," contains five essays written in the 1990s. The first of these is a historical monograph written for *A New Handbook of Political Science* (Goodin and Klingemann, 1996). It presents an "eclectic," progressive view of the history of political science, a view that counts as progress the accumulation of evidence about things political as well as our increasing capacity to draw inferences from that evidence. Classical, medieval, Renaissance, Enlightenment, nineteenth-century, and modern political science are surveyed according to these two criteria. Four alternative views are identified—an anti-science view as in Straussianism, a post-science view as in "constructivism," and two rejections of eclecticism as in scientific monism (rational choice theory) and various forms of Marxist monism.

Chapter 3, taken from a centenary volume (Shils, 1991) celebrating the "great teachers of the University of Chicago's first century," is a biographical sketch of Charles Merriam, founder of the "behavioral" political science movement. It makes the important point that Merriam was an intellectual participant in the "behavioral revolution" as well as its political founder. Chapter 4, taken from *Biographical Memoirs* (National Academy of Sciences, 1987), shows how truly wondrous was the creativity of Harold Lasswell in his twenties and thirties. What reading these two biographical essays in tandem shows is that Merriam was very much a part of the "take-off" of both Lasswell's psychological and Gosnell's quantification part of the behavioral revolution. Merriam, in other words, was both idea man and facilitator. Lasswell, Gosnell, and V. O. Key Jr. did not invent themselves.

Chapter 5, "A Voice from the Chicago School," recounts my career in comparative politics, the origins of this program at the University of Chicago, and its influence on the first book published under the auspices of the Committee on Comparative Politics, *The Politics of the Developing Areas* (Almond and Coleman, 1960), as well as on my early chairship of the committee. It describes the central role of Lucian Pye in the committee's nine-volume Studies in Political Development series. It also accords credit to scholars who independently made important contributions to comparative and development studies during these decades. This chapter is taken from Hans Daalder's *Comparative European Politics: The Story of a Profession* (1997), a collection of the "autobiographies" of the scholars who made significant contributions to European political studies of the post–World War II decades.

Chapter 6, "Area Studies and the Objectivity of the Social Sciences," seeks to recover for the contemporary political science generation some of the great debate on the problem of "objectivity" in the social sciences. Can history, historical sociology, and political science really be objective, or are they fated ultimately to be "constructed" by subjective motivation, by social structure, by ideology? In these modern, postmodern, structuralist, and constructivist polemics, the early classical discussions of the theme of objectivity in the social sciences at the turn of the century, articulated in the great methodological essays of Max Weber and Karl Mannheim, have been lost sight of, and a great metatheoretical theme has been bowdlerized. This chapter spells out what Weber and Mannheim actually had to say about the problems of objectivity, and dispels the obfuscation surrounding these issues.

The five chapters of Part 2 deal with aspects of democratic theory. Chapter 7, "Capitalism and Democracy," was delivered as a lecture in Moscow at a seminar on the market (October 28–November 2, 1990). It was subsequently published in *PS: Political Science and Politics* (September 1991). The director of the seminar was the American economist, Nobelist Gary Becker, and the principal contributors were economists. All of the economists made the case for the "shock therapy" approach to transforming the economies of the socialist countries. My lecture reviewed the substantial historical and social science literature on the interaction of government and the economy, and supported an argument for a safety net, for a balanced approach to the introduction of the market.

Chapter 8, "The Appeals of Communism and Fascism," compares the findings of two early political culture studies—one of "fascist-authoritarian" attitudes (Adorno et al., 1950), and one of the appeals of communism

(Almond, 1954). They are relevant to the theory of democracy in that they suggest explanation for anti-democratic attitudes of the left and of the right. Delivered as a paper at the annual meeting of the American Political Science Association in 1962, this chapter may be viewed as an early step in the development of modern political psychology.

Chapter 9 is a study of democracy overloaded and in crisis, seeking explanation of the "cultural revolution" of the late 1960s and early 1970s in the United States and parts of Europe. Social scientists were thoroughly surprised by the extraordinary mobilization of young people at this time. This chapter explains this youth activism and cultural experimentalism as the product of an overlarge, thinly socialized "baby boom" generation mobilized by the Vietnam War, the military draft, and the African-American mobilization of these years. It shows the U.S. democratic system under great stress, functioning outside normal channels, reversing tried political traditions, and modifying what had been long-established moral standards.

Chapter 10, "The Civic Culture: Retrospect and Prospect," attributes the original stimulus for the *Civic Culture* study to Merriam's Comparative Civic Training project in the University of Chicago's Department of Political Science in the 1920s. The shortfall from expectations of this project left me with a challenge that I sought to meet some two decades later in collaboration with Sidney Verba, when we were both members of the Princeton Center for International Studies and had access to resources to fund such a project. The study succeeded in launching what now amounts to a subdiscipline of political culture studies, and has enhanced our ability to explain stability and change in political institutions and public policy. This chapter was originally given in the form of two lectures under the auspices of the Center for the Study of Democracy in the University of California–Irvine's School of Social Sciences. The chapter deals not only with the background of the theory, but also with the prospects of its survival as an explanation of democratic stability.

Chapter 11 states the theory of civic culture in its essentials, and was originally published in the *International Encyclopedia of the Social and Behavioral Sciences* (Smelser and Baltes, 2001).

# Part 1

---

# Historical Perspectives

# 2

# The History of Political Science: An Essay

IF WE WERE TO MODEL THE HISTORY of political science in the form of a curve of scientific progress in the study of politics over the ages, it would properly begin in Greek political science, make some modest gains in the Roman centuries, not make much progress in the Middle Ages, rise a bit in the Renaissance and the Enlightenment, make some substantial gains in the nineteenth century, and then take off in solid growth in the twentieth century as political science acquires genuine professional characteristics. What would be measured by this curve is the growth and qualitative improvement in knowledge concerned with the two fundamental questions of political science: the properties of political institutions, and the criteria we use in evaluating them.

We would record three rising blips in the twentieth-century growth curve. There was the Chicago blip in the interwar decades (1920–1940), introducing organized empirical research programs, emphasizing psychological and sociological interpretations of politics, and demonstrating the value of quantification. A second, much larger blip in the decades after World War II would measure the spread of "behavioral" political science throughout the world, improvements in the more traditional subdisciplines, and professionalization in the sense of the establishment of multi-

From *A New Handbook of Political Science,* edited by Robert E. Goodin and Hans-Dieter Klingemann (Oxford and New York: Oxford University Press, 1996). Reprinted, with minor revisions, with permission of Oxford University Press.

membered, meritocratically recruited, relatively nonhierarchal departments, the establishment of associations and specialist societies, refereed journals, and so forth. A third blip would register the entry of deductive and mathematical methods, and economic models in the "rational choice–methodological individualist" approach.

We might call this view of disciplinary history the "progressive-eclectic" view. It would be shared by those who accept as the criterion of political science scholarship the search for objectivity based on rules of evidence and inference. This criterion would be applicable not only to studies we call "behavioral," but also to political philosophy, both historical and normative, empirical case studies, historical and contemporary, systematic comparative studies, statistical studies involving survey and aggregate quantitative data, as well as research involving formal mathematical modeling and simulated and real experiments. In this sense it is an eclectic, nonhierarchal view, rather than an integral, standard one.

It is "progressive" in the sense that it imputes the notion of improvement to the history of political studies, both in the sense of insight into political phenomena, which is an old, well-established standard, the quantity of knowledge, and its "quality" in the sense of rigor. With respect to the first criterion most colleagues would agree that Michael Walzer (1983) has a better grasp of the concept of justice than did Plato; and with respect to the second Robert Dahl (1989) gives us a better theory of democracy than did Aristotle.

There are four opposing views of the history of political science. Two of them would challenge its scientific character. There is an "anti-science" position as well as a "post-science" position. Two of them would challenge its eclecticism in favor of a purist monism, or hierarchalism—the Marxists and the "rational choicists." The Straussians express the "anti-science" view, that the introduction of scientific methodology is a harmful illusion, that it trivializes and clouds understanding, and that the basic truths about politics are to be uncovered through direct colloquy with the classics and old texts. The "post-empirical, post-behavioral" approach to disciplinary history takes a deconstructive view; there is no privileged history of the discipline. There is a pluralism of disciplinary identities, each with its own view of disciplinary history.

The Marxist/neo-Marxist "critical theory" approaches challenge our eclecticism, arguing that political science or rather social science (since there can be no separable political science) consists of the unfalsifiable truths discovered and stated in the works of Marx and elaborated by his associates and followers. This view rejects the notion of a political science separable from a science of society. The science of society reveals itself in the course of its own dialectical development. Rational choice theory rejects our eclecticism in favor of a hierarchal model of political science as moving toward a parsimonious set of formal, mathematical theories applicable to the whole of social reality, including politics.

This chapter also assumes that political science has both scientific and humanistic components, both governed by the same imperatives of scholarly inquiry—the rules of evidence and inference. Contributions to knowledge may come from great insight or great virtuosity. We also assume from the ontological perspective of the family of sciences that it is on the "cloud" side of Karl Popper's "clouds and clocks" continuum (1972). This is to say that the regularities it discovers are probabilistic rather than lawlike, and that many of them may have relatively short half-lives.

The essential object of political science, which it shares with all of scholarship, is the creation of knowledge, defined as inferences or generalizations about politics drawn from evidence. As Gary King, Robert Keohane, and Sidney Verba put it, "Scientific research is designed to make . . . inferences on the basis of empirical information about the world" (1993, p. 7). This criterion is evident even in such explicitly "anti-scientific" work as that of the Straussians. That is, they consider evidence, analyze it, and draw inferences from it. It is impossible to conceive of a scholarly enterprise that does not rely on this evidence-inference methodological core. It would include Marxist and neo-Marxist studies, even though these studies are based on assumptions about social processes that are unfalsifiable and hence not fully subject to the rules of evidence, or logical inference. It would include Clifford Geertz's "thick description" kind of political science (1973), exemplified by John Womack's study (1968) of the Mexican peasant leader Zapata at the simple display of the evidence extreme, and the work of Anthony Downs (1957), William Riker (1962), and Mancur Olson (1965) at the inferential-deductive extreme. In *Zapata* we seem to have only evidence without inference; and in *The Economic Theory of Democracy,* inference without evidence. But Albert Hirschman (1970) tells us that the biography of the peasant leader is teeming with explanatory and policy implications; and the axioms and theorems of Downs generate a whole family of propositions testable by evidence. Both are falsifiable through contrary evidence, or logical flaws.

## A Historical Overview

### The Greeks and Romans

Though heroic efforts have been made to include writings of the ancient Near East in the political science chronicle, they are more properly viewed as precursors. Love for the Bible cannot convert the advice given to Moses by his father-in-law as to how he might more efficiently adjudicate the conflicts among the children of Israel, or the Deuteronomic doctrine of kingship into serious political science. But when we reach the Greece of Herodotus (c. 484–425 B.C.E.), we are in a world in which analysis of political ideas and ideals, and speculation about the properties of different kinds of polities and the nature of statesmanship and citizenship, have become part of conventional wisdom. Informed Greeks of the fifth century B.C.E.—living in the many independent Greek city-states, in which the same language is spoken, and the same or similar gods are worshipped, sharing common historical and mythological memories, engaged in inter-city trade and diplomacy, forming alliances and carrying on warfare—provided an interested audience for information and speculation about varieties of governmental and political arrangements, and economic, defense, and foreign policies.

The history of political science properly begins with Plato (428–348 B.C.E.), whose *The Republic, The Statesman,* and *The Laws* (Sabine and Thorson, 1973, chaps. 4–5; Strauss and Cropsey, 1987, pp. 33 ff.) are the first classics of political science. In these three studies, Plato sets out theories of justice, of political virtue, of the varieties of polity, and their transformation, which have survived as political theories well into the nineteenth century, and even until the present day. His theory of political stability and his theory of performance optimization, modified and elaborated in the work of Aristotle and Polybius, anticipate contemporary speculation about democratic transition and consolidation. In his first political typology, in *The Republic,* Plato presents his ideal regime based on knowledge and possession of the truth, and hence exemplifying the rule of virtue; and then presents four other developmentally related regimes in descending order of virtue—timocracy, oligarchy, democracy, and tyranny. Timocracy is a corruption of the ideal state in which honor and military glory supplant knowledge and virtue; oligarchy is a corruption of timocracy replacing honor with wealth as the principle of recruitment; democracy arises out of the corruption of oligarchy, and in turn is corrupted into tyranny.

In *The Statesman,* written much later than *The Republic,* and in *The Laws,* written in his old age—after the sobering experiences of the Peloponnesian War, and the failure of his mission to Syracuse—Plato distinguishes between the ideal republic and the realistically possible varieties of polity. To classify real regimes he introduces the famous three-by-two table, the marriage of quantity and quality—the rule of the one, the few, the many, in their pure and impure versions—which generated the sixfold classification of regimes—monarchy, tyranny, aristocracy, oligarchy, democracy, ochlocracy—which Aristotle perfected and elaborated in *Politics,* and which has served as a basic taxonomy through the ages and into the nineteenth century.

In *The Laws,* Plato presented the first version of the "mixed constitution" as the realistically best and most stable regime, designed to halt the cycle of development and degeneration implicit in the sixfold scheme. The mixed constitution, as formulated by Plato, attains stability by combining principles that might otherwise be in conflict—on the one hand the monarchic principle of wisdom and virtue, with the democratic principle of freedom on the other. This scheme was adopted and improved upon by Aristotle. It is the first explanatory theory in the history of political science, in which institutions, attitudes, and ideas are related to process and performance. It is the ancestor of separation of powers theory.

Aristotle (384–322 B.C.E.) spent twenty years as a member of Plato's Academy and then, after a period of tutoring Alexander of Macedon, returned to Athens and formed his own Lyceum, a teaching institution cum library-museum and research institute. The method of the Lyceum was inductive, empirical, and historical in contrast to the predominantly idealist and deductive approach stressed in Plato's Academy. The Lyceum is said to have collected 158 constitutions of Greek city-states, only one of which—that of Athens—has survived. The lectures that make up Aristotle's *Politics* (Barker, 1958) were apparently drawn from the analyses and the interpretations of these data.

While Plato's metaphysics led him to depreciate the real world and the human capacity to perceive and understand it, and to posit a world of ideal forms of which reality was a pale approximation, Aristotle, in contrast, was more of a hands-on empiricist, viewing political reality as a physician might view illness and health. Ernest Barker points out:

> It is perhaps not fanciful to detect a special medical bias in a number of passages of the *Politics.* This is not merely a matter of the accumulation of "case records," or of the use of the writings of the school of

Hippocrates such as the treatise of "Airs, waters, and places," It is a matter of recurring comparison between the art of the statesman and the art of the good physician; it is a matter of the deep study of the pathology of constitutions, and of their liability to the fever of sedition, which we find in Book V of the *Politics;* it is a matter of the preoccupation with therapeutics which we also find in the same book—a preoccupation singularly evident in the passage (at the end of chapter XI) which suggests a regimen and cure for the fever of tyranny. (1958, p. xxx)

While in his theory of the polity Aristotle begins from Plato's sixfold classification of states, from a realistic point of view he argues that there are really four important types: oligarchy and democracy, into which most of the Greek city-states might be classified; "polity," constitutional, or "mixed" government, which is a combination of oligarchy and democracy and which (because it reconciles virtue with stability) is the best attainable form of government; and tyranny, which is the worst. To back up his argument he points out that while the social structures of cities vary according to the economies, occupations, professions, and statuses contained in them, these differences are reducible into different distributions of rich and poor citizens. Where the rich dominate we have oligarchy; and where the poor dominate we have democracy. Where the middle class dominates we may have "mixed" or constitutional government, tending to be stable, since extreme interests are outweighed by moderate ones. Political structures and patterns of recruitment are classified according to the arrangements of the deliberative, magistrative, and judicial organs, and the access of different classes to them.

To a modern political scientist—a Dahl, Rokkan, Lipset, Huntington, Verba, or Putnam—Aristotle's analysis in *Politics* and *Ethics* (Barker, 1958; Rhys, 1934) of the relation of status, occupation, profession, and class to varieties of political institutions on the one hand, and of the relation between political socialization and recruitment to political structure and process on the other, would be quite familiar ground. The metaphysics and ontology would be shared. But if these chapters, or something like them, had been submitted by contemporary graduate students in search of dissertation topics, one can visualize marginal comments of a Dahl or Verba, as: "What cases are you generalizing about?" "What about using a scale here?" "How would you test the strength of this association?" and the like. Aristotle presents a whole set of propositions and hypotheses on what makes for political stability, and what makes for breakdown, on developmental sequences, on educational patterns and political performance, that cry out for research designs and careful quantitative analysis. The Aristotelian method consists essentially of a clinical sorting out of specimens, with hypotheses about causes and sequences, but without systematic tests of relationships.

The Greek political theory of Plato and Aristotle was a combination of universalistic and parochial ideas. The world about which they generalized was the world of the Greek city-states. They were generalizing about Greeks and not about humankind. Citizens were differentiated from slaves, alien residents, and foreigner barbarians. With Alexander's conquests, and the intermingling of Greek and oriental cultures, two notions generated by the Stoic philosophical school gained in authority. These were the idea of a universal humanity and the idea of an order in the world based on natural law. These ideas were first advanced by the Stoic philosopher Chrysippus in the last third of the third century B.C.E. Their clearest formulation was in the work of Panaetius (185–109 B.C.E.) and Polybius (203–120 B.C.E.), two Stoic philosophers of the second century B.C.E. who in turn transmitted these ideas to the Roman intellectual elite of the late republic. While Panaetius developed the philosophical and ethical aspects of late Stoicism, Polybius adapted Platonic and Aristotelian ideas to the history of Rome, and to the interpretation of Roman institutions.

Polybius attributes the remarkable growth and power of Rome to its political institutions. He makes more explicit the developmental ideas of Plato and Aristotle, offering simple sociopsychological explanations for the decay of the pure forms of monarchy, aristocracy, and democracy, and their degeneration into the impure forms of tyranny, oligarchy, and ochlocracy. The Roman state builders, according to Polybius, through a process of trial and error had rediscovered the virtues of the mixed constitution—the combination of the monarchic, aristocratic, and democratic principles implemented in the Consulate, the Senate, and the Assembly. It was these institutions that made possible the conquest of the world in the course of half a century, and that, according to Polybius, guaranteed a future of stable and just world rule under Roman law (Sabine and Thorson, 1973, chaps. 4–9).

Three-quarters of a century later the Roman lawyer Cicero (106–43 B.C.E.) applied "mixed constitution" theory to Roman history at a time when the institutions of the Roman Republic were already in deep decay. This part of his work was an appeal for a return to the structure and culture of the earlier Roman Republic prior to the populist and civil war decades of the Gracchi, Marius, and Sulla. More significant and lasting was his development of the Stoic doctrine of natural law. This was the belief that there is a universal natural law resulting from the divine order of the cosmos and the rational and social nature of humanity. It was his formulation of this natural law idea that was taken up in the Roman law, and passed from it into Catholic church doctrine and ultimately into its Enlightenment and modern manifestations (Sabine and Thorson, 1973, chaps. 9–10).

Thus we find formulated in Greek thought by the end of the third century B.C.E., and in Roman thought in the following centuries, the two great themes of political theory, themes that carry through the history of political science into the present day. These are: What are the institutional forms of polity? and, What are the standards we use to evaluate them? The answer to the first was the Platonic and Aristotelian sixfold classification of pure and impure organizational forms, and the "mixed constitution" as the solution to the problem of degeneracy and cyclicalism. And the answer to the question of evaluation—legitimacy, justice—was the doctrine of natural law. These ideas were transmitted to Rome by the late Stoics—particularly Panaetius and Polybius—and from the work of Romans such as Cicero and Seneca into Catholic political theory.

### Mixed Constitutions and Natural Law Theory in History

Mixed constitution theory and the theory of law receive their fullest medieval codification in Thomas Aquinas (1225–1274), who relates the mixed constitution to justice and stability through its conformity to divine and natural law. His exemplars of the mixed constitution are the divinely ordained political order of the Israel of Moses, Joshua, and the judges, balanced by elders and tribal leaders; and the Roman Republic in its prime—with its mix of Assembly, Senate, and Consulate. He follows the arguments of Aristotle on the weaknesses and susceptibility to tyranny of the pure forms of monarchic, aristocratic, and democratic rule. Combining the pure forms is the antidote to human weakness and corruption (Blythe, 1992, chap. 3).

In the late Middle Ages and in the Renaissance, mixed government and natural law provide the theoretical coinage according to which governments were valued. Just as Israel of the premonarchic period, and Rome of the Republican age were viewed by Thomas Aquinas and those whom he influenced as approximating the ideal of mixed government in the past, for the Italian political theorists of the late Middle Ages and the Renaissance, Venice was the exemplar, with its monarchic Doge, its aristocratic Senate, and democratic Great Council. The stability, wealth, and power of Venice were taken as proof of the superiority of the mixed system.

The variety of principalities and republics in northern Italy in these centuries, the overarching and rival claims of church and empire, the warfare, conquest, revolution, diplomatic negotiation, and institutional innovation in which they were constantly engaged, stimulated several generations of political theorists who reflected and wrote on this political experience (Blythe, 1992; Pocock, 1975; Skinner, 1978). Central to their discussions were the ideas of the mixed constitution as expressed in Aristotle and Thomas Aquinas. In the sixteenth century, with the translation of his *History of Rome,* Polybius became influential particularly in Florence and in the work of Machiavelli (1469–1527). In the Florentine crises of the late fifteenth and early sixteenth centuries Machiavelli engaged in a polemic with the historian Guicciardini in which the principal authorities cited were Aristotle, Polybius, and Thomas Aquinas, and the issues turned on which countries were the best exemplars of the mixed constitution. Luigi Guicciardini favored an Aristotelian, Venetian-Spartan aristocratic bias, and Machiavelli favored a somewhat greater role for the popular element, and relied more on Polybius for support (Blythe, 1992, pp. 292 ff.).

The breakthrough of Renaissance political theory lay in Machiavelli's treatment of the legitimacy of regimes and political leaders. Prior to *The Prince* and the *Discorsi* (Machiavelli, 1964, chap. 17; Skinner, 1978, pp. 131 ff.), writers treated political regimes dichotomously as pure and corrupt, normative or nonnormative, in the original Platonic and Aristotelian senses. Machiavelli, viewing politics as practiced in Italy in the fifteenth and sixteenth centuries, legitimized nonnormative politics as unavoidable, as survival-related, as part of reality. A prince who failed to employ problematic means when necessary to survival would be unable to do good when that was possible. Machiavelli touched the nerve of political science with this "value-free" orientation, and his name became a synonym for moral indifference and political cynicism. And the issues raised by this venture into realism are still fluttering the dovecotes of political philosophy.

The theory of sovereignty, so important a theme in the Middle Ages, the Renaissance, and the Enlightenment, receives its first full formulation in the work of Jean Bodin (1529–1596). His doctrine of absolutism as a solution to the problem of instability and disorder is formulated in polemic with the theory of the mixed constitution. Employing a realistic, historical method, he makes the argument that the classic cases of mixed government—Rome and Venice—were actually concentrated and centralized regimes, that, indeed, every important and long-lasting regime concentrated the legislative and executive powers under a central authority. His appreciation of the influence of environmental and social structural conditions on the characteristics of states anticipates Montesquieu in its anthropological sensitivity (Sabine and Thorson, 1973, chap. 21).

While there was substantial progress in the development of political science in the Enlightenment, such writers as Hobbes, Locke, Montesquieu, Hume, Madison, and Hamilton were pursuing the same themes that concerned Plato, Aristotle, Polybius, Cicero, Aquinas, Machiavelli, and Bodin—the forms and varieties of rule, and the standards by which one judged them. In considering the progress made by the Enlightenment philosophers, we look for improvements in the gathering and evaluation of evidence and in the structure of inference.

The first scholarly project completed by Thomas Hobbes (1588–1679) was a translation of the *Peloponnesian Wars* of Thucydides, a history of a disorderly and tragic epoch, just as England of the seventeenth century was disturbed by civil war, regicide, dictatorship, and exile. Hobbes's view of the state of nature, of the reasons for humankind's consent to be governed, the nature of political obligation, and the legitimacy of different forms of government, was influenced by reflections on the fall of Athens, and the violence and moral confusion of seventeenth-century England. In his later books he concluded that sovereign authority in a society is required if the deliverance of its members out of a disorderly and violent state of nature is to be secured. The relation between the sovereign and the people is contractual. In exchange for obligation and obedience, the subject gets safety and security. The best form of government, logically derived from these premises, because it is rational and unambiguous, is monarchic absolutism limited by the ruler's obligation to provide for the security and welfare of the members of the society. Hobbes's achievement was his logical derivation of conclusions about the best form of government from what he viewed as material conditions and human needs. He advanced the argument by restricting assumptions to what he viewed, and what he thought history confirmed, as "material" evidence of the human condition. He drew uncompromising logical inferences from these assumptions (Hobbes, 1914, intro.; Sabine and Thorson, 1973, chap. 24; Strauss and Cropsey, 1987, pp. 396–420).

John Locke's conclusions about the origins and legitimacy of government are derived from a different set of contractual assumptions than those of Hobbes. People consent to government to ensure their welfare and liberty. The Lockean state of nature is not so abysmal as that of Hobbes. There are inconveniences and costs, and the consent to government is a conditional one, measured by the extent to which government performs these limited functions. In moving from the state of nature, "people give up to the community the natural right of enforcing the law of reason, in order that life, liberty, and property may be preserved" (Locke, 1924, pp. xi ff.). There are the beginnings of separation of powers theory in John Locke. The power granted to the community is divisible into three components—the legislative, the executive, and the federative, the last a relatively unspecified power pertaining to foreign relations. In Locke as well as in Hobbes the progress in political science scholarship lies in the logical derivation of the nature and forms of government, and of the bases of authority, liberty, and obligation, from sociological and psychological assumptions. Their strength lies in their logical rationalism, rather than in the gathering of evidence.

Though it is an exaggeration to describe Montesquieu's evidence as rigorously gathered and accumulated, surely he takes this step beyond Hobbes and Locke. While he recognizes laws of nature, and derives the formation of government from these laws, he emphasizes above all the variety of human political experience and the pluralism of causation. Montesquieu goes to "Persia," and back in time to Rome, so to speak, to Venice, to many other European countries, and especially to England, to compare their institutions with those of France. He is a comparativist and causal pluralist. To explain varieties of polity and public policy, he considers climate, religion, customs, economy, history, and the like. He founds the best form of government in his notion of separation of powers, and a kind of Newtonian balance among these powers, which he views as most likely to preserve liberty and promote welfare. And he finds his best exemplification of separation of powers in post–Petition of Right England (Montesquieu, 1977, bk. 11).

Montesquieu's classification of governments includes republics, monarchies, and despotisms; and the republican category is divisible into aristocracies and democracies. He finds exemplified in the government of England the ideal of mixed government combining democratic, aristocratic, and monarchic institutions in a dialectic-harmonic balance. His political theory is an explanatory, system-functional, conditions/process/policy theory (1977).

It had great influence on the framers of the U.S. Constitution. And it may have been in Hamilton's mind when he wrote in *Federalist* 9, "The science of politics . . . has received great improvement. The efficacy of the various principles is well understood, which were either not known at all, or imperfectly known to the ancients," and in *Federalist* 31, "Though it cannot be pretended that the principles of moral and political knowledge have, in general, the same degree of certainty with those of the mathematics, yet they have much better claims in this respect than . . . we should be disposed to allow them" (Hamilton et al., 1937, pp. 48, 189). What led Madison and Hamilton to view themselves as such good political scientists, was through having tested the theories of Montesquieu, Locke, and other European philosophers against the experience of the thirteen colonies, and the United States under the Articles of Confederation. They had the confidence of engineers applying laws of politics, derived from empirical and laboratory-like examinations of individual cases. Separating executive, legislative, and judicial power, which they had learned from Montesquieu, and mixing powers through checks and balances, which they had learned from practical experience with the thirteen colonies, had enabled them to treat politics in equation-like form: Separation + checks and balances = liberty.

## The Nineteenth Century

In the seventeenth and eighteenth centuries the philosophers of the Enlightenment forecast the improvement in the material, political, and moral condition of humanity as a consequence of the growth of knowledge. In the nineteenth and twentieth centuries, scholars and intellectuals elaborated this theme of progress and improvement, predicting different trajectories and causal sequences. In the first part of the nineteenth century there were the great historicists, or historical determinists—Hegel (1770–1831), Comte (1798–1857), and Marx (1818–1883)—who, in the Enlightenment tradition, saw history as unilinear development in the direction of freedom and rational rule. In Hegel, reason and freedom are exemplified in the Prussian bureaucratic monarchy. In Comte, the constraints of theology and metaphysics are broken by science as it enables humanity to exercise rational control over nature and social institutions. In Marx, capitalism supplants feudalism, and in turn is supplanted first by proletarian socialism, and then by the truly free, egalitarian society.

Hegel departs from Enlightenment notions by his dialectical view of history as the clash of opposites and the emergence of syntheses. The Prussian bureaucratic monarchy, as it rationalized and modernized in the post-Napoleonic decades, was viewed by Hegel as the exemplification of an ultimate synthesis (Sabine and Thorson, 1973, chap. 17; Strauss and Cropsey, 1987, pp. 732 ff.). In Marx the Hegelian dialectic became the principle of class struggle leading to the ultimate transformation of human society. The nature of the historical process was such, according to Marx, that the only social science that is possible is one that is discovered in, and employed in, political action. In Marxism this science of society became a fully validated, economy/ideology/polity–driven scheme. Armed with this powerful theory, an informed vanguard would usher in a world of order, justice, and plenty (Sabine and Thorson, 1973, chap. 34; Strauss and Cropsey, 1987, pp. 802 ff.).

Auguste Comte, the originator with Saint Simon (1760–1825) of philosophical positivism, inaugurated the new science of "sociology" in his six-volume *Cours de Philosophie Positive* (Konig, 1968, vol. 3, pp. 201 ff.). He made the argument that all the sciences went through two stages—(1) the theological and (2) the metaphysical—before becoming (3) scientific or positive. Thus, argued Comte, astronomy first passed through these three stages, then physics, then chemistry, then physiology, and finally social physics (the social sciences inclusive of psychology), and was then in process of maturing as a science. Comte saw this new scientific sociology as furnishing a blueprint for the reform of society.

There was a wave of empiricism in reaction to these sweeping, abstract, and monistic theories, which produced a large number of descriptive, formal legal studies of political institutions, and several monumental, pedestrian, descriptive political ethnographies such as Theodore Woolsey's *Political Science: The State Theoretically and Practically Considered* (1892); Wilhelm Roscher's *Politik: Geschichtliche Naturlehre der Monarchie, Aristokratie, und Demokratie* (1892); and Woodrow Wilson's *The State: Elements of Historical and Practical Politics: A Sketch of Institutional History and Administration* (1895). These were essentially ponderous classificatory exercises, employing some variation of the Platonic-Aristotelian system of classification.

Related to historicism, but more empirical in approach and more pluralistic in explanation, were a group of writers in the second half of the nineteenth century who might be characterized as "evolutionists" and who influenced modern sociology in a variety of ways. These included Herbert Spencer (1820–1903), Sir Henry Maine (1822–1888), and Ferdinand Tonnies (1855–1936). Spencer, an early post-Darwinian social evolutionist, avoids a simple unilinearism (1965). He is concerned with accounting for cultural and political variation, as well as generic improvement. He explains political decentralization and centralization by physical features of the environment as mountainous versus open prairie terrain. He also makes the argument, backed up by historical example, that democratization is the consequence of socioeconomic changes resulting in urban concentration, and the proliferation of interests due to the growth of manufactures and the spread of commerce.

There was a common dualistic pattern among the later nineteenth-century writers on the historical process. Maine (1963) distinguishes ancient from modern law in terms of the shift from status relationships of a diffuse character, to specific contractual ones. Tonnies (1957) introduces the distinction between *Gemeinschaft* and *Gesellschaft* (community and society). At the turn of the century, Weber (1864–1920) and Durkheim (1858–1917) contrast modern rationality with traditionality (Weber, 1968, vol. 1, pp. 24 ff.), and organic with mechanical solidarity (Durkheim, 1960). This theme of "development," of "modernization," continues into the twentieth century, and into the present day with efforts at defining, operationalizing, measuring, and interpreting socioeconomic/sociopolitical "modernization," as I suggest below.

It was common throughout the nineteenth century to speak of the study of politics and society as sciences, for knowledge about politics to be described as consisting of lawful propositions about political institutions and events based on evidence and inference. John Stuart Mill (1806–1873) was a philosopher and methodologist of social science (1961) as well as democratic theorist (1962). Alexis de Tocqueville (1805–1859) wrote two great books—*Democracy in America* (1945) and *The Old Regime and the French Revolution* (1955)—that developed the theme of the historic spread of equality and democracy, but through in-depth historical and empirical methodologies.

All these nineteenth-century social and political theorists readily fall under our organizing concept of the advancing rigor and logical coherence of the study of political phenomena defined as the properties and legitimacy of rule. The holders of the chairs in politics at both Oxford and Cambridge at the turn of the century—Frederick Pollock (1890) and John Seeley (1886)—both wrote introductions to political "science."

For Mill, Tocqueville, Moissaye Ostrogorski, Woodrow Wilson, and Roberto Michels, democracy as an alternative to other regimes is a major preoccupation. Each in his own way continues the debate about "mixed government." Mill wants the educated, the informed, the civically responsible to play a preeminent role in democracy to avoid the corrupt and mass potentialities in democracy. Tocqueville found in the U.S. legal profession an aristocratic admixture to moderate the "leveling" propensities of democracy. Ostrogorski (1964, vol. 2, concl.) and Michels (1949) both see fatal flaws in democracy, and inevitable oligarchy resulting from the bureaucratization of mass political parties.

Linking European political theory with U.S. political science of the first decades of the twentieth century was the concept of "pluralism," a variation on the "mixed government" theme. The concept of state sovereignty associated with the ideology of absolutist monarchy was challenged in the late nineteenth and early twentieth centuries by "pluralists" of both the right and the left. Otto Gierke (1868) in Germany, and Leon Duguit (1917) in France, question the complete authority of the central state. Conservative political theorists such as John Figgis (1896) assert the autonomy of churches and communities; left-wing theorists such as Harold Laski (1919) made such claims for professional groups and trade unions.

With the seminal figures of Marx and Freud, and the great sociological theorists of the end of the nineteenth century—Pareto, Durkheim, Weber—and with the polemic about sovereignty and pluralism, we are already in the immediate intellectual background of twentieth-century political science.

## The Professionalization of Political Science in the Twentieth Century

In the latter half of the nineteenth century, and the first decades of the twentieth, the rapid growth and concentration of industry and the proliferation of large cities in the United States, populated in considerable part by immigrants from the countryside, or from foreign countries, created a situation prone to corruption on a major scale. It took political entrepreneurs with resources to organize and discipline the largely ignorant electorates who swarmed into such urban centers as New York, Boston, Philadelphia, Chicago, St. Louis, Kansas City, and the like. The "boss" and the "machine" and intermittent reform movements were the most visible U.S. political phenomena of the late nineteenth and early twentieth centuries. Reform movements inspired by an ideology of efficiency and integrity and supported by urban business and professional elites drew on the talents of journalists of the quality media and on academic communities. The corruption of politics by business corporations seeking contracts, franchises, and protection from governmental regulation became the subject of a journalistic "muckraking" literature that brought to public view a political infrastructure and process—

"pressure groups" and the "lobby"—deeply penetrative and corrupting of local, state, and national political systems.

In the interwar years, American political scientists were challenged by this political infrastructure, and by the muckraking literature that exposed it, and began to produce serious monographic studies of pressure groups and lobbying activities. Peter Odegard (1928) wrote on the American Anti-Saloon League, Pendleton Herring (1929) on pressure groups and the Congress, Elmer Schattschneider (1935) on politics and the tariff, Louise Rutherford (1937) on the American Bar Association, and Oliver Garceau (1941) on the American Medical Association. There were many others, and all put their stamp on the political science of the interwar years. The realism and empiricism of these early students of what some called "invisible" or "informal" government drew on the ideas of an earlier generation of American political theorists including Frank Goodnow (1900) and Woodrow Wilson (1887).

## *The Chicago School*

Thus in the first decades of the twentieth century the notion of a "scientific" study of politics had put on substantial flesh. Europeans such as Comte, Mill, Tocqueville, Marx, Spencer, Weber, Durkheim, Pareto, Michels, Mosca, Ostrogorski, Bryce, and others had pioneered, or were pioneering, the development of a political sociology, anthropology, and psychology in which they moved the study of politics into a self-consciously explanatory mode. Empirical studies of governmental and political processes had made some headway in American universities. But in major part the study of politics in American universities in these decades was still essentially legal, philosophical, and historical in its methodology. The significance of the University of Chicago's School of Political Science (c. 1920–1940) lay in its demonstration through concrete, empirical studies that a genuine enhancement of political knowledge was possible through an interdisciplinary research strategy, the introduction of quantitative methodologies, and through organized research support. Other writers spoke a language similar to Merriam's in "The Present State of the Study of Politics" (1970, chap. 1) (e.g., Catlin, 1964). But the school that Merriam founded in the 1920s and staffed in part with his own students made a quantum leap in empirical investigative rigor, inferential power in the study of things political, and institutional innovation.

What led Merriam to become the great political science entrepreneur of his generation was the dynamic setting of the city of Chicago booming with wealth and aspiring toward culture in the early decades of the twentieth century, and the interplay of his academic life and his political career. His hopes for high political office had been dashed by his defeat in the Chicago mayoral campaign in 1919. It was no longer possible for him to aspire to become the "Woodrow Wilson of the Middle West" (Karl, 1974, chap. 4). At the same time he was unable to settle for a quiet academic career. His years in municipal politics, and his wartime experience with foreign affairs and propaganda, sensitized him to "new aspects" in the study of politics. Not long after returning to the University of Chicago from his "public information" post in Italy, he issued his "New Aspects" declaration, and began his buildup of the Chicago department, and the various research programs that identified it as a distinctive "school." He was an institutional innovator, first creating the Social Science Research Committee at the University of Chicago to dispense financial support for promising research initiatives among the Chicago social science faculty, and then pioneering the formation of the Social Science Research Council (SSRC) to provide similar opportunities on the national scale.

The first major research program to be initiated at Chicago was built around Harold Gosnell, who received his doctorate under Merriam in 1921 and was appointed to an assistant professorship in 1923. He and Merriam (1924) collaborated in a study of the attitudes toward voting of a selection of some 6,000 Chicagoans in the mayoral election of 1923. The selection was made prior to the introduction of "probability sampling," and was carried out through "quota control," which sought to match the demographic characteristics of the Chicago population by quotas of the principal demographic groups. Quota control, discredited in the Truman-Dewey election of 1948, was then the "state-of-the-art" approach to the sampling of large populations. The interviewers were University of Chicago graduate students trained by Merriam and Gosnell. Gosnell followed up this study with the first experiment ever to be undertaken in political science. This was a survey of the effects on voting of a nonpartisan mail canvass in Chicago that was intended to get out the vote in the national and local elections of 1924 and 1925. The experimental technique Gosnell devised was quite rigorous: there were carefully matched experimental and control groups, different stimuli were employed, and the results were analyzed according to the most sophisticated statistical techniques then available. Follow-up research was done by Gosnell in Britain, France, Germany, Belgium, and Switzerland. Nothing like this had ever been done by political scientists before.

Lasswell's accomplishments when he was in his twenties and thirties were extraordinary. Between 1927 and 1939 he produced six books, each one innovative, exploring new dimensions and aspects of politics. The first, *Propaganda Technique in the First World War* (1927), introduced the study of political communication (to be followed in 1935 by a book-length annotated bibliography called *Propaganda and Promotional Activities* [Lasswell with Casey and Smith]), identifying the new literature of communications, propaganda, and public relations. The second book, *Psychopathology and Politics* (1930), explored the depth psychology of politics through the analysis of the case histories of politicians, some of them mentally disturbed. The third book, *World Politics and Personal Insecurity* (1935b), speculated about the psychological bases and aspects of individual political behavior, different kinds of political regimes, and political processes. The fourth book, the celebrated *Politics: Who Gets What, When, and How* (1936b), was a succinct exposition of Lasswell's general political theory, emphasizing the interaction of elites competing for such values as "income, deference, and safety." In 1939 he published *World Revolutionary Propaganda: A Chicago Study* (Lasswell and Jones), in which he examined the impact of the world depression on political movements among the Chicago unemployed, exemplifying the interaction of macro and micro factors in politics at the local, national, and international levels. Lasswell also published some twenty articles during these years in such periodicals as *The American Journal of Psychiatry, The Journal of Abnormal Psychology, Scientific Monographs, The American Journal of Sociology, The Psychoanalytical Review,* and the like. He was the first investigator of the interaction of physiological and mental-emotional processes to use laboratory methods. He published several articles during these years reporting the results of his experiments in relating attitudes, emotional states, verbal content, and physiological conditions as they were reported or reflected in interview records, pulse rates, blood pressure, skin tension, and the like.

While Gosnell and Lasswell were the full-time makers of the Chicago revolution in the study of political science, the senior scholars in the department, including Merriam himself and his colleagues Quincy Wright in international relations and Leonard White in public administration, were also involved in major ways in the making of the reputation of the Chicago school. Merriam sponsored and edited a series of books on civic education in the United States and Europe, a forerunner of contemporary studies of political socialization and culture (1931). During these same years Wright (1942) carrried on his major study of the causes of war, which involved the testing of sociological and psychological hypotheses by quantitative methods. White took on James Bryce's problem of why in the United States the "best men do not go into politics" (1908). White's book, *The Prestige Value of Public Employment,* based on survey research, appeared in 1929.

## *World War II and the Postwar Behavioral Revolution*

The Chicago school continued its productivity up to the late 1930s, when the Hutchins administration attacked the value of empirical research in the social sciences. Several of the leading professors in the Department of Philosophy, including George Herbert Mead, as well as several of the department's leading "pragmatists," resigned and went to other universities. In political science Lasswell and Gosnell resigned, and Merriam's retirement brought the productivity of the Chicago Department of Political Science almost to a halt. However, the Chicago school had reached a mass that ensured its future in the country at large. Herman Pritchett continued his innovative work in public law at the University of Chicago; Lasswell continued his work at Yale, inspiring Dahl, Charles Lindblom, and Robert Lane in their transformation of the Yale department. V. O. Key Jr. at Harvard produced several generations of students with empirical and quantitative research interests in political parties, elections, and public opinion. David Truman and Avery Leiserson brought the study of interest groups to theoretical fruition. William T. R. Fox, Klaus Knorr, and Bernard Brodie and their students, and I and mine, brought University of Chicago international relations and comparative politics to Yale, Princeton, MIT, and the Rand Corporation.

World War II turned out to be a laboratory, and an important training experience for many of the scholars who would seed the "behavioral revolution." The problems of how to ensure the high rate of agricultural and industrial production on the part of a reduced labor force, how to recruit and train soldiers, sailors, and airmen, and later how to discharge and return them to civilian life, how to sell war bonds, how to control consumption and inflation, and how to monitor internal morale and the attitudes of allies and enemies, created demand for social science personnel in all the branches of the military and civilian services. The war effort created pools of social science expertise that on the conclusion of the war were fed back into the growing academic institutions of the postwar decades.

Working for the Department of Justice, Lasswell developed systematic quantitative content analysis for the monitoring of the foreign-language press, and the study of allied and enemy propaganda in the United States.

He also participated with social scientists such as Hans Speier, Goodwin Watson, Nathan Leites, and Edward Shils in the work of an analysis division in the Foreign Broadcast Intelligence Service of the Federal Communications Commission, which among other things analyzed the content of Nazi communications for information on internal political and morale conditions in Germany and Occupied Europe. Survey research techniques, other kinds of interviewing methods, and statistical techniques, especially sampling theory, were brought to bear on the war-related problems of the various military services, the Departments of Agriculture, Treasury, and Justice, and such agencies as the Office of Price Administration and the Office of War Information. Anthropology, then in its psychiatric-psychoanalytic phase, was similarly drawn into the war effort. The causes of Fascism and Nazism, the reasons for the French political breakdown, the cultural vulnerabilities of Russia, Britain, and the United States, were sought in family structure, childhood socialization, and cultural patterns. The Office of War Information and the War Department drew on the anthropological and psychological expertise of Ruth Benedict, Margaret Mead, Cora Dubois, Clyde Kluckhohn, Ernest Hilgard, Geoffrey Gorer, and others. Social psychologists and sociologists specializing in survey research and experimental social psychology, including Rensis Likert, Angus Campbell, Paul Lazarsfeld, Herbert Hyman, Samuel Stouffer, and Carl Hovland, were employed by the army, navy, and air force in dealing with their personnel problems, by the Department of Agriculture in its effort to increase food production, by the Treasury in its effort to market bonds, and by the various intelligence services, including the Office of Strategic Services. A younger generation of political scientists working in these various agencies during the war years experienced something like postdoctoral internships under the supervision of leading scholars in the social science disciplines.

The rapidly growing academic enterprise in the post–World War II and Cold War world drew on these wartime interdisciplinary experiences. The curriculum of political science, and departmental faculties as well, expanded rapidly in response to this broadened conception of the discipline and the spread of higher education. The study of international relations stimulated by the important U.S. role during this time was fostered in mostly new research institutes at Yale, Princeton, Columbia, MIT, and Harvard, spreading into the middle-western and western universities in the 1950s and 1960s. New subspecialties such as security studies, international political economy, public opinion, and political culture studies joined with the older subspecialties of international law, organization, and diplomatic history in the staffing of these research institutes and political science departments. The new and developing nations of Asia, Africa, the Middle East, and Latin America, now seen as threatened by an aggressive Soviet Union, required area specialists, and specialists in economic and political development processes and problems. Departments of political science expanded rapidly to accommodate these new area specialties and international relations programs.

The survey research specialists of World War II found themselves to be in great demand. Business wanted to know how best to market and merchandize their products; and politicians wanted to know the susceptibilities and intentions of their constituents. From small beginnings in the 1930s and 1940s, the field of survey and market research exploded in the postwar decades. It had both commercial and academic components. The main academic institutions involved in this development were the University of Michigan with its Institute of Social Research and its Survey Research Center, founded by psychologists Rensis Likert, Angus Campbell, and Dorwin Cartwright; the Bureau of Applied Social Research at Columbia, founded by sociologists Paul Lazarsfeld and Robert Merton; and the National Opinion Research Center at the University of Chicago, headed in its early years by sociologist Clyde Hart. These three organizations in the postwar decades produced a literature and a professoriat that contributed substantially to the "behavioral revolution."

Among these three university centers, the University of Michigan turned out to be the most important in the recruitment and training of political scientists. Its Institute of Social Research established a Summer Training Institute in the use of survey methods open to young political and other social scientists as early as 1947. Over the years this program has trained hundreds of American and foreign political scientists in survey and electoral research techniques. In 1961 it established an Interuniversity Consortium for Political and Social Research supported by subscribing universities and maintaining in machine-readable form a rapidly growing archive of survey and other quantitative data. This archive has served as the database for a large number of doctoral dissertations, articles in learned journals, and important books illuminating various aspects of the democratic process. It has administered its own summer training program in quantitative methods.

In 1977 the University of Michigan's Survey Research Center Election Studies became the American National Election Studies supported by a major grant from the National Science Foundation, with an independent national board of overseers drawn from American universities. This organization, based at the Center of Political Studies of the University of Michigan's Institute of Social Research and directed by Warren Miller, with its board of overseers chaired by Heinz Eulau of Stanford University, has regularly conducted national election studies with input from the larger national political and social science community, and its findings are available to the scholarly community as a whole (Miller, 1994, vol. 25, pp. 247–265).

If we can speak of the University of Chicago's School of Political Science as the agency that sparked the scientific revolution in the study of politics in the two interwar decades, surely the University of Michigan's Institute of Social Research deserves a major credit for the spread of this scientific culture in the post–World War II decades into most of the major academic centers in the United States and abroad. Several hundred young scholars have been trained in survey and statistical methods in its Summer Training Institutes; scores of articles and dozens of books have been produced by scholars using its archival materials; the Michigan election studies have served as models for sophisticated election research in all the rest of the world.

The spread and improvement in empirical political theory involved more than election research technique and theory. Such fields as international relations and comparative politics grew as rapidly as did the field of American politics, and its newer growth involved quantification and interdisciplinary approaches. The major university centers of graduate training during the postwar decades—Yale, the University of California at Berkeley, Harvard, the Universities of Michigan, Wisconsin, and Minnesota, Stanford, Princeton, MIT, and others turned out hundreds of political science Ph.D.'s to staff the proliferating and growing political science departments in American and in many foreign colleges and universities. Most of these centers of graduate training provided instruction in quantitative methods in the decades after World War II (Somit and Tannenhaus, 1967; Crick, 1959; Eulau and Prewitt, 1976).

The SSRC, under the leadership of Pendleton Herring in the 1940s–1960s, facilitated and enriched these developments through its graduate, postdoctoral fellowship, and research support programs. Two of its political science research committees—the Committee on Political Behavior, and its spin-off, the Committee on Comparative Politics, were particularly active in spreading these ideas and practices. The Committee on Political Behavior provided direction and support in U.S. election and legislative studies. The Committee on Comparative Politics led in the development and sophistication of area and comparative studies. While most of the participants in these programs were American political and social scientists, around one-fifth of the participants in the conferences of the Committee on Comparative Politics during the years 1954–1972 were foreign scholars. Some of these—Stein Rokkan, Hans Daalder, Samuel Finer, Richard Rose, Giovanni Sartori, among others—were in turn leaders in movements in Europe and in their particular countries to expand and improve the quality of the work in political and social science (Committee on Comparative Politics, 1971).

The discipline of political science was becoming a modern "profession" over these years. "Political science," "government," and "politics" departments had first come into existence at the turn of the twentieth century, when they began to be formed by an alliance of historians, lawyers, and philosophers. By the first decades of the twentieth century there were freestanding departments in many U.S. universities. The American Political Science Association was formed in 1903, with a little more than 200 members. It reached around 3,000 members at the end of World War II, exceeded 10,000 in the mid-1960s, and now includes more than 13,000 individuals. Most of these members are instructors in institutions of higher education, organized in a large number of subspecialties. Most political science teachers and researchers have obtained degrees as doctors of philosophy in political science, at one of the major centers of graduate training. Qualifications for the degree normally involve passing a set of field and methodological examinations, and the completion of a major research project. Scholarly reputations are based on the publication of books and articles screened for publication by "peer review." Advancement in scholarly rank normally requires evaluation by external reviewers specialized in the field of the candidate. There are more than a dozen political science journals specialized by field, and governed by the processes of peer review.

The half century of political science training and research since the end of World War II has created a major academic profession with many subspecialties, and made many substantive contributions to our knowledge and understanding of politics in all its manifestations. Area studies—research on Western and Eastern Europe, East, Southeast, and South Asia, the Middle East, Africa, and Latin America, carried on by literally thousands of trained scholars, organized in centers in scores of universities and colleges, with their own professional organizations and journals, have produced libraries of informative and often sophisticated monographs.

A quick and selective review of substantive research programs may help us appreciate this growth of political knowledge. We have already described the spread and sophistication of election research. Its forecasting record may be compared with that of meteorology, and of seismology. We have made major progress in our understanding of political culture as it affects political institutions and their performance, as well as the cultures of important elite and other social groups. Examples from survey research come from Almond and Verba (1963), Verba (1987), Alex Inkeles and David Smith (1974a), Ronald Inglehart (1977, 1990), Samuel Barnes and others (1979), and Robert Putnam (1973, 1993). More descriptive-analytical studies of political culture are exemplified in the work of Lucian Pye (1962, 1985, 1988; Pye and Verba, 1965). Our understanding of political participation has been brought to a high level through a series of studies carried on over the last decades by Verba, Ahmed, and Anil Bhatt (1971), Verba and Nie (1972), Verba, Nie, and Kim (1977), Schlozman and Verba (1979), and Schlozman, Verba, and Brady (1995).

In the early decades of the postwar period, Talcott Parsons and others (Parsons, 1951; Parsons and Shils, 1951; Parsons and Smelser, 1956) developed "system" frameworks for the comparison of different types of societies and institutions, drawing on the work of such European sociological theorists as Weber and Durkheim. Drawing on these and other sources, David Easton pioneered in the introduction of the "system" concept into political science (Easton, 1953, 1965, 1990; Almond and Coleman, 1960; Almond and Powell, 1966). While these theoretical frameworks have been questioned as to their utility, and have been criticized for an alleged conservative "equilibrium" bias, these systemic-functional concepts have entered into general usage and into the institutional vocabulary of political science.

Through aggregate statistical methods our understanding of the processes of modernization and democratization (Lerner, 1958; Deutsch, 1961; Lipset, 1959, 1994; Diamond and Plattner, 1993) and governmental performance (see Hibbs, 1978; Cameron, 1978; Alt and Chrystal, 1983) have been vastly improved. Our understanding of interest groups and of "corporatist" phenomena has made significant progress (Schmitter and Lehmbruch, 1979; Berger, 1981; Goldthorpe, 1984); as has our appreciation of the key importance of political parties in the democratic process (Lipset and Rokkan, 1967; Sartori, 1976; Lijphart, 1968, 1984; Powell, 1982).

Theories of representation and of legislative behavior and process have been explored and codified in studies by Wahlke and Eulau (1962, 1978), Hannah Pitkin (1967), and Eulau and Prewitt (1973). Herbert Simon (1950, 1957, 1958), James March (1958, 1965, 1988), and others, beginning from studies of governmental organizations, have created a new interdisciplinary field of organization theory generally applicable to all large-scale organizations, including business corporations. Public policy research, pioneered jointly in Europe and the United States, has taken off in recent decades, and promises the development of a new political economy (see Wildavsky, 1986; Flora and Heidenheimer, 1981; Heidenheimer, Heclo, and Adams, 1990; Castles, 1989).

The theory of democracy has been significantly advanced by the work of Robert Dahl (1956, 1961, 1966, 1970, 1971, 1973, 1982, 1985), Arend Lijphart (1968, 1984), and Giovanni Sartori (1987); and that of democratization has been developed by Linz and Stepan (1978), Diamond and Plattner (1993), Schmitter, O'Donnell, and Whitehead (1986), Samuel Huntington (1991), and others. The lifelong dedication of Robert Dahl to the study of democracy is an example of how normative and empirical political theory may mutually enrich each other (1989).

While I have stressed the growth and spread of empirical, explanatory, and quantitative political science in this essay, there has been "progress" in the older traditions of the discipline as well. The propositions and speculations of the political historians, political philosophers, and legal scholars have been increasingly based on improvements in scholarly methodology—rigorous accumulation of information, and refinements in the logic of analysis and inference. Comparative political history has made important contributions to the theory of the state, political institutions, and public policy (Moore, 1966; Skocpol, 1979, 1984). Refinements in case study methodology have been made by Harry Eckstein (1975) and Alexander George and Andrew Bennett (1997), and these have increased the rigor of historical studies in comparative politics and foreign policy (George and Smoke, 1974; George, 1980; George and McKeown, 1982; George and Simons, 1994). The methodology of comparison has been refined and improved through the work of Almond and Coleman (1960), Almond, Flanagan, and Mundt (1973), Przeworski and Teune (1970), Neil Smelser (1976), Dogan and Pelassy (1990), David Collier (1993), and King, Keohane, and Verba (1993).

With the work of John Rawls (1971), Robert Nozick (1974), Brian Barry (1970), Michael Walzer (1983), James Fishkin (1992), and others, normative political philosophy has made substantial progress, and not entirely without influence from empirical studies. William Galston (1993), in *Political Science: The State of the Discipline,* points out that political philosophy and theory are moving in the direction of increasing reliance on empirical evidence, much of it drawn from the research of political science and the other social science disciplines. Galston urges political theorists to take on the task of codifying the findings of empirical research as they may bear on political philosophy, as Robert Dahl (1956), Dennis Thompson (1970), and James Wilson (1993) have done.

Martin Shapiro's evaluation of the contemporary study of the courts and public law (1993) similarly urges a closer integration of legal studies with institutional and processual political science. Political science without legal analysis is seriously lacking in explanatory power; and legal analysis without the political institutional and processual context is formalistic and sterile. The work of Shapiro and that of a growing band of students of the courts and public law demonstrates the validity of this proposition.

Thus, my account of the history of political science is inclusive of progress made by the earlier traditional subdisciplines, measured by the same criteria. As the scientific revolution of the twentieth century has impinged on the study of politics, the response of the discipline of political science has been multivocal and ambivalent. Some parts of the discipline responded earlier to these challenges; and some parts saw the face of science as lacking in all compassion and empathy, and as a threat to humane scholarship. One ought not overlook the fear of obsolescence generated by the introduction of statistics, mathematics, and diagrammatic virtuosity. But the newer generations cultivating the study of political history, philosophy, and law have overcome these anxieties, discovered the vulnerabilities and shortcomings of the behavioral approach, developed their own arsenal of mystifications, and proven to be quite as competent in the employment of smoke and mirrors as their behavioral brethren.

## Political Science in Europe

While political science had its origins and first growth in the Mediterranean world of antiquity, in medieval Catholic, Renaissance, Reformation, Enlightenment, and nineteenth-century Europe (and indeed in Indian antiquity, and in medieval Islam [Rangavajan, 1987; Rabi, 1967]), this was a matter of individual scholarship, whether in institutional settings as the Greek academies, or in the European universities of the Middle Ages and later. Many early political philosophers and theorists operated as part-time scholars within the framework of the Church, its bureaucracy and orders, supported by kingly and aristocratic patrons, or were themselves aristocrats or persons of wealth. In the nineteenth century with the growth of European universities, scholarship on the state, administration, politics, and public policy was increasingly based in universities. The typical unit of European universities until recently consisted of a single professorial chair held by a single scholar surrounded by lesser docents and assistants. In the postwar decades some of these university chairs have been broadened into departments with a number of professorial billets assigned to different teaching and research specialties.

The *European Journal of Political Research* (Valles and Newton, 1991) devoted an issue to the postwar history of European political science. An introductory essay by the editors argues that the progress of political science in Europe has been associated with democratization for obvious reasons, and with the emergence of the welfare state because an activist, open, penetrative state requires large amounts of information about political processes and political performance. On the question of the impact of U.S. political science on that of Europe, while recognizing that this has been very substantial, they point to the fact that there already was a "behavioral" election study tradition in Europe prior to World War II (Siegfried, 1930; Duverger, 1965) in France (Tingsten, 1963) and Sweden. The great nineteenth- and early-twentieth-century figures in the social sciences who inspired the creative developments in the United States were European, as I have suggested. Richard Rose (1990) points out that while the major development of modern political science took place in the United States after World War II, the founders of U.S. political science—the Woodrow Wilsons, the Frank Goodnows, the Charles Merriams—took their degrees or spent postgraduate years at European universities, principally the German ones. Learning, culture, and professional skill were concentrated in the Old World, and it thinned out as one went west. In the period prior to World War I, American scholars still viewed themselves as provincials. In the interwar years, and in such an innovating center as the University of Chicago, Merriam still urged his most promising students to spend a postgraduate year in Europe, and provided the financial support to do so.

The conquests of Nazism and Fascism and the devastation of World War II disrupted university life in continental Europe for almost a decade. Much of German social science scholarship was effectively transplanted to the United States, where it contributed to the U.S. war effort, and enriched U.S. sociological, psychological and political science teaching and research. There was an entire "exiled" graduate faculty in the New School for Social Research in New York; and hardly a major university was without one or more "exiled" professors in its social science faculties. Scholars such as Paul Lazarsfeld, Kurt Lewin, Wolfgang Kohler, Hans

Speier, Karl Deutsch, Hans Morgenthau, Leo Lowenthal, Leo Strauss, Franz Neumann, Henry Ehrmann, Otto Kircheimer, and Herbert Marcuse made important contributions to the "behavioral" revolution in the United States, as well as to the various trends that attacked it. Hence the political science that was planted in Europe after World War II was in part the product of a political science root-stock that had originally come from Europe.

In the first decades after World War II as the physical plant of Europe was renewed, and its institutions put back in place and staffed, what was new in the social sciences was mostly American in origin. The break from legalism and the historical approach in the study of governmental institutions, political parties and elections, interest groups, public opinion, and communications had been accomplished in U.S. universities and research centers. Along with the Marshall Plan for the shattered European economy, American scholars backed up by American philanthropic foundations were missionaries for the renewal of European scholarship, and for the assimilation of the American empirical and quantitative approaches. Young European scholars supported by Rockefeller and other foundation fellowships visited and attended U.S. universities by the dozens. U.S.-based research programs—the SSRC Committee on Comparative Politics, the University of Michigan election studies, the Inglehart studies of political values—sought out European collaborators, trained them, and often funded them.

This one-sided dependency only lasted for a short period of time. Social science scholarship and traditions were too deeply rooted in European national cultures to have been thoroughly destroyed in the Nazi period. By the 1960s old universities had been reconstituted, and many new ones had been established. European voices were increasingly contributing to the significant research output in the social sciences. The Committee on Political Sociology of the International Sociological Association, though joining American with European efforts, was predominantly European in participation. Its impact in Europe was much like that of the American Committee on Comparative Politics before it. Comparative European studies such as the Smaller European Democracies project, led by Dahl, Lorwin, Daalder, and Rokkan, helped contribute to the development of a European political science professionalism. The Survey Research Center of the University of Michigan began its active role in the development of sophisticated election research in Europe with a study in England in the early 1960s, followed by other European countries. Each such national election study left a cadre of trained professionals to carry on future work in election research.

A European Council on Political Research (ECPR) was founded in 1970 (Rose, 1990) with funds from the Ford Foundation and with an agenda similar to that of the political science committees of the American Social Science Research Council. It provided funds for the establishment of a summer-school training program in social science methodology (located at the University of Essex), workshops held in different national centers concerned with particular research themes, and actual joint research projects. Among the activities it has fostered are a data archive and a professional journal, the *European Journal of Political Research.* Membership in the ECPR is by department and institution. By 1989 the ECPR had 140 department members. By 1985 the *Directory of European Political Scientists* listed just under 2,500 members. The strength of political science in individual European countries is suggested by the number of national departments affiliated with the ECPR. Of the 140 members as of 1989, 40 were in the United Kingdom, 21 in Germany, 11 in Italy, 13 in the Netherlands, and only 5 in France (Rose, 1990, p. 593). The influence of American political science on European and international political science is reflected to some extent by the number of foreign members of the American Political Science Association (APSA), and hence subscribers to the *American Political Science Review.* The United Kingdom, Germany, and Japan each have well over 100 members. Israel, South Korea, and the Netherlands each have around 50 members. Norway, Sweden, and Taiwan have around 30 members, while France has only 27 (APSA, 1994, pp. 327 ff.).

By the 1990s, the profession of political science, along with a common conception of scholarship, was well established globally, being organized in the International Political Science Association, in various national and subnational organizations, as well as in many different functional specializations.

## Opposing Perspectives on Disciplinary History

Those who would disagree with this progressive-eclectic account of the history of political science may be sorted out in four groups. There are those who reject the notion of a progressive political science—from an anti-science perspective (the Straussians), or from a post-science, deconstructive perspective. And there are those who reject the eclecticism of our position—the Marxists and neo-Marxists, who argue that the basic laws of human society have been discovered by Marx and his associates and that these laws show that historical economic, social, and political processes, as well as the human action influencing these processes, are one inseparable unity. Hence the Marxists would reject both the progressiveness and the eclecticism of our approach. The second group rejecting the methodological eclecticism of our approach are the maximalists among the "rational choice" political scientists, whose view of disciplinary history is one that culminates in a parsimonious, reductive, formal-mathematical stage.

## Anti-Science

The Straussian version of the history of political science harks back to the German intellectual polemics of the late nineteenth and early twentieth centuries. As a young German Ph.D. in the immediate post–World War I years, Leo Strauss shared in the general admiration of Max Weber for "his intransigent devotion to intellectual honesty . . . his passionate devotion to the idea of science" (1989, p. 27). On his way north from Freiburg, where he had heard the lectures of Heidegger in 1922, Strauss describes himself as having experienced a Damascan disillusionment with Weber, and a conversion to Heideggerian existentialism. Strauss's mode of coping with the pessimism of the Heidegger view of the nature of "being" was through an affirmative political philosophy seeking the just society and polity through the recovery of the great exemplars of the canon of political philosophy, through dialogue and deliberation, and through the education of a civic elite.

According to Strauss, Weber was the problematic intellectual figure who legitimated modern positivistic social science, its separation of fact and value, its "ethical neutrality," its effort to become "value-free." Strauss attributes to Max Weber the belief that all value conflicts are unsolvable:

> The belief that value judgments are not subject, in the last analysis to rational control, encourages the inclination to make irresponsible assertions regarding right and wrong or good and bad. One evades serious discussion of serious issues by the simple device of passing them off as value problems. [This search for objectivity produces an] emancipation from moral judgments . . . a moral obtuseness. . . . The habit of looking at social or human phenomena without making value judgments has a corroding influence on any preferences. The more serious we are as social scientists, the more completely we develop within ourselves a

state of indifference to any goal, or of aimlessness and drifting, a state which can be called nihilism. [A bit later Strauss qualifies this statement:] Social science positivism fosters not so much nihilism, as conformism and philistinism. (1959, pp. 21 ff.)

This attack on Weber has been extended by Strauss and his followers to the contemporary social sciences, and in particular to the "behavioral" trends in political science, which Weber is said to have inspired. In contrast to this "positivistic," Weberian social science, Strauss presents a model of a "humanistic social science" in which scholarship is intimately and passionately engaged in dialogue with the great political philosophers over the meaning of the central ideas and ideals of politics—justice, freedom, obligation, and the like. The history of the political science timeline that the Straussians offer in the place of the one presented here, characterizes contemporary "behavioral" political science as the product of a heresy that assumed palpable form in the nineteenth century, and was fully formulated in the work of Max Weber at the turn of the century.

Its characterization of Weber as the arch-positivist and separator of fact and value, and of "behavioral political science as pursuing this erroneous course of ethical neutrality," is mistaken with respect both to Max Weber and to most of the contemporary practitioners of so-called behavioral political science. Weber's views of the relation between "fact and value" are much more complex, and involve a deeper concern for value issues, than the caricature contained in the writings of Strauss and his students. I draw attention to two contexts in which Weber deals with these questions—in his lecture "Politics as a Calling," and in his essay "Objectivity in Social Science" (1949, 1958). In the lecture "Politics as a Calling" he refers to two kinds of ethically oriented political action—the ethics of absolute ends, and the ethics of responsibility (*Gesinnungsethik und Verantwortungsethik*). Science would have little to contribute to the ethics of absolute ends, other than examining the adequacy of the relation of means to ends. Since the chosen end is sacred or absolute, there can be no opportunity-cost analysis of the consequences of pursuing this end for other ends. But if one takes a rationally responsible view of the effect of means on ends, scientific analysis makes possible an "opportunity-cost" analysis of political action, that is, how a given choice of policy or action may on the one hand transform the end one is seeking, and on the other hand preclude the choice of other options. "We can in this way," says Weber, "estimate the chances of attaining a certain end by certain available means . . . we can criticise the setting of the end itself as practically meaningful . . . or as meaningless in view of existing conditions" (1949, p. 152). Elaborating his argument about the ways in which means may affect ends in "unintended ways," Weber says:

> [W]e can answer the question: what will the attainment of the desired end "cost" in terms of the predictable loss of other values. Since in the vast majority of cases, every goal that is striven for does "cost" . . . something in this sense, the weighing of the goal in terms of unintended consequences cannot be omitted from the deliberation of persons who act with a sense of responsibility. [Science can make one] realize that all action and naturally . . . inaction, imply in their consequences the espousal of certain values, and . . . what is so frequently overlooked, the rejection of certain others. (1958, p. 152)

But in addition to this twofold means-end analysis, Weber points out that science can enable us to clarify our goals, comprehend their meaning: "We do this through making explicit and developing in a logically consistent manner the 'ideas' which . . . underlie the concrete end. It is self evident that one of the most important tasks of every science of cultural life is to arrive at a rational understanding of these 'ideas' for which men . . . struggle" (1958, p. 152). Weber goes on:

> [T]he scientific treatment of value judgments may not only understand and empathically analyze the desired ends and the ideals which underlie them; it also can judge them critically [according to their internal consistency]. The elevation of these ultimate standards . . . to the level of explicitness is the utmost that the scientific treatment of value judgments can do without entering into the realm of speculation. . . . An empirical science cannot tell anyone what he *should do* but rather what he *can* do—and under certain circumstances—what he *wishes* to do. (1958, p. 152)

The reality of the Weberian fact-value formulation is as far from the Straussian caricature as is its depiction of the state of contemporary empirical political science. I therefore reject the view of the history of the discipline implied in the Straussian perspective. On the other hand, I would include much of the substantive work done by these political theorists, and that of Strauss himself, in the work that I include in the progressive-eclectic account given here, to the extent that it has increased the body of logically drawn inferences about politics from reliable accumulations of evidence.

*Post-Science, Post-Behavioralism*

Among contemporary political scientists, there is a prevailing, perhaps dominant view of the history of the discipline, that we are now in a "post-positivist, post-scientific, post-behavioral" stage. Arlene Saxonhouse speaks of the "demise of positivism and the demands for verification as the only philosophic stance for the human sciences, with the rejuvenation of normative discourse in a society concerned with the dangers of an unleashed science. . . . [P]olitical scientists in general and political theorists in particular are no longer willing to adopt uncritically the distinction of fact and value that controlled the social sciences for several generations" (1993, p. 9).

A small subdiscipline in political science specializing in the "history of political science" pursues this theme. David Ricci, in a book called *The Tragedy of Political Science* (1984), argues that the naive belief in political "science" that had emerged in U.S. political science in the 1920s–1960s had been thoroughly discredited in the disorders of the 1960s and 1970s. He concludes that political science as empirical science without the systematic inclusion of moral and ethical values and alternatives, and a commitment to political action, is doomed to disillusion. Political science has to choose sides or become a "precious" and irrelevant field of study. Even more sharply, Raymond Seidelman rejects political science professionalism. Modern political science must bridge this separation of knowledge and action "if [these professional] delusions are to be transformed into new democratic realities" (1985, p. 241).

There has been a substantial exchange of ideas about the "identity" and history of political science in the decade bounded by the two editions of Ada Finifter's *Political Science: State of the Discipline* (1983, 1993). In the first edition, John Gunnell presents a picture of the history of political science marked by a "scientistic" revolution in the half century from the 1920s until the 1970s, followed by a "post-empiricist" period continuing into the present (1983, pp. 12 ff.). In the second edition, Arlene Saxonhouse makes the comments about the "demise of behavioralism" that I quoted above. In the interval between these two volumes there has been a further exchange of views in the *American Political Science Review* among a number of historians of political science. In an article appearing in the December 1988 issue titled "History and Discipline in Political Science," John Dryzek and Stephen Leonard conclude that "there is no neutral stance for evaluating, accepting, or rejecting disciplinary identities. Rather, standards can only emerge in the conflicts and debates within and between traditions of inquiry. It is in this conflict and debate that the relationship between disciplinary history and identity crystallizes. . . . [P]lurality is going to be the essence of, rather than an obstacle to, the progress of political science" (p. 1256). The view expressed here is that there will be as many disciplinary histories as there are "disciplinary identities" and that there is no "neutral" way of choosing among them.

A flurry of responses to this pluralist approach to the history of political science appeared in the June 1990 issue of the *Review,* under the general title "Can Political Science History Be Neutral?" with contributions from Raymond Farr, John Gunnell, and Raymond Seidelman, and a reply by Dryzek and Leonard. All three of the respondents support the "pluralist" view of disciplinary history expressed by Dryzek and Leonard, with some qualifications. In two collections of articles and papers treating the history of political science, Raymond Farr and his associates codify this pluralist perspective (Farr and Seidelman, 1993; Farr, Dryzek, and Leonard, 1995).

We have to conclude from these exchanges that there is a consensus of *expressed* opinion that while each one of the major competing schools of political science history—the so-called behavioral or political "science" perspective, the anti- and post-science perspectives, and the Marxist and rational choice ones—makes claim to being the valid approach to disciplinary history, there is no way of arbitrating among these claims. The treatment offered here of a progressive-eclectic history is rejected by this apparent consensus. My account of the growth of political knowledge, defined as the capacity to draw sound logical inferences from an increasing body of reliable evidence, would only be one of several accounts no one of which would have any special claim to validity.

## Integralism and Maximalism: Anti-Pluralism

### *Theory and Praxis*

There are several schools that would challenge the approach to the history of political science as the progress of "objective" scholarship, on the grounds that objectivity is both impossible to achieve, and if sought leads to "scientism" and the embrace of the status quo. From this point of view even the search for professional objectivity is to be eschewed. One has to choose political sides, and self-consciously employ scholarship in the service of good political goals. For the various neo-Marxist schools this meant hooking scholarship up to socialism.

In the history of Marxist scholarship there was a point at which one branch of this tradition rejected this dialectical view of scholarship. Karl Mannheim, in *Ideology and Utopia* (1949), concluded that objectivity in political science was possible: "The question, whether a science of politics is possible and whether it can be taught, must if we summarize all that we have said thus far, be answered in the affirmative." He attributes to Max Weber the demonstration that objective social science scholarship is possible (p. 146). But while objectivity becomes possible for Mannheim, this capacity is only likely to be developed "by a relatively classless stratum which is not too firmly situated in the social order. . . . This unanchored, relatively classless stratum is, to use Alfred Weber's terminology, the 'socially unattached intelligentsia'" (p. 171). For contemporary political science scholarship, "professionalism" has taken the place of Mannheim's "unattached intelligentsia" as the guarantor of the obligation of the search for objectivity—professionalism in the sense of affiliation to professional associations, peer accreditation and reviewing of recruitment and scholarship, and the like. At the time that Weber and Mannheim were presenting these ideas, professional associations in the social sciences and particularly in political science and sociology were in their infancy. And it is of interest that it is precisely this notion of the search for objectivity through professionalism that continues to be the target of both contemporary neo-Marxist and other "left" critics.

This polemic against "ethical neutrality" and the "search for objectivity" has been carried on from a number of perspectives. The "Frankfurt school" out of which "critical theory" emerged, inspired by the Marxist theorist Georg Lukacz, and led by Max Horkeimer, Theodor Adorno, Herbert Marcuse, and currently by Jurgen Habermas, view the conduct of political inquiry as an aspect "of a total situation caught up in the process of social change. . . . Positivists fail to comprehend that the process of knowing cannot be severed from the historical struggle between humans and the world" (Held, 1980, pp. 162 ff.). Theory and theoretical labor are intertwined in social life processes. The theorist cannot remain detached, passively contemplating, reflecting, and describing "society" or "nature." A formulation by Habermas (1992, pp. 439 ff.) reaffirms this unity of theory and "praxis" perspective. The influence of this point of view was reflected in the deep penetration of views such as these into Latin American, African, and other area studies under the name of "dependency theory" during the 1970s and 1980s (Packenham, 1992).

How may we treat Marxist and neo-Marxist scholarship in this progressive-eclectic account of the history of political science? These literatures are very substantial indeed, running into the many hundreds of volumes, and learned articles in very large numbers. Exemplary of the very important place some of this work must have in the history of political science are the important empirically based studies of class and politics that were largely the product of Marxist and neo-Marxist scholarship (Hill, 1982; Hilton, 1990; Thompson, 1963). Nevertheless, while Marxism directed attention to the explanatory power of economic development and social structure, it also diverted scholarly attention away from other important explanatory variables such as political institutions, religion, ethnicity, the international setting, individual leadership, contingency, and chance. Its conception of economic development was oversimplified and primitive. As the modern economy produced an increasingly diversified and internationalized labor force, the capacity of Marxist scholarship to perceive and properly weight economic, social, and political variables attenuated. Thus while these various Marxist schools greatly increased the quantity and kind of evidence available to historical and social science scholarship, their inferential logic was seriously faulty and not properly open to falsification. Eric Hobsbawm (1962, 1987, 1994) and other Marxist historians (Hill, 1982; Hilton, 1990; Thompson, 1963) make a great contribution to the historical scholarship on the nineteenth and earlier centuries, but have difficulties in their efforts to interpret and explain the twentieth (Judt, 1995).

## Scientific Maximalism: The Rational Choice Approach

The rational choice approach, variously called "formal theory," "positive theory," "public choice theory," and "collective choice theory," is predominantly a lateral entry into political science from economics. While economic metaphors had been used by political scientists such as Pendleton Herring, V. O. Key Jr., and Elmer Schattschneider (Almond, 1980, pp. 32 ff.), it was the economists Kenneth Arrow (1951), Anthony Downs (1957), Duncan Black (1958), James Buchanan and Gordon Tullock (1962), and Mancur Olson (1965) who first applied economic models and methods in the analysis of such political themes as elections, voting in committees and legislative bodies, interest group theory, and the like. In the 1993 edition of *Political Science: The State of the Discipline,* the chapter dealing with "formal rational choice theory" describes this approach as promising "a cumulative science of politics." Its coauthors claim that "rational choice theory has fundamentally changed how the discipline ought to proceed in studying politics and training students" (Lalman, Oppenheimer, and Swistak, 1993).

This approach holds out the prospect of a unified, cumulative, political science theory, part of a unified, formal social science theory, based on common axioms or assumptions derived essentially from economics. These assumptions are that human beings are rational, primarily short-term, material self-interest maximizers. Its advocates argue that from such premises it is possible to derive hypotheses regarding any sphere of human activity—from decisions about what to buy and how much to pay for it, or whom to vote for, to decisions about whom to marry, how many children to have, how political parties should negotiate and form coalitions, how nations should negotiate and form alliances, and the like. The theory is parsimonious, logically consistent, mathematical, and prefers experimental methods to observational and inductive ones for the testing of hypotheses.

This is the maximal, aspirational version of the approach, encountered in the Lalman, Oppenheimer, Swistak contribution to the *State of the Discipline* volume cited above, in Peter Ordeshook's "The Emerging Discipline of Political Economy" (1990), in William Riker's "Political Science and Rational Choice" (1990), in Mancur Olson's "Toward a Unified View of Economics and the Other Social Sciences" (1990), as well as in other writers in this genre. This approach argues a discontinuity in the history of political science, in which everything that went before had to be viewed as prescientific. Its vision of the future of the discipline is of a cumulating body of formal theory, internally logical and consistent, capable of explaining political reality with a relatively small number of axioms and propositions.

Some very eminent writers in this movement do not share in these maximal expectations. On such a question as the content of utility, some economists reject the model of Economic Man as the rational, material self-interest maximizer. Milton Friedman (1953) long ago took the position that it made no difference whether this assumption was correct or incorrect; just as long as it produced valid predictions. Just as long as it proved relevant at all, it could serve a heuristic function in testing the usefulness of different versions of utility. It is interesting that one of the pioneers of rational choice political theory, Anthony Downs, has long since moved away from Political Man modeled on Economic Man, and is engaged in a major work on social values and democracy that assumes the importance of political institutions in shaping political choices, and the importance of the political socialization of elites and citizens in the utilization and improvement of political institutions (1991). Having lost contact with institutions through the reductionist strategy followed by this movement, now most of its practitioners are in search of institutions.

Robert Bates, a pioneer in the application of rational choice theory in the study of developing countries, now favors an eclectic approach to political analysis: "Anyone working in other cultures knows that people's beliefs and values matter, so too do the distinctive characteristics of their institutions." Bates wants to combine the political economy approach with the study of cultures, social structures, and institutions: "A major attraction of the theories of choice and human interaction, which lie at the core of contemporary political economy, is that they offer the tools for causally linking values and structures to their social consequences" (1988).

This less heroic version of rational choice theory is quite continuous with so-called behavioral political science. And it is so viewed in this version of the history of political science. Its formal deductive approach to generating hypotheses has distinct uses, but it is not inherently superior to the process of deriving hypotheses from deep empirical knowledge, as some of its devotees claim. Donald Green and Ian Shapiro argue that "formalism is no panacea for the ills of social science. Indeed, formal exposition does not even guarantee clear thinking. Formally rigorous theories can be inexact and ambiguous if their empirical referents are not well specified. Formalization, moreover, cannot be an end in itself; however analytically tight and parsimonious a theory might be, its scientific value depends on how well it explains the relevant data" (1994, p. 10).

In a major critique of the empirical literature produced by the rational choice approach, Green and Shapiro conclude that

> exceedingly little has been learned. Part of the difficulty stems from the sheer paucity of empirical applications: proponents of rational choice seem to be most interested in theory elaboration, leaving for later, or others, the messy business of empirical testing. On our reading, empirical failure is also importantly rooted in the aspiration of rational choice theorists to come up with universal theories of politics. As a consequence of this aspiration, we contend, the bulk of rational-choice-inspired empirical work is marred by methodological defects. (1994, p. 10)

To escape from this sterility, Green and Shapiro advise rational choice theorists to resist the theory-saving impulses that result in method driven research. More fruitful than asking "How might a rational choice theory explain X?" would be the problem driven question: "What explains X?" This will naturally lead to inquiries about the relative importance of a host of possible explanatory variables. No doubt strategic calculation will be one, but there will typically be many others, ranging from traditions of behavior, norms, and cultures to differences in peoples' capacities and the contingencies of historical circumstance. The urge to run from this complexity rather than build explanatory models that take it into account should be resisted, even if this means scaling down the range of application. Our recommendation is not for empirical work instead of theory; it is for theorists to get closer to the data so as to theorize in empirically pertinent ways. (1994, p. 10)

John Ferejohn and Debra Satz, responding to the Green-Shapiro critique, tell us that "The aspiration to unity and the quest for universalistic explanations have spurred progress in every science. By ruling out universalism on philosophical grounds, Green and Shapiro surrender the explanatory aspirations of social science. Such a surrender is both premature and self-defeating" (1995, p. 83). On the other hand, a member of the more moderate, eclectic camp of the rational choice school, Morris Fiorina, in answer to the Green-Shapiro critique, minimizes the extent of universalism and reductionism in the rational choice community. He acknowledges, "Certainly, one can cite rational choice scholars who write ambitiously—if not grandiosely—about constructing unified theories of political behavior" (1995, p. 87). But these, according to Fiorina, are a small minority. And in making extravagant claims, rational choicers are no different in their overselling from the functionalists, systems theorists, and other innovators in the social sciences and other branches of scholarship.

The polemic regarding the larger aspirations of the rational choice approach leads us to subsume its accomplishments under our progressive-eclectic view of disciplinary progress, rejecting its maximal claims and view of political science, and recognizing its positive contribution of a formal deductive approach to the arsenal of methodologies, hard and soft, that are available to us in our efforts to interpret and explain the world of politics. The movement to penetrate political science, laterally so to speak, without in many cases acquiring knowledge of the substantive fields they propose to transform, has led inevitably to a method-dominated strategy, and an illustrative record of accomplishment, rather than a problem-focused strategy in which formal, deductive methods find their appropriate place.

## Conclusion

The recent historians of political science, cited above, ask us to adopt a *pluralist* view of political science. The *methodenstreit*—the methodological war—of the 1970s and 1980s, they tell us, has ended in a stalemate. The idea of a continuous discipline oriented around a shared sense of identity has been rejected. There are as many histories of political science, they say, as many distinct senses of identity, as there are distinct approaches in the discipline. And the relations among these distinct approaches are isolative. There is no shared scholarly ground. We are now, and presumably into the indefinite future, according to these writers, in a post-behavioral, post-positivist age, a discipline divided, condemned to sit at separate tables.

What I propose in this essay on the history of political science is a view based on a search of the literature from the ancients until the present day, demonstrating a unity of substance and method, and cumulative in the sense of an increasing knowledge base and improvements in inferential rigor. There is pluralism in method and approach, but there is only one scholarship, distinctive from other forms of intellectual activity by its commitment to rules of evidence and inference.

# 3

# Charles Edward Merriam

CHARLES EDWARD MERRIAM (1874–1953) was the founder and leader of the "Chicago school" of political science. He was an active member of the University of Chicago faculty for almost half a century. He began his career as a "docent," then the lowest faculty rank at the University of Chicago, in the academic year 1900–1901, and retired from active service as the Morton Dennison Hull Distinguished Service Professor of Political Science in 1940. He continued to occupy his office in retirement, offer seminars, and meet students for the better part of the 1940s.

He was born in the small town of Hopkinton, Iowa, the second son of a storekeeper of New England Scottish Presbyterian background. He was educated in the local Lenox Academy and the University of Iowa. Beginning with an interest in a career of law and politics, he shifted to the discipline of government, then just in process of separating from history in U.S. universities. He took his Ph.D. at Columbia, with a year in Germany at the University of Berlin, studying the Staatswissenschaften. At Columbia he studied public law and political theory. He was a young graduate student at the time of the Seth Low reform campaign against Tammany Hall in 1897. Seth Low was then president of Columbia University, and a large part of the

Reprinted, with minor revisions, from *Remembering the University of Chicago: Teachers, Scientists, and Scholars,* edited by Edward Shils (Chicago: University of Chicago Press, 1991). Copyright 1991 by the University of Chicago. All rights reserved.

student body entered the campaign, including Merriam, who gave campaign speeches from the back of a wagon. He brought to his University of Chicago career this mix of influences and experiences—a boyhood in post–Civil War, small-town, middle-western America; an exposure to Scottish Covenanter Presbyterianism particularly through his mother; an encounter with Tammany Hall and the urban reform movement; and Germanic scholarship (Karl, 1974, chaps. 1–2).

He inspired and edified many generations of undergraduates by his example of combining teaching and doing (Karl, 1974, chap. 4), and he sent several dozens of Ph.D.'s to the faculties of other major universities. The political science department, which he shaped in the 1920s and 1930s, largely from his own ideas and experiences, and which he staffed with his own graduate students, significantly shaped the model of modern political science in the United States, spreading to Europe post World War II, and to China and the Soviet Union (Karl, 1974, chap. 8).

As the leading figure in the founding of the Social Science Research Council, and as the chairman of its board of directors in its early years, he made an important contribution to the modernization of the social sciences (Karl, 1974, chap. 7). It was this organization that spread the culture of rigorous empirical research to the various social science disciplines, and to the centers of higher education both here and abroad.

As a young man teaching municipal government at the university, and serving as Alderman of the Fifth Ward, he fought for civic reform and for the professionalization of municipal government. He left a lasting legacy here in the establishment of professional associations of local government officials, located in the "1313" building on the university campus. As his reputation grew, he played a similar role at the national level, serving on such bodies as Hoover's Commission on Recent Social Trends, and Roosevelt's Committee on Administrative Management, and the National Resources Planning Board, agencies that were concerned with bringing modern science and knowledge to bear on social policy, and with the development of honest and effective management practice. The unifying theme of his professional career was the development of the sciences of politics and society in the service of democracy and the public welfare (Karl, 1974, chap. 12).

He was a politician and statesman in both academic and public life in the very best sense of those terms. Though he spent much time first in city hall in Chicago, and later at meetings of the Social Science Research Council, foundations, and various commissions in New York, Washington, D.C., and elsewhere on the East Coast, he was always available to students, and maintained an intimate and active university and departmental life. By the time I came to know Merriam, first in 1930 as an undergraduate member of one of his seminars in political theory, he had already passed the scholarly "point of no return," though he cherished the belief throughout his career that he would return to creative scholarship in his later years. He suffered the fate of multiply-talented persons. His students could implement his dreams and designs of creative scholarship. But once he and others became aware of his gifts in human relations especially with the rich and the powerful, and his imagination and energy as a builder of institutions, he was drawn away from scholarship and toward these essentially political roles—evangelist of political and social science, coalition builder in the university and in the national life of the social science disciplines; and reformist, progressive, and liberal ideologist and coalition builder in local and in national politics (Karl, 1970).

He was active in the "Bull Moose" wing of the Republican Party, in the short-lived interlude of the Progressive Party, and he became one of the intellectual stalwarts of the New Deal. For a brief period during his mayoral campaign in 1911, people thought of him in presidential terms, as the "Woodrow Wilson of the West." The frequency and length of his long-distance telephone calls waxed and waned as election days neared and receded. During Prohibition years he kept two bottles of Johnny Walker Black Label in a filing cabinet to toast an influential visitor, or a successful colleague.

The idea of the scholar in politics ran into conflict with trends toward graduate training and professionalization in U.S. universities at the turn of the century. Merriam's department chairman and then president of the university, Henry Pratt Judson, actively opposed Merriam's ventures into politics. Merriam had been hired on the basis of his early work on the history of political theory as reflected in his doctoral dissertation on theories of sovereignty, and in his early book on the history of American political theory. There was the promise of productivity and originality in these early studies.

The first book in the empirical "behavioral" type of political science that he began to foster in the 1920s was a study of "nonvoting" in Chicago, based upon a large-scale survey that included some 6,000 respondents. It was a departmental venture employing graduate students as interviewers. It was coauthored with Harold Gosnell, and the first chapter, which dealt with survey and sampling methods, and questionnaire construction, was written by Merriam. Harold Lasswell's studies of communication and propaganda and political psychology were foreshadowed by

Merriam's wartime service in directing the U.S. information program in Italy, and by Merriam's fascination with the phenomena of leadership.

The Merriam whom I encountered from 1933 to 1938 as a graduate student in the department was surrounded by his former students—then assistant and associate professors. These included Lasswell, Gosnell, Frederick Schuman, and Carroll Wooddy. Closer to being peers were Leonard White and Quincy Wright, the first a specialist on public administration, and the second a specialist on international relations. But Merriam had no real peers in the department. His friends and colleagues referred to him affectionately but respectfully as the "chief."

The department was patriarchal in structure. Merriam served on many dissertation committees, but the actual detailed supervision was done by Lasswell, Gosnell, White, and others. Merriam would approve the topic, and have some general idea of the drift of the project. There was an initiation rite after one's dissertation orals, when Merriam would invite the neophyte to have a drink at the Shoreland Bar. I recall a long walk with the "chief" in the hot sun of the late spring, up Fifty-ninth Street to Lake Shore Drive, and along the drive to the then stylish Shoreland Hotel with its beautiful view of the lakefront. It had the only air-conditioned bar in Hyde Park. I still have a letter that he sent me in 1939, a few months after I received my degree, addressed for the first time to "My Dear Doctor Gay."

He prided himself on being a good judge of people. His patronage was extensive. He touched the lives of many, if not most, of the scholars who became prominent in the social sciences in the 1920s to the 1950s. Within our own department he was curious about everybody and treasured little bits of information that he could use to tease us. When I first presented him with the plans for my doctoral dissertation on the elites of New York City, he smiled and said, "The desert is full of bones." He went to many weddings, including mine. It pleased him to be instrumental in helping the children of immigrants to mainstream careers, and he shared in the joy of parents. He was sensitive to the pain of immigrant parents as their children assimilated in an alien culture. He urged us to be our brothers' keepers. If we were successful we were reminded that "so-and-so" had a writer's block or other troubles and needed help. As I left the university in 1939, he gave me such an assignment, and reminded me of it intermittently over the years.

He was a man who combined courage and prudence. He turned the notion of political prudence into a political science concept. It came out of the historical experience of the populist and progressive movements in which he had participated, which had minimized the importance of political institutions as parties, and such governmental arrangements as separation of powers. The notion of political prudence to Merriam was very much like Max Weber's "ethics of responsibility," the idea that politicians had to assume responsibility for the consequences of the causes and goals they advocated, whether these consequences were intended or not. The social sciences, and political science in particular, had the job of anticipating the consequences of different political structures, political decisions, and public policies.

As to his courage, it was Merriam who went to the home of W. I. Thomas, a sociology colleague and author of the *Polish Peasant in Europe and America,* when he was in disgrace because of a sexual scandal, and took him by the arm to the Quadrangle Club to reunite him with his friends. And it was Merriam who defended his young colleague Frederick Schuman and others accused of subversion in the mid-1930s. It was he along with others who prevailed on the drugstore millionaire Charles R. Walgreen, who had been hounding the university for harboring left-wingers, to fund a lectureship on U.S. institutions instead.

Merriam was a tall man with a shambling walk. He spoke with something of a nasal twang, a bit out of the side of his mouth. He enjoyed recalling childhood experiences with another colleague, Louis Brownlow, who also had a midwestern, small-town background, even imitating the accents and repeating the homilies to which they had been exposed. He used to walk up the stairs, scorning the elevator, to his third-floor office. He had a private office, with his personal library and an old typewriter on which he typed his manuscripts. He did a lot of writing during the summers, and used to come to his office to work in the cool of the early morning. V. O. Key Jr., who occupied the office next to him, was an even earlier riser, and had done a day's work before nine or ten o'clock. There was an office for the departmental secretary, another office for a research associate, occupied at different times by such honored figures (to the younger graduate students) as V. O. Key Jr., Herman Pritchett, and Albert Lepawsky. He had in addition a large office occupied by three or four younger research assistants who, while working on their dissertations, might be employed part-time in research for the Recent Social Trends study, the Committee on Administrative Management, or the National Resources Planning Board. He would come out of his office at odd moments, to banter with his students, pass on a political confidence, or tell a story. He had periods of self-doubt and melancholy when he was especially needy of affection and response.

He ran an evening advanced seminar where we read our chapters as we worked on our dissertations, and where Merriam would occasionally read or discuss projects on which he was engaged. In whimsical and melancholy moments, he presented his thoughts and moods as though authored by his dog, Carlo. Carlo was the name of a pet dog of Merriam's early boyhood who had to be left in Hopkinton when the family tried living in California for a few years in the 1880s. The legend was that the dog languished and died of loneliness. Carlo seemed to have become a vehicle for Merriam's fantasies and regrets.

The local stage on which Merriam performed was the Social Science Research Building facing the Midway on Fifty-ninth Street and University Avenue. It was built around the same time that the social sciences were acquiring a national identity through the formation of the Social Science Research Council. Merriam had been largely responsible for soliciting the gift from the Laura Spelman Rockefeller Fund for the construction of this first building on a university campus solely devoted to the social sciences.

A younger colleague in sociology, William Fielding Ogburn, chaired a committee to decide upon the appropriate symbolism—iconography, mottoes, and quotations. Recommendations were solicited from all the social science departments. There was a battle over this symbolism reflecting differences in social science philosophy among the departments and scholars in the social sciences. The most popular motto for the lintel over the entrance was Aristotle's "Anthropos Zoon Politikon" (man is a political animal), but Ogburn, a strongly statistical brand of sociologist, preferred a quotation from the British physicist Lord Kelvin: "When you cannot measure, your knowledge is meagre and unsatisfactory." Such a strong identification with quantification was foreign to Merriam's view of the social sciences. He was abroad at the time these decisions were being made, and the chairman of the committee on symbolism won the day. Merriam's wrath on his return when he found the Kelvin motto carved in stone was unavailing, as anyone passing the front of the building can witness.

This five-floor building, gothic in style and appurtenances, housed the departments of anthropology, economics, political science, sociology, and parts of social service administration, education, philosophy, and psychology most closely associated with the social sciences. There was a lecture hall on the first floor (where recorded classical music was played during the noon hour), seminar and class rooms, and a statistical laboratory presided over by Ogburn on the fifth floor.

It was an intimate setting. In the course of a graduate career spanning four or five years, one would encounter all the faculty at one time or another in the halls, on the stairs, in the elevator, or in a large seminar room on the second floor where tea and cookies were served every afternoon at four o'clock. Graduate students in political science shared offices and mingled with sociology, anthropology, and economics students. The building suited and fostered the interdisciplinary culture that Merriam cherished.

The productivity of the department accelerated from the early years of Merriam's chairmanship to the final ones. The first half of the 1920s was the period of the pioneers identified with the quantitative voting turnout studies of Harold Gosnell, the psychoanalytic and sociological studies of Harold Lasswell, Frederick Schuman's innovative work in international relations, and the studies of attitudes toward public employment of L. D. White. The more visible leaders of the second generation were V. O. Key Jr., at work in the early 1930s on the techniques of "graft" in U.S. politics; Herman Pritchett, who made an early field study of the organization and politics of the Tennessee Valley Authority; and Albert Lepawsky, who led a cohort of graduate students in studies of the politics of the metropolitan region of Chicago, with Lepawsky specializing on the judicial system of the region.

Among the Ph.D.'s of the later 1930s were Victor Jones and John Vieg, who were at work on the government of the metropolitan region of Chicago, and the mode of governance of its educational system; William T. R. Fox, who was associated with Quincy Wright in his studies of war; and David Truman and Avery Leiserson, later important contributors to the theory of political parties and pressure groups, whose dissertations were supervised by L. D. White. Leo Rosten did his celebrated study of the Washington, D.C., press corps under Merriam's and Lasswell's supervision in these years. The later Nobel laureate Herbert Simon came in at the end of this cohort, and was already pioneering in the measurement of administrative performance in the late 1930s. My own work in the early and middle 1930s dealt with the politics of the unemployed during the depression, which I did in association with Harold Lasswell, and with the social and political characteristics of the business elites in New York City, which I did under the supervision of Gosnell and Lasswell.

The "myth" of the Chicago school has somewhat exaggerated its innovativeness. Some of the dissertations that were done during these decades were rather conventional descriptive studies of governmental institutions, political processes, and political ideas. But for just about every one of the graduate students of that time, the boundaries of the discipline of political science had been broadened and deepened. We were aware that we were members of an innovative department, and most had feelings of pride in breaking new ground, and entertaining unconventional insights into the explanation of political behavior. Early anxieties that the University of Chicago label would not fare well in the political science job market because of this reputation for innovation were quickly allayed after the war years, when a University of Chicago degree acquired a special cachet.

During its best years it was a harmonious department, and this could be attributed to the personality and management style of Merriam. The department encouraged risk, rewarded merit, eschewed stuffiness, and mocked a bit at conventionality. Envy and malice, not unusual in academic settings, were mitigated by Merriam's combination of generosity and optimism (White, 1942).

Merriam's political science department did not survive his retirement. Even before that event, Lasswell, Gosnell, and Schuman had left for other universities or government service. The department that emerged in the 1940s and 1950s was sharply divided between a humanist wing led by the refugee political philosopher Leo Strauss, and survivors of the Merriam department. It is ironic that just as Merriam's type of political science was waning at the University of Chicago, it was becoming the cutting edge of the discipline nationally. What was missed at the University of Chicago (even as the first atomic pile was being tested in Stagg Field) was that the post–World War II decades were to become the era of "big science," and that the social sciences and political science would not escape the powerful draft of the great discoveries and developments in physics and biology. What Merriam had pioneered in the 1920s and 1930s—the idea of research as having an equal, or greater, claim on the university with teaching, securely funded team research and research programs, reductionist strategies in research designs, and quantification—rapidly became the dominant model to emulate at leading universities. Though Merriam never referred to his type of political science as "behavioral" political science, and actually would have been uncomfortable with the term, it was under this name that the Chicago school diffused in the post–World War II period to other major universities.

The Chicago school is generally acknowledged to have been the founding influence in the history of modern political science, and Charles E. Merriam is generally recognized as the founder and shaper of the Chicago school. Hence there may be a point in elaborating a bit on the kind of "science" Merriam thought he was fostering back in the early 1920s when he began to prophesy and exhort. I draw on Merriam's 1925 book *New Aspects of Politics,* and on the second and third editions, published in 1931 and 1970, which contained other writings from this early period and later.

He spoke and wrote in the rhetoric and logic of prophecy. But though he was a prophet, he was not of the desert breed, not an ascetic. As a major entrepreneur of social science funding, and one of the inventors of the weekend conference, he appreciated worldly enjoyments. Like the prophets he attacked his complacent colleagues for cultivating the forms rather than the spirit of their calling. He exhorted them to live up to their enlightenment obligations, spelled out the rewards of virtue, and specified the professional way of life leading to these rewards.

The false prophets were scholars like Harold Laski and Charles Beard, who ridiculed Merriam's emphasis on political psychology, organized research, and quantification. In his manifesto of the early 1920s, he wrote:

> I am not unmindful of the significance of the study of the history of human experience; nor, trained in public law, am I unmindful of the value of the juristic approach to the problems of political theory and practice. . . . In suggesting that politics sit around the table with psychology and statistics and biology and geography, I am not suggesting that we ask our older friends to go. Only this: politics must follow its problem wherever the problem leads. (1970, p. 57)

Merriam was a believer in the "enlightenment" and "progress." Science was to be the instrument of professional progress. Political science was to move beyond its historical, legal, and philosophical methods, cultivated by individual scholars in their libraries, and become a more powerful explanatory discipline, drawing on the other sciences—social, natural, mathematical. These emerging sciences of politics and society would lead to a new "political prudence" that would make possible "the conscious control of human evolution toward which intelligence steadily moves in every domain of human life" (1970, p. 60).

He saw these transformations of political science as in continuity with the tradition of the discipline. He offered the solace to the political theorists and the more conservative political scientists of his generation, of a new political theory. He wrote in 1931:

> It may reasonably be expected that a new synthetic philosophy will emerge, fusing the material now found scattered throughout the natural

sciences, the social sciences, the humanities, into a new interpretation with perhaps a new logic. But "science" will be inside, not outside, this new philosophy when it appears. . . . [H]ere the adventurous political theorist may find full sweep for his analytic and synthetic faculties weaving together the new data developed by modern research. (1931, p. 41)

Merriam's view of the contributions that the other sciences would make to political science recognized the dangers of reductionism. The logic of his prophecy began with the argument that political theorists had always been concerned with the effects of psychological, sociological, economic, biological, and geographic variables on the characteristics of states, statesmen, and citizens. Given these concerns in the traditions of political science, it was really not much to suggest that as our knowledge increased, political science would replace its primitive and intuitive psychology, sociology, anthropology, biology, and the like, with more reliable insights resulting from their more recent scientific achievements. He specified the various aspects of political science that might be illuminated and hardened by the introduction of this knowledge. At the end of each such analysis he confronted the danger that political scientists going deeply into the various social sciences might become lost, tending to reduce political phenomena to the terms of the contributing sciences. He answered this fear by arguing, "better be lost for a while in order to return to the discipline and enrich it" (1970, pp. 182 ff., 218 ff.).

Merriam was especially positive about the possible contributions of psychology to the new political science. But he did not view psychology as the primary science and politics the secondary one. "What we are really striving to achieve," he wrote in 1924, "is neither psychology nor psychiatry as such, nor biology as such, nor history as such, nor economics as such, but the development of scientific method in the observation, measurement, and comparison of political relations" (1970, p. 183). Psychology held out special promise for Merriam.

In counseling colleagues and graduate students to take risks in their research, he openly acknowledged the possibility of having to take a few casualties: "It may be said that the lines of inquiry suggested are not appropriate for political scientists, because they carry us out of our accustomed territory, and we may be lost in the desert. . . . [A] certain number of explorers must always be lost, especially if they advance too far or too fast" (1970, p. 182).

In his treatment of quantification, Merriam makes the point that modern statistics had its origins in the study of affairs of state, so that the complaints of some of his contemporaries at his urging that political science move in quantitative directions, were really quite inappropriate. He spoke of the census as a revolutionary invention making possible a surer grasp of social structure, social change, and of the performance of government. Acquiring skills in quantification forced social scientists and political scientists to relate their conceptualizations to the real phenomena to which they were supposed to refer. He understood the importance of "operationalization," though he never used the word. He saw in the development of correlational analysis the possibility of generating testable theories of the relationship between various social properties such as sex and economic status, and political opinion and voting behavior. He took great pride in what must be the first modern behavioral studies in political science—the "nonvoting" studies of Harold Gosnell (Merriam and Gosnell, 1924), and the "prestige value of public employment" studies of Leonard White (1929) (and Lasswell's trail-breaking clinical case studies in *Psychopathology and Politics* [1930]). He particularly relished the experimental aspects of the Gosnell study, and the depth psychological ventures of Lasswell.

In his argument for the self-evident character of the importance of quantification in the study of politics, he pointed to such measurable phenomena as the vote, the legislative roll call, judicial decisions, various aspects of the administrative process, the military services, and the educational system as

> teeming with definite facts susceptible of relationship to other sets of social facts. In the case of public institutions, experiment may be carried out and situations varied for the purpose of determining the effect of the various factors in behavior. No richer material is found than in the domain of political operations. Furthermore when the minute study of political operations and traits is begun, the number of feasible statistical relationships is of course very largely increased. (1970, p. 214)

Merriam confronted those colleagues concerned that political science might be lost in number crunching with the answer: "Possibly so. It may well be that politics must lose its way before it finds itself again in the modern world of science" (1970, p. 214). If Merriam were alive today and a regular reader of the *American Political Science Review,* I am not quite sure what conclusions he might reach about the present state of the study of politics from the point of view of quantification. Would he say, "It is wholly improbable that politics will be absorbed in statistics" (1970, p.

214), or would he say, "It may be disastrous if political investigators rush into the collection and quantitative measurement of facts without preliminary consideration and statement of what we call 'the problem,' and without certain hypotheses . . . which the proposed examination of facts might be expected to prove or disprove" (1970, p. 215). These two statements—one confident and one apprehensive—appear in adjoining pages of the same chapter on "Politics and Numbers" in *New Aspects of Politics.*

Rereading these documents of the early history of the scientific movement in the study of politics, one cannot escape an impression of an age of innocence. The writing had a simple and wholesome quality about it. The growth of scientific knowledge held out the prospect of increasing humanity's capacity for understanding, explaining, and improving the political process. When the first edition of *New Aspects* appeared in 1925 the Bolshevik Revolution had not as yet taken on its sinister Stalinist form, and Italian Fascism was still being admired for its enforcement of railroad timetables. The depression was a few years off, and National Socialism was not as yet taken seriously. When the second edition of *New Aspects* was published in 1931, a sense of menace appears in some of the more recent writings included in the book, but the basic optimism persists.

In the 1990s, a century after the founding of the University of Chicago, and half a century after Merriam's retirement, we recognize that there was a naive quality in his prophecy, just as there was naivete in the whole thrust of science and technology as it developed in Merriam's time. It was a pre–nuclear threat, pre-overpopulation, pre–pollution and toxic waste, pre–ozone depletion version of science and progress. The descendants of Merriam in the university both here and abroad pursue his combination of scientific research and responsible public policy analysis, but without his unequivocal confidence that it would result in "the conscious control of human evolution toward which intelligence steadily moves in every domain of human life" (1970, p. 60).

This essentially was the vision of Charles E. Merriam, whose activities in the first half of the twentieth century left a deep imprint on the University of Chicago, and on the political science profession as it developed nationally and internationally in the subsequent decades.

# 4

# Harold Dwight Lasswell

HAROLD D. LASSWELL RANKS AMONG the half dozen creative innovators in the social sciences in the twentieth century. Few would question that he was the most original and productive political scientist of his time. While still in his twenties and early thirties, he planned and carried out a research program demonstrating the importance of personality, social structure, and culture in the explanation of political phenomena. In the course of that work he employed an array of methodologies that included clinical and other kinds of interviewing, content analysis, para-experimental techniques, and statistical measurement. It is noteworthy that two decades were to elapse before this kind of research program and methodology became the common property of a discipline that until then had been dominated by historical, legal, and philosophical methods.

Lasswell was born in 1902 in Donnellson, Illinois (population c. 300). His father was a Presbyterian clergyman, his mother a teacher; an older brother died in childhood. His early family life was spent in small towns in Illinois and Indiana as his father moved from one pulpit to another, and it stressed intellectual and religious values. Although the regional milieu of his childhood and adolescence might suggest that Lasswell was raised in an intellectual backwater, in fact it was an unusually rich environment. He was especially influenced in adolescence by a physician uncle who

Reprinted with minor revisions from National Academy of Sciences, *Biographical Memoirs* (Washington, D.C.: National Academy of Sciences, 1987).

was familiar with the works of Freud; by an English teacher in the Decatur, Illinois, high school he attended who introduced him to Karl Marx and Havelock Ellis; and by a brilliant young teacher of high school civics, William Cornell Casey, who later became a professor of sociology at Barnard College in Columbia University. He excelled in high school, edited the school newspaper, gave the valedictory address at graduation, and was awarded a scholarship to the University of Chicago after winning a competitive examination in modern history and English (Marvick, 1977; Rogow, 1969).

When Lasswell entered the University of Chicago in 1918—at age sixteen—the university was in the third decade of its remarkable growth. At a time when sociology as a curriculum did not yet exist at most universities, Chicago had a major department that was staffed by such gifted theorists and researchers as W. I. Thomas, Albion W. Small, and Robert Park. Its philosophy department was dominated by realists and pragmatists such as James Tufts and George Herbert Mead. Its economics department, in which Lasswell majored, included Jacob Viner, John M. Clark, Harry Alvin Millis, and Chester Wright. Its political science department was soon to begin its dramatic rise, but in Lasswell's undergraduate years the department was in transition, with Henry Pratt Judson soon to retire and Charles Edward Merriam in the wings. Lasswell was a member of a graduate cohort that included Robert Redfield, Louis Wirth, and Herbert Blumer (Karl, 1974, chaps. 3–8).

His graduate years in the Department of Political Science at Chicago coincided with the publication of Merriam's manifesto, *The Present State of the Study of Politics* (1921, reprinted in 1970), and with Merriam and Gosnell's survey study of nonvoting in Chicago (1924). In *The Present State,* Merriam proposed that two steps be taken to make the study of politics more scientific: (1) the exploration of the psychological and sociological bases of political behavior, and (2) the introduction of quantification in the analysis of political phenomena. The nonvoting study was a demonstration of the uses of sociopsychological hypotheses and quantitative methods in the explanation of political phenomena. It was a survey of the "political motives" of some 6,000 nonvoters in the Chicago mayoral election of 1923; individuals to be surveyed were selected by a "quota control" sampling procedure that was intended to match the census demographic distributions. In the immediate aftermath of this study and during Lasswell's graduate student days, Harold Foote Gosnell (then a first-term assistant professor of political science) conducted the first experimental study in political science—and what may very well have been the first experimental study (1926) in the social sciences outside of psychology. This was a survey of the effects on voting of a nonpartisan mail canvass in Chicago that was intended to get out the vote in the national and local elections of 1924 and 1925. The experimental technique Gosnell devised was quite rigorous: there were carefully matched experimental and control groups, different stimuli were employed, and the results were analyzed with the most sophisticated statistical techniques then available. Reflecting the programmatic and comparative vision of these researches, follow-up studies of voting turnout were made by Gosnell in Britain, France, Germany, Belgium, and Switzerland.

While Harold Gosnell was chosen by Merriam to develop the statistical component of his early 1925 vision, it was Harold Lasswell who was encouraged to develop the clinical, psychological, and sociological components. As a young graduate student, Lasswell published an article in 1923 titled "Chicago's Old First Ward," and in collaboration with Merriam he published another in 1924 on public opinion and public utility regulation.

Merriam threw out two challenges to the brilliant and ambitious young political scientist. The first came out of Merriam's wartime experience as chief American propagandist in Rome; the second arose from Merriam's interest in the characteristics of political leaders and the uses of the study of the abnormal and the psychopathological in explaining normal and typical behavior. Merriam's first interest—the importance of morale, propaganda, and civic training in the explanation of political behavior—led to Lasswell's 1927 doctoral dissertation, *Propaganda Technique in the First World War,* and ultimately to his invention of systematic content analysis and its uses in World War II. Merriam's second interest—the psychological and personality aspects of leadership and the uses of the abnormal in the explanation of the normal—led to a series of articles by Lasswell on political psychology and personality in politics, culminating in *Psychopathology and Politics* (1930).

Lasswell's doctoral dissertation on propaganda in the 1914–1918 war was a systematic effort to place World War I propaganda experience in the context of a theory of politics. Although there was something of antiwar muckraking in its tone, it also had the marks of rigorous scholarship: careful operational definitions, specification of the techniques of propaganda, and conditions that limit or facilitate their effectiveness. Lasswell had done field research in Europe for the study, interviewing scholars and governmental officials regarding aspects of the propaganda experience and the Great War. He also anticipated his later invention of content analysis in a simple quantitative study, "Prussian Schoolbooks and International Amity" (1925), which was carried out in connection with his dissertation (in the study, Lasswell counted and evaluated the significance of the references to national superiority, military glory, foreign inferiority, military heroes, and the like, in textbooks approved by the Prussian Ministry of Education after the establishment of the Weimar Republic).

Lasswell was appointed assistant professor of political science at Chicago in 1926 and soon embarked on researches in political psychology. Papers that he published from 1925 to 1929 showed him to be engaged in a search of the literature concerned with political psychology and political personality. One paper published in the *American Journal of Psychiatry* in 1929 recommended that psychiatrists keep adequate personality records and make them available to bona fide researchers; another published in *American Political Science Review* the same year argued the case for the use of data on mentally ill persons with some involvement in politics as one approach to the analysis of the relationship between personality and politics. This literature search and his concern with the improvement of psychiatric record-keeping were incidental to Lasswell's extraordinary book *Psychopathology and Politics,* which appeared in 1930, when he was twenty-eight.

Lasswell's work in preparing the book was extensive. He had been granted a postdoctoral fellowship by the Social Science Research Council for 1927–1928 and spent most of that academic year in Berlin undergoing psychoanalysis at the hands of Theodor Reik, a student of Freud. There is a report that he made a presentation at a Freud seminar urging that psychiatric records be kept in order to facilitate research. He also discussed these ideas with leading psychiatrists in Vienna and Berlin. In late 1928 and 1929 he consulted with the psychiatric directors of the most important mental institutions on the eastern seaboard, tapping their memories of cases of politician patients. With their permission he examined psychiatric records at St. Elizabeth's in Washington, D.C.; Sheppard and Enoch Pratt Hospital near Baltimore; Pennsylvania State Hospital in Philadelphia; Bloomingdale Hospital of White Plains, New York; and Boston Psychopathic Hospital. He also gave depth-psychiatric interviews to a number of "normal" volunteers.

*Psychopathology and Politics* was the first relatively systematic, empirical study of the psychological aspects of political behavior, and it coincided with the very beginnings of the culture and personality movement in anthropology and psychiatry. Lasswell was already in communication with anthropologist Edward Sapir, then a colleague at the University of Chicago, as well as with the New York psychiatrist Harry Stack Sullivan. The three of them began to plan an ambitious program of culture and personality research in middle and late 1925. Margaret Mead's *Coming of Age in Samoa* appeared two years before *Psychopathology and Politics,* and Ruth Benedict's *Patterns of Culture* appeared four years later. The first publication of the authoritarian personality research of the Frankfurt school—*Studien über Autorität und Familie*—appeared in 1936, and the *Authoritarian Personality* of Theodor Adorno, Else Frenkel-Brunswik, Sanford Levinson, and Nevitt Sanford only appeared in 1950.

Chapters 6 through 9 of *Psychopathology and Politics* report Lasswell's case materials. These are not, and are not represented as being, findings or scientific explanations of political behavior. They are presented as clinically supported hypotheses regarding the personality-etiological bases of recruitment to different kinds of political roles and attitudes. Thus Lasswell draws on clinical material and his own depth-psychiatric interviews to suggest why some individuals become agitators and others become administrators. Similarly he illuminates the relationship between personality variables and ideological propensities such as ultrapatriotism, internationalism, pacifism, socialism, and anarchism.

The rest of the book deals with methodological and theoretical issues. Among the methodological issues he treats are the uses of life histories in political science; the uses of the study of the deviant or the abnormal for the understanding of the normal; the dimensions used in typologies of politicians; the prolonged "depth" or psychoanalytic interview as a mode of research in the psychological bases of social behavior; and the technique of free association as method of getting data on politically relevant feelings and attitudes. He also presents a general theory of political behavior derived from a review of the various propositions of the psychoanalytic movement. This proposition, presented in the form of an equation, reduces political behavior—in the sense of choice of political roles and ideologies—to displacements of private, essentially "oedipal" and "libidinal" motives as rationalized in terms of political ideas and issues. It is a matter of some contention among Lasswell students as to whether this equation was literally intended or was a rhetorical exaggeration to draw attention to the importance of psychological motivation in the explanation of political phenomena. Supporting the reductionist position is the fact that the Freudian movement at this time took a similarly reductionist stand in the explanation of social, political, and aesthetic phenomena. Supporting the rhetorical interpretation is the fact that in this as in later work, Lasswell interprets unconscious oedipal and libidinal tendencies as powerful constraints on rational, object-oriented behavior, constraints that can be mitigated by psychotherapy. This was to be a theme of Lasswell's entire intellectual career—that professional political science had the obligation of discovering or inventing a "politics of prevention" of war and other evils; that there was a "commonwealth of human dignity" to which it ought to aspire; and that both of these required substantial psychotherapeutic inputs.

This dualism and ambivalence of reductionism and therapeutic optimism in some sense characterized the three principal influences on Lasswell's thought: the Presbyterianism of his family and childhood background, which deals with the question of how good may be wrested from an intractable evil; the Marxist-sociological background, which deals with the necessarily revolutionary confrontation of the traditional and reactionary with progressive forces; and the Freudian-psychoanalytic background, which deals with the confrontation of neurosis with psychotherapy. Lasswell's later contributions to political psychology took the constraint rather than the reductionist perspective. It is of interest that in an "Afterthoughts" he wrote for the 1960 edition of *Psychopathology and Politics,* he makes no reference to his equation; instead he tells us that at the time of writing the book he already shared in a revisionist ego-psychology trend, a movement in psychoanalysis that affirmed the importance of rational and cognitive processes.

In addition to the empirical and methodological parts, *Psychopathology and Politics* included a theoretical or meta-methodological part. Chapters 12 and 13—"The Personality System and Its Substantive Reactions" and "The State as a Manifold of Events"—presented Lasswell's framework of politically relevant variables and a strategy of political explanation, which moves from intrapsychic processes and their etiology, to interpersonal and social processes, to domestic and international political processes, and back again. Personality, economy, society, and politics are considered and dealt with as interacting systems.

What Lasswell presented as a theoretical framework and set of hypotheses in *Psychopathology and Politics* became his research program during the decade of the 1930s. Consider the intellectual balls he was juggling during these years. For the psychiatrists whom he had been urging to keep records of their interviews in the interest of scientific research, he set up a model laboratory in his own offices in the Social Science Research Building at the University of Chicago. Advised and encouraged by psychiatrists, Harry Stack Sullivan of Sheppard and Enoch Pratt Hospital and William A. White of St. Elizabeth's, he devised a procedure under which skin conductivity, pulse rate, respiration, and body movements of experimental subjects were measured as the spoken word was recorded. Three articles describing this procedure and reporting preliminary results appeared in psychoanalytic journals in 1935, 1936, and 1937. Unfortunately these research records were destroyed in 1938 in an accident that befell the vans moving Lasswell's effects to Washington, D.C., on his departure from Chicago. This project, if not the first, was certainly one of the earliest efforts to link psychological, autonomic, and behavioral variables with communications and personality processes.

If this laboratory research was an effort to implement the methodological message of *Psychopathology and Politics,* then *World Politics and Personal Insecurity* (1935b) was an elaboration of the theoretical perspectives spelled out in the final chapters of *Psychopathology and Politics.* Lasswell called his approach to political explanation "configurative analysis." In configurative analysis the political process is defined as conflict over the definition and distribution of the dominant social values—income, deference, and safety—by and among elites. In his first paragraph he proposes the formula long associated with his name: "Politics is the study of who gets what, when, and how." Political science research hence requires the analysis of the social origins, skills, personal traits, attitudes, values, and assets of world elites, and their changes over time. Proper understanding of political processes calls for a combination of equilibrium and developmental analysis and the adoption of contemplative and manipulative attitudes toward political change. Equilibrium analysis emphasizes the systemic, the recurrent, the stable interaction of economic, social, political, and personality variables; developmental analysis stresses the dynamic, the dialectical and transformative aspects of social change. The contemplative attitude contributes to the discovery of "regularities," "laws," principles of social behavior. The manipulative attitude subjects these regularities to the test of imagination, tracing the consequences of changes in conditions and policies, extrapolating trends and the like.

What Lasswell had in mind by the manipulative attitude is not fully clear in these passages. From the beginning he had a commitment to a moral and consequential political science, but his earlier work focused on politics and power. In his early schematization of political values as income, deference, and safety, he describes them rather casually as illustrative and representative values—not a complete set of political goals. He did not begin to deal explicitly with the political value and public policy realm until his association with Myres McDougal and the Yale School of Law in the late 1930s.

The bulk of *World Politics and Personal Insecurity* illustrates his method and approach. In chapters 2 through 6, conflicts among and within nations are related to human aggressive propensities, as well as the structural conditions of international relations and domestic societies. The consequences of economic and class structure, cultural diffusion, and the media of communication are the topics of chapters 7, 8, and 9. In chapter 10, politics, culture, and personality are related in an interesting discussion of trends in U.S. society: he treats the possibilities of the emergence of right-wing extremism and fascism and the approach of political psychiatry in a politics of prevention. A final chapter deals—in sociological and psychoanalytic terms—with the prospects of peace and social justice.

A briefer book, *Politics: Who Gets What, When, and How,* was published in 1936; it presented much of what was argued in *World Politics* but in a more succinct and more schematic form. If Lasswell has written a textbook, then this is it. It defined politics as the struggle among elite groups over such representative values as income, deference, and safety. The actors in these conflictual processes are groups organized around skill, class, personality, and attitude characteristics; they employ in different ways and with different effects the political instrumentalities of symbol manipulation, material rewards and sanctions, violence, and institutional practices.

These three books, which were written over a six-year period, constitute Lasswell's most important contributions to political theory. In this same productive decade of the 1930s, Lasswell was involved in two other major enterprises. He consolidated his earlier interest in propaganda research by collaborating with R. D. Casey and B. L. Smith in the preparation of an annotated bibliography of some 4,500 items. It was published in 1935 as a book—*Propaganda and Promotional Activities: An Annotated Bibliography*—with an introduction on the theory of propaganda by Lasswell. Later editions continued to guide and codify the field of communications and public opinion research. In an effort to implement the research program laid out in *World Politics,* Lasswell and a number of his graduate students carried out a field study of propaganda and political agitators and organizers among the unemployed in the city of Chicago during the depression and New Deal years. A book coauthored with Dorothy Blumenstock Jones first reported these findings in 1939.

The first phase in Lasswell's career came to an end in 1938. He left the University of Chicago to join forces with psychiatrist Harry Stack Sullivan and Yale anthropologist Edward Sapir, under the auspices of the William Alanson White Psychiatric Foundation. There was both "push" and "pull" behind these plans to leave. Under the presidency of Robert Hutchins, the hospitality of the University of Chicago to the empirical social sciences had notably cooled. Merriam's department came under criticism on grounds of "number crunching" and "psychologizing" as well as internal recruitment. Hutchins's conception of political science was humanistic, deductive, even Aquinian. Although Lasswell had tenure—as did Gosnell—both men left the university: Lasswell in 1938 for Washington, D.C., and the William Alanson White Psychiatric Foundation; Gosnell a few years later, also for the Capital but for government service. Merriam himself was approaching retirement and was unable to defend his younger men.

The "pull" of the eastern seaboard on Lasswell had an earlier origin. During the mid-1920s when he was preparing for his study of psychopathology and politics, Lasswell encountered the maverick psychiatrist Harry Stack Sullivan during his visits at eastern psychiatric hospitals. He also made the acquaintance of Dr. William Alanson White, the director of St. Elizabeth's, who was strongly interested in research and in collaboration with the social sciences. (Lasswell, because of his association with Merriam, was in a position to facilitate access for Dr. White to the early organizational meetings of the Social Science Research Council, then being held in Hanover, New Hampshire.) During these same years, Sullivan had come to know the cultural anthropologist Edward Sapir, then a colleague of Lasswell's at the University of Chicago. The three men, although of different ages—Sapir was born in 1884, Sullivan in 1892, and Lasswell in 1902—were attracted to one another out of the strongest interest in culture personality themes. They dreamed of a research institute that would combine the study of culture, society, and personality and contribute to a better and happier world. The research institute never came to fruition, but these encounters surely influenced Lasswell's program at the University of Chicago, Sapir's Institute of Human Relations at Yale, and Sullivan's William Alanson White Psychiatric Foundation in Washington, D.C.

In 1938, however, it appeared that these plans for a social science cum psychiatry institute in either New York or Washington, D.C., with Sapir, Sullivan, and Lasswell as the full-time core research faculty, were about to mature. In April 1938 the trustees of the William Alanson White Foundation decided to seek funds to support a full-time permanent research staff in psychiatry and the social sciences. And the three men were ready to move: Lasswell was pessimistic about prospects at Chicago, Sapir was acutely uncomfortable at Yale, and Sullivan looked forward to creative research collaboration under the most favorable of auspices.

It was in this mood of high hopes that in the spring of 1938 Harold Lasswell packed and shipped his files and belongings in two moving vans that were fated to collide and burn on a lonely Indiana highway. But this was only the beginning of misadventure and tragedy. The fundraising plans were unsuccessful, and relations between Sullivan and Lasswell deteriorated. Sapir died in early 1939.

Lasswell thus began the second phase of his career at age thirty-six, in Washington, D.C., with uncertain prospects. He improvised for a while, giving educational radio broadcasts on "Human Nature in Action" over NBC and consulting to foundations. Beginning in the academic year 1938–1939 he taught seminars as a visiting lecturer in association with Myres McDougal at the Yale School of Law; he was appointed professor of law there in 1946. As the international crisis deepened, he became involved in research programs at the Library of Congress and the Department of Justice. The Library of Congress, at Lasswell's recommendation, established a "war communications research project," drawing on his experience with World War I propaganda. And the Department of Justice set up a special war policies unit to help administer the Foreign Agents Registration Act and the Sedition Act. Both of these tasks involved content analysis of the media of communication: on the world scale, as the propaganda war heated up in 1939 and 1940, and on the domestic organizational scale, as Nazis and Fascists infiltrated foreign-language groups and media in the United States. Lasswell gave expert testimony in a number of trials under this legislation; he was also instrumental in the effort to have quantitative content analysis admitted as evidence in the federal courts.

During the war years he played an active role as a consultant to the Office of Facts and Figures and its successor organization, the Office of War Information; to the Office of Strategic Services; to the Foreign Broadcast Monitoring Service of the Federal Communications Commission; and to the army's Psychological Warfare Branch. For the social sciences these various research divisions of the government departments constituted advanced training centers for young social scientists. Leading scholars such as Lasswell, Paul Lazarsfeld, Samuel Stouffer, and Carl Hovland trained groups of specialists in survey research, experimental small-group research, propaganda and content analysis, and the like.

The methodological and substantive payoffs of Lasswell's wartime research are reported in *The Language of Politics: Studies in Quantitative Semantics* (1949), which was jointly edited with one of Lasswell's most brilliant students, Nathan Leites. This volume places mass communications content in the context of domestic and international politics, offers solutions for the principal methodological problems of quantitative content analysis, and reports on a number of successful uses of content analysis, both as a judicial tool and as a technique of intelligence gathering.

It had been Lasswell's ambition during World War II to set up what he termed a "world attention survey": a continual quantitative analysis of the content of the principal print and broadcast media of the major nations—friend, neutral, and enemy. It was a project of immense proportions and was set aside in the war years in favor of a much more modest program of propaganda analysis located in the Office of War Information and the Federal Communications Commission.

But in the aftermath of the war and working with wartime collaborators—particularly sociologist Daniel Lerner and political scientist Ithiel Pool—Lasswell pursued these research themes. Based now as a professor in the Yale School of Law, in collaboration with Lerner, Pool, and others at the Hoover Institute and Library at Stanford, he undertook a series of comparative studies of elites and political symbols. Several volumes reporting the findings of these researches appeared in the 1950s. But one of the most important products of these Stanford years was *The Policy Sciences* (1951), a state-of-the-art analysis of social science methodology as of the early 1950s that Lasswell coedited with Daniel Lerner, with coauthors Ernest R. Hilgard and others.

The third phase of Lasswell's career began in 1946 when he joined the Yale Law School faculty as a professor of law. He had been teaching part-time at Yale in association with Myres McDougal since 1938, and was a visiting research associate in the Institute of International Studies during the war years. His permanent location in New Haven in 1946 made possible a fruitful collaboration between Lasswell and McDougal in teaching, research, and contributions to legal and political theory, a collaboration that continued for the next several decades.

In a major monographic contribution to the *Yale Law Journal* of March 1943, Lasswell and McDougal recommended the fundamental reform of law school curricula. The monograph argued that lawyers were the principal policymakers in modern democratic societies and that traditional law school curricula failed to provide training for the variety of policymaking roles lawyers were called upon to perform. In this seminal article, Lasswell and McDougal sought to remedy these shortcomings. They formulated a curricular philosophy based on the assumption that law had to be understood as a process of authoritative decision by which the members of a community clarify and secure their common interests. They then elaborated a sequence of seminars and courses that would effectively implement this philosophy. Prominent in this and later collaborations with McDougal and other law school colleagues were two theoretical innovations—components of an "institutional and value map"—that are properly associated with Lasswell's Yale career. The first innovation was a functional scheme for the analysis of decisionmaking. This became in its final form a seven-phase process beginning with intelligence, in the sense of knowledge, and proceeding to promotion, prescription, invocation, application, termination, and evaluation. The second innovation was a classification of goals or base values that included power, wealth, respect, well-being, affection, skill, rectitude, and enlightenment. These two theoretical schemes enabled the legal scholar to locate his research in the policy process and to specify its substantive value aspects. The theoretical categories served to place in context the various legal and other studies that Lasswell carried on in the next decades.

One of Lasswell's most influential contributions to legal studies was *Power and Personality* (1948), in which he presented a series of case histories of judges to demonstrate the connection between personality characteristics and patterns of legal decisionmaking. Other Lasswell contributions to legal research and analysis are contained in such volumes as *Studies in World Public Order* (with McDougal, 1960); *In Defense of Public Order: The Emerging Field of Sanction Law* (with Richard Arens, 1961); *Law and Public Order in Space* (with McDougal and Ivan A. Vlaslc, 1963); and *Human Rights and World Public Order: The Basic Policies of an International Law of Human Dignity* (with McDougal and Lung-chu Chen, 1980). A final volume, titled *Jurisprudence for a Free Society: Studies in Law, Science, and Policy* and coauthored with McDougal, is still to appear.

Lasswell became Ford Professor of Law and Social Science Emeritus at Yale in 1970. The last seven years of his life were spent in New Haven, where he continued his research interests, and in New York City, where he was affiliated with the Policy Sciences Center, which he had helped to found in the 1940s.

Quantitatively, Lasswell's productivity was enormous. He wrote, coauthored, edited, and coedited some sixty books. He also contributed more than 300 articles to a wide range of journals: political science, sociological, psychiatric and psychological, legal, journalism, and public opinion. His publications also include several hundred reviews and comments. Among the important works that have not yet been mentioned are *Power and Society* (with Abraham Kaplan, 1950); "Democratic Character" (1951); *The Decision Process: Seven Categories of Functional Analysis*

(1956); *The Future of Political Science* (1963); *The Sharing of Power in a Psychiatric Hospital* (with Robert Rubenstein, 1966); *Peasants, Power, and Applied Social Change: Vicos as a Model* (with Henry F. Dobyns and Paul L. Doughty, 1971); and *The Signature of Power: Buildings, Communication, and Policy* (with Merritt B. Fox, 1979).

These titles suggest the enormous range of Lasswell's interests, which he maintained throughout his life. *Power and Society,* which was written in collaboration with the philosopher Abraham Kaplan, was a propositional inventory and conceptual handbook for political science. Among its noteworthy contents was the elaborated version of Lasswell's classification of base values (see above). Lasswell's monograph "Democratic Character" was an important addendum to a 1951 reprint of *Psychopathology and Politics* and *Politics: Who Gets What, When, and How,* neither of which dealt with the psychological aspects of democracy. This monograph sought first to define the value orientations that would be supportive of democratic institutions and then to spell out "democratic" personality characteristics and the social and family conditions that were likely to produce them. His monograph on the decision process (1956) spelled out more clearly his theoretical framework for the phases of policymaking and implementation discussed above.

In *The Future of Political Science,* evocative of earlier visions of a world in which social science research has reached high influence, he draws on two social science research projects in which he was engaged in the 1960s. The first of these was an anthropological study of a hacienda in Peru. In this effort Lasswell collaborated with Allan Holmberg of Cornell and later produced the book *Peasants, Power, and Applied Social Change.* The experiment involved giving increasing initiative in decisionmaking to the peasants in the hacienda and attempting to measure the consequences of these and other experimental inputs of modernization and democratization. The second, done collaboratively with Robert Rubenstein, was a study of an experiment at the Yale Psychiatric Institute involving the participation of patients with staff and psychiatrists in decisionmaking on the ward. The research was concerned with the effects of this participation on the effectiveness of the ward and on the therapeutic goals of the institute. *The Sharing of Power in a Psychiatric Hospital* documented this study.

*The Future of Political Science* proposes that the political science profession develop the capacity to administer comprehensive surveys of world political change in order to advise effectively in the avoidance of war and other social evils. Such a survey would be informed by Lasswell's decision-process and goal-value conceptualizations. He also describes the kind of professional education that would be required to administer this kind of research program and cultivate the creativity essential for effective intervention.

Finally, in *The Signature of Power,* published after his death, Lasswell explores the relations between the architecture of public buildings, their public functions, and the surrounding political culture. Using photographs of public buildings and monuments from all over the world to illustrate his points, he demonstrates that the functions of buildings—civil or military, judicial, legislative, and bureaucratic—influence their structures. These structures in turn are influenced by national cultures, which produce their own structural variations.

Lasswell received many honors in the course of his career. He served as president of the American Political Science Association in 1956 and of the American Society of International Law from 1966 to 1968. He received honorary degrees from the University of Chicago, Columbia University, the University of Illinois, and the Jewish Theological Seminary. He was actively associated as officer, board member, or consultant to the Committee for Economic Development, the Commission on the Freedom of the Press, the Rand Corporation, the American Association for the Advancement of Science, and many other organizations. He was a fellow of the American Academy of Arts and Sciences and was inducted into the National Academy of Sciences in 1974.

Harold Lasswell suffered a massive stroke on December 24, 1977, from which he never recovered. He died of pneumonia in his apartment in New York City on December 18, 1978.

*       *       *

I wish to acknowledge the help I have received from a number of sources: from Dwaine Marvick's introduction to his anthology *Harold D. Lasswell on Political Sociology* (1977); from the various contributions to Harold Lasswell's festschrift—*Politics, Personality, and Social Science in the Twentieth Century* (Arnold Rogow, 1969), the memorial volume *Harold Dwight Lasswell, 1902–1978,* which was published by the Yale Law School under the editorship of Myres McDougal, and Helen Swick Perry's *Psychiatrist of America: The Life of Harry Stack Sullivan* (1982), which contains information on the early collaboration of Lasswell with Sapir and Sullivan; and from personal communications and accounts provided by William T. R. Fox, Bruce L. Smith, Andrew R. Willard, Rodney Muth, and Myres McDougal.

# 5

# A Voice from the Chicago School

I RECALL A WALK WITH HAROLD LASSWELL sometime in 1931, in my senior year at the University of Chicago. We were discussing my prospects for graduate work in political science. Lasswell thought that the Rabbinic background of my family, and my training in biblical studies, would be a plus, something like having a second cultural experience in addition to growing up in Chicago. This was very reassuring to me, the first time anyone had told me that being Jewish might have some positive career advantages, or that growing up in Chicago was a cultural experience.

## Graduate Training at the University of Chicago

I was an Americanist during my graduate years at the University of Chicago during 1933–1938, as were almost all of the graduate students except the international relationists. While Samuel Harper lectured on nineteenth-century Russian history and the Bolshevik Revolution in those years, and we had the occasional foreign visitor such as Harold Laski, or Herman Finer, who lectured on European politics, we had no foreign area studies to speak of, and no dissertations focused on the European area.

---

From *Comparative European Politics: The Story of a Profession,* edited by Hans Daalder (London and New York: Pinter, 1997). Reprinted, with minor revisions, with permission of the Continuum International Publishing Group.

While we were not parochial, the faculty of the department was entirely American-born, and the dominant accent was midwestern, in Merriam's case quite twangy.

The curricular structure was functional rather than geographical. L. D. White taught a course on comparative public administration, and Gosnell one on comparative political parties. Lasswell's public opinion course included a lot of European material. The Ph.D. in international relations was interdisciplinary and included diplomatic history, as well as international economics, and a Lasswell-given psycho-anthropology of international relations.

One of the research programs going on during my University of Chicago years—Merriam's Civic Training series (1931)—included volumes on the Soviet Union, Britain, France, Germany, and Italy. We students were not aware of the battle going on between Charles Merriam and Roberto Michels regarding the latter's contribution on Italy to the Civic Training series. Merriam wanted the Italian study to include the story of the Fascist effort at controlling what we would now call the socialization processes. Michels, then in process of becoming a Fascist himself, and wanting to avoid writing anything critical of Fascism, insisted on doing a historical monograph on the rise of Italian nationalism (Karl, 1974). Merriam invited Michels to spend a summer teaching in the Chicago summer quarter, when he hoped that Harold Lasswell could prevail on Michels to do a revision of the Italian case study. Nothing came of it, and Michels's manuscript went unpublished.

Thus, though we had no professor of comparative government who taught courses under that label or specialized on Europe during my graduate years, we were exposed to European scholarship and encountered European scholars as lecturers or as fellow students. I wrote my dissertation on wealth and politics in New York City under the supervision of Harold Lasswell and Harold Gosnell. It was indicative of the mood then prevailing in graduate studies at the University of Chicago that I could select a Marxist theme as the topic of my thesis—the relation between economic and political power as reflected in the changing social composition of the economic and political elites in New York City from the colonial period until the then (1936) present day.

Bernard Crick (1959) did not get the Chicago school right. We were not "progressives" and "Bull Moosers," though Merriam had been such early in his career. The ideology of the department in my years was a mix of political and administrative reform directed against inefficiency and corruption and opposition to the evils of capitalism, then so manifest in the world depression, large-scale unemployment, and the suppression of the labor movement. The more adventurous students among us were exploring a heady mix of Marx and Freud.

During my graduate years I shared an office with Edward Shils. He introduced me to Max Weber, whose methodological writings he was then translating in collaboration with Louis Wirth, and more generally to European sociology. He encouraged me to improve on my college German and French by translating Weber's "Politik als Beruf" (1921), and parts of Pareto's "Les Systemes Socialistes" (1965).

I spent my dissertation year in New York City in 1935–1936 as a predoctoral field fellow for the Social Science Research Council (SSRC), at the time that the "University in Exile" was getting under way at the New School for Social Research. I believe I was one of the first nonlocal students to seek them out. Hans Speier was my mentor there. I took a reading course in Max Weber under Albert Salomon's supervision. I took the subway out to Spuyten Duyvil one evening a week, where I spent an hour or two trying to construe Weber's complex prose.

More significantly, Hans and Lisa Speier introduced me to Dorothea Kaufmann—my future wife—a young refugee and child psychologist from Cologne. I acquired added incentives to improve on my German. My first teaching assignment at Brooklyn College put me deep in Americana. I taught five sections of American government for fifteen hours per week. To alleviate the boredom I read almost the whole of the monographic and historical literature on American political institutions. I aspired to break out of the American monotony and introduce a course in comparative political parties, but as a young instructor I could not introduce a new, elective course into the curriculum.

## A World War II Postdoctoral

My German stood me in good stead at the outbreak of war. Lasswell was widely consulted in the gearing up of the U.S. government for World War II, particularly by the Department of Justice and the various information services. Two months after Pearl Harbor I was hired as head of the Enemy Section of the Bureau of Intelligence of the Office of Facts and Figures, the predecessor of the Office of War Information. I had to build up a small staff of specialists on Nazi Germany and Occupied Europe to inform our own propaganda people of morale problems in enemy areas. I hired Herbert Marcuse to report on developments in Germany, and Henry

Ehrmann to report on Occupied France. Marcuse, in the aftermath of Stalingrad, wrote a lovely memo on a Goebbels speech on the theme of "Stimmung und Haltung" (loosely translated as "mood and behavior"), a distinction the Nazi propaganda minister drew in an effort to downplay the defeatism that was beginning to show among German workers and troops. Marcuse then appealed to me as an ironic Hegelian Marxist. He became a cultural guru much later.

I spent the last few months of the war, and the first months after VE (Victory in Europe) Day in Germany, working for the U.S. Strategic Bombing Survey (of the U.S. Air Force), interrogating German Gestapo and other Nazi intelligence personnel in the various internment camps of northern and central Germany about the effects of bombing on German morale. Moving as a small mobile team in the lee of the advancing armies, we were able to interview surviving members of small resistance movements as they met our advancing divisions. Though my official mission was to study the effect of strategic bombing on German morale, I was more interested in the extent and the character of oppositional activity in Germany during the last years and months of the war.

## The Anti-Nazi Resistance and European Political Parties

As I returned to academic life in the fall of 1945, I began a study of resistance movements in the various occupied countries of Europe, and within Germany as well. During my last August days at our headquarters in Bad Nauheim, Supreme Headquarters Allied Expeditionary Forces (SHAEF) issued a regulation against looting by U.S. troops, including documents among the prohibitions. I had precious copies of my interviews with resistance survivors, and other materials such as leaflets, along with some Gestapo arrest statistics. I took a chance and packed these documents in my footlocker and shipped them home, along with my spoils of war—two fencing foils that I had found in an abandoned Gestapo office, a set of carpenter's files, and a wonderfully long editor's shears, which I took out of a German army supply depot, and which I have been using until the present day.

Hence I was able in 1945–1946 to complete a study titled "The Resistance and the Political Parties of Western Europe" with some unique in-depth data on the German case, as well as materials on the other European countries. I was particularly interested in the Christian parties of

Germany, Italy, and France, then led by religious elements with bona fides through having kept free of, or having actively opposed, Nazism-Fascism (Almond, 1947, 1948a, 1948b, 1949). These parties, along with the Social Democrats and the Communists, created a brief political entente cordiale in some European countries, which fell apart with the onset of the Cold War.

## The Market Value of a University of Chicago Ph.D.

On my return to Brooklyn College and civilian life in 1945, I was already retooled as a European specialist. But my having taught American government more than thirty times in the prewar years at Brooklyn College left me with a sense of being an Americanist as well. Or rather, I could never accept the disciplinary convention that "comparative government" excluded the American case. In another sense I was a somewhat unusual kind of comparativist. My University of Chicago graduate training meant that I had political sociological and psychological training as well.

When I came out of graduate school in 1938, a University of Chicago Ph.D., particularly of a Lasswellian flavor, was a bit on the flaky side. There was some doubt about our qualifications as specialists on the nuts and bolts of political science—the study of governmental and legal institutions. But within a few years the market demand for the University of Chicago interdisciplinary training exemplified in the visibility of such Chicago Ph.D.'s as V. O. Key Jr., Herman Pritchett, David Truman, and Herbert Simon, among others, improved greatly. It resulted in my being hired at the Institute of International Studies at Yale in 1946, and receiving tenure in the Yale Department of Political Science in 1949.

The reigning texts in comparative government as the United States returned to civilian life in the late 1940s were Herman Finer's *Theory and Practice of Modern Government* (1932, 1949) and Carl J. Friedrich's *Constitutional Government and Politics* (1937). American political studies were more "advanced." Although as time went on Finer and Friedrich included chapters on such themes as parties and elections, pressure groups, public opinion, and political communication, the analytic treatment was largely historical, legal, and philosophical. American studies in the first decades of the twentieth century had begun to be more sociological, psychological, processual, and functional. The innovative empirical research on American politics being carried on by such scholars as Charles Merriam, Harold Gosnell, Harold Lasswell, Peter Odegard, Pendleton

Herring, Elmer Schattschneider, and others during the 1930s had brought to light a complex political infrastructure and process.

Europe in the post–World War II years was primarily preoccupied with rebuilding its economy and social structure. It was threatened and divided by the Cold War. Both conservative and Marxist ideology depreciated research on the political infrastructure. For Marxists, pressure groups were reduced to class phenomena—the trade unions were part of the working class, and business, professional, and farm groups were the agents of capitalism. For the conservatives—anti-democratic, or distrustful of democracy—such institutions as political parties, to say nothing of pressure groups, were viewed as subversive of the sovereign authoritarian state. In some European countries debate still raged on the question of whether the political realm was plural or monist, whether sovereignty could be divided. In the United States this ideological issue had been settled as early as the founding decades and the *Federalist Papers.*

The great social and political science traditions of the continental Europe of the late nineteenth and early twentieth centuries—exemplified by Marx and his followers, Freud and his social science interpreters, Pareto, Weber, Durkheim, Gaetano Mosca, Ostrogorski, Michels, and others—had been thoroughly disrupted by World War II. England's six-year-long World War II burden was a serious but not so thoroughgoing interruption. In Germany, and to a somewhat lesser extent in Italy, much of the academic social science community had gone into exile, primarily to the United States, where it enriched the American academy, particularly in the social sciences.

In the 1940s–1950s there was a widely shared view that the United States and Britain stood almost alone in the world as trustees for humane civilization, and Britain was exhausted from its six-year-long wartime exertions. The United States had an enormously productive economy. Its universities were in process of expanding in order to assimilate the millions of GIs returning from the wars. For the social scientists and political scientists of those years it was "great to be alive," with large hopes of discovery, important and profound messages to convey, and large resources to back it all up.

I was four times fortunate to be in that generation of American social scientists. From my University of Chicago background I had a unique methodological product line to sell; chance had placed me at the junction of European and American studies; I was in a strong research setting, first at Yale and then at Princeton; I was already known to the Social Science Research Council, then about to embark on its greatest years under

Pendleton Herring. The SSRC could draw on the strong commitment to the social sciences by the Rockefeller and Carnegie Corporations under the iconoclastic eyes and in the steady hands of Samuel Willets, Charles Dollard, Frederick Keppel, and John Gardner.

## The SSRC Committee on Comparative Politics

In 1954, I became the first chairman of the SSRC Committee on Comparative Politics, having been "seconded" from the Committee on Political Behavior. We were a "young" committee selected with an eye to escaping from American and European parochialism, and intellectual conservatism. Thus we had a number of specialists on what came to be called "third-world" countries (Lucian Pye on China and Southeast Asia; James Coleman on Africa; Myron Weiner on India), and Europeanists already researching the European political "infrastructure" (Sigmund Neumann, Joseph LaPalombara, and Almond). In what follows I will first treat the work of the Committee on Comparative Politics in which I shared, and then turn to my own work in comparative politics.

The first program of the new committee might have been forecast from the personnel of the founding Committee on Political Behavior, which included Pendleton Herring, V. O. Key Jr., David Truman, Avery Leiserson, and Oliver Garceau—all of them students of interest groups and the democratic process. A grant from the Carnegie Corporation enabled us to embark on a "retail" grant program for the study of political groups in foreign countries (1957–1958). What we proposed to do was to bring foreign area studies up to "state-of-the-art," encouraging scholars to delve into the political infrastructure of European and other foreign countries. Our funds enabled us to assemble our grantees for the discussion of research plans in advance of fieldwork. A number of political scientists made significant research contributions on the basis of these grants—Henry Ehrmann's study of French interest groups (1957), Joseph LaPalombara's study of Italian interest groups (1964), Juan Linz's study of Spanish authoritarianism (1970), Myron Weiner's study of Indian pressure groups and political parties (1962), Edward Banfield's study of attitudes toward groups in southern Italy (1958), S. M. Lipset's *Political Man* (1960), Samuel Beer's study of British collectivism (1965), and the like.

In these early post–World War II years there was much theoretical speculation and programmatic discussion. The SSRC had sponsored a conference on the state of comparative government studies, which was held at Northwestern University in 1952. Out of this had come a report published in the *American Political Science Review* (1953), and Roy C. Macridis's *The Study of Comparative Government* (1955), critiques of the state of the field, and proposals for improvement. My early structural-functional contributions, stimulated by the research programs and conferences of the committee, appeared during these years (Almond, 1956; Almond and Coleman, 1960). Lucian Pye's early contributions to modernization theory also appeared during these years (1962, 1966), as did Henry Ehrmann's comparative study of interest groups (1958) and Edward Shils's *Political Development in the New States* (1960), which had been produced for one of our early conferences.

Another major grant, for the period 1960–1963, this time by the Ford Foundation, enabled the committee to embark on a series of conferences on the general theme of political modernization and development. Lucian Pye assumed the committee chairmanship in 1963, and directed the program that eventuated in the nine-volume Political Development series published by Princeton University Press over the period 1963–1978. Five of the first six volumes dealt with important aspects and institutions of development—the communications media (Pye, 1963), bureaucracy (LaPalombara, 1963), education (Coleman, 1965), political culture (Pye and Verba, 1965), and political groups and political parties (LaPalombara and Weiner, 1966). A sixth volume compared the developmental experience of two relatively modernized, non-European countries, Japan and Turkey (Ward and Rustow, 1964). Finally, three volumes turned to the analysis of development in history. The first of these, *Crises and Sequences in Political Development,* by six of the committee members (Binder, Coleman, LaPalombara, Pye, Verba, and Weiner, 1971), argued that developmental patterns—centralized-decentralized, democratic-authoritarian, and the like—could be explained by the way in which different countries had been confronted historically by, and coped with, problems of political centralization and authority, collective political participation, national identity and legitimacy, and economic and social welfare. In the ninth volume, a test of the usefulness of this framework was made by a group of ten historians reviewing European and American experience in terms of these "crises" (Grew et al., 1978). The eighth volume (1976), which I shared in planning with Charles Tilly, drew a number of European and American historians and political scientists into doing original historical research on European state-building in the sixteenth to nineteenth centuries. The book differed from earlier studies that emphasized the development of institutions. Tilly proposed dealing with policy areas as causative, as the so-called independent variables, with differences in institutional development as the dependent ones. One part of the volume treated the interplay of historical strategic and security variables with the formation of armed forces, and associated state agencies; another the interaction of economic development, strategic interests, and the formation of the revenue-collecting institutions of the state. Another part of the volume dealt with different patterns of recruitment and training of bureaucratic personnel, as they influenced the structure and culture of West European states.

This was an extraordinary period of intellectual activity over an interval of some two decades. The actual number of scholars participating in committee activities was 245, 199 of them American and 46 foreign, mostly European (Wood, 1971). The topics opened up and stressed by the committee were on the frontiers of political science research.

## Other Centers of Creativity

But while the committee's programs were highly visible and influential both in the United States and abroad, they were only one of the creative centers in comparative politics in the post–World War II decades. The Institute for Social Research and the Survey Research Center at the University of Michigan were major catalysts in the diffusion to Europe and elsewhere of survey research–based election studies. Wherever these University of Michigan studies touched, they left cadres trained in political sociology, psychology, and statistics. Robert Dahl at Yale during the late 1960s and early 1970s carried out his own program of comparative studies, focused on the theme of "opposition," producing two important volumes of theoretical analysis and country studies (1966, 1973). Dahl's venture into comparative politics culminated in *Polyarchy* (1971), a major contribution to comparative democratic theory. Samuel Huntington at Harvard anticipated the critique of American political science in its pluralistic 1950s decade, with his studies of the role of the military in politics (1957), his collaborative work with Zbigniew Brzezinski comparing the United States and the USSR (Brzezinski and Huntington, 1963), and, most important, his trail-breaking *Political Order in Changing Societies* (1967).

The "political mobilization" studies also developed quite independently of the work of the Committee on Comparative Politics. This research program was initiated by Daniel Lerner (1958), Karl Deutsch (1961), and S. M. Lipset (1960, 1994) and was based on aggregate statistical analysis of the influence of industrialization, urbanization, the spread of education, and mass communications on political mobilization and democratization.

The creative scholars in comparative politics in the 1960s–1970s were heavily overcommitted. I recall an encounter at the Center for Advanced Study in the Behavioral Sciences in 1967 with Robert Dahl, Val Lorwin, Hans Daalder, and Stein Rokkan, then planning a collaborative study of the "small democracies" of Europe. European studies tended to be dominated by "Great Powers" examples and data. Most Europeanists specialized in England, France, or Germany. A study of the small European countries—the four Scandinavian ones, Ireland, Belgium, and the Netherlands, Austria, and Switzerland, with their different combinations of ethnic, linguistic, religious, economic, and strategic variables—held out great theoretical promise. The later work on "consociationalism" and "neocorporatism" shows this to have been the case.

## Overtones of Max Weber

I welcomed the opportunity to engage in theoretical speculation in the early years of the committee's activities. Ever since graduate student days I had nurtured Weberian aspirations—to know just about everything there was to know, and to write with apodictic confidence about its meaning. I had completed my study *The Appeals of Communism* in the same year in which the committee was established. I had no major research commitments at the time, and the beginning of the committee's activities was an invitation to theorize. The immediate post–World War II generation of social scientists was challenged to encompass the variety of political phenomena, which were then emerging. How could one grasp and comprehend this immense and unstable reality? Europe and its great civilization and cultural tradition were in a shambles; it was an open question whether democracy would survive on the European continent. We were the heirs to that civilization. (I recall a visit—or should I say a pilgrimage with another aspiring social scientist in uniform—in the summer of 1945 to visit Marianne Weber. We exchanged a few words about Max Weber, nothing much. She was old and frail and spoke faintly. She appreciated our gift of several packages of Lucky Strike cigarettes, which were then exchangeable for scarce items like coffee.)

Two theoretical papers came out of these early years on the Committee on Comparative Politics. "Comparative Political Systems" was written as a discussion paper for the first conference of the committee, held at Princeton in the spring of 1955. (As I write about this first gathering sponsored by the committee, I recall that Stein Rokkan, then a Rockefeller Fellow, attended and took an active part in this first encounter, wearing a heavy overcoat. June in Bergen was different from June in Princeton, but Stein didn't seem to notice the heat. Stein was with the committee from the start, giving as well as receiving.)

The paper I presented was an early formulation of the "Functional Approach," suggesting that different political systems could be systematically compared according to their structural and cultural characteristics. Structure was defined in Weberian-Parsonian terms as action, behavior, with legal and normative aspects treated insofar as they influenced actual behavior; culture was defined as psychological orientation, again in Weberian-Parsonian terms. The essay simply proceeded to compare four "sorts" of political systems—(1) the Anglo-American, (2) the continental European "immobilist" systems, (3) the Scandinavian and Low Country "working multiparty systems," and (4) the totalitarian systems—according to these structural and cultural criteria. It delights me to recall that it was this crude sorting of political systems that Arend Lijphart critiqued in 1968, and which was followed by his trail-breaking democratic studies, beginning with his "Typologies of Democratic Systems" in 1968 and culminating in his definitive *Democracies* in 1984.

## Bringing the Rest of the World into Comparative Politics

In its early effort to break out of the Europe-centeredness of comparative politics, the Committee on Comparative Politics sponsored, as its first major work, a comparative study of the developing areas. This was a collaboration between Lucian Pye (Southeast Asia), Myron Weiner (South Asia), James Coleman (sub-Saharan Africa), Dankwart Rustow (the Near East), and George Blanksten (Latin America), with James Coleman joining me in the editing of the volume. I wrote the introductory chapter presenting the framework of comparison, and James Coleman wrote a concluding chapter summarizing the findings of the various area studies and presenting a typology of developing systems.

Looking back at this product of the late 1950s I would defend it as the first effort to provide an analytical scheme for political scientists embarking on field research in the developing areas. It codified and combined a number of research traditions. The first of these—the European sociological tradition of Pareto, Durkheim, and Weber—was then being transmitted through the writings of Talcott Parsons. Parsons called his research approach "the action frame of reference," after Weber's ontological view of the subject matter of the social sciences as *Soziale Handlung* or "social action." In my introductory essay to *The Politics of the Developing Areas,* I conclude that an empirical theory of comparative politics would consist of observations about the variety and properties of political systems conceived as functional-structural statements of probability. I subsequently realized that what I had sought to produce in the late 1950s to help my colleagues decide what questions to ask when they went into the field to study exotic political systems was a "comparative political statics." Some years later, as I suggest below, I confronted the problem of comparative political dynamics.

The systemic and functional concepts that I introduced in *The Politics of the Developing Areas* were drawn from anthropological, sociological, and political theory. The system-environment input-output model came from Parsons and David Easton, the first drawing on biological system models, the second on mechanical ones; the recruitment function came from Pareto and Lasswell, socialization from the psycho-anthropologists (Margaret Mead, Ruth Benedict, Florence and Clyde Kluckhohn, Lasswell, and Erik Erikson), communication from the social psychologists (Paul Lazarsfeld, Elihu Katz), and the media people, interest articulation, and aggregation from the American political scientists of the 1920s–1950s (Merriam, Gosnell, V. O. Key Jr., David Truman, and others); rule making, rule implementation, rule adjudication came from separation of powers theory. I review this conceptual history in my presidential address to the American Political Science Association (1966).

Rereading this essay, spelling out the various political functions and illustrating them with examples from the modern world of European and American, as well as "third-world" and primitive societies, my mood varies between pride and embarrassment. My embarrassment arises out of its pedantry and pretentious lapses. My models, of course, were Weber's *Wirtschaft und Gesellschaft* (1922), and Parsons and Shils's *Toward a General Theory of Action* (1951). The input-output-system model that I crafted at that time did indeed combine and codify European sociological theory, and Freudian psycho-anthropological theory, as well as the new primarily American "political process" approach. This recipe was concocted at the Center for Advanced Study in the Behavioral Sciences, where I spent 1956–1957 working with a group of imaginative and playful anthropologists (Evon Vogt, John Roberts, John Whiting, Kimball

Romney, and others) who helped me think about functions, structures, and social systems.

I was aware of some of the shortcomings of this essay as I composed it in the late 1950s, and was made aware of more shortcomings as critics were quick to fault it in subsequent years. The argument that it was a static theory was not really damaging; it was indeed a comparative political statics. The appropriate response was to complement it with a political dynamics. This, indeed, became my main interest in the late 1960s and the early 1970s when the work for *Crisis, Choice, and Change* (with Flanagan and Mundt, 1973) was being done.

## The Structural-Functional Approach

As I taught comparative politics at the graduate level at Stanford in the 1960s in the revolutionary and countercultural mood of the time, a more sophisticated functional model began to take shape, taking into account the "postmodern" and "deconstructive" mood that swept the discipline of political science in those years. I recognized that one had to distinguish "system functions" from "process functions," and both of these from "policy functions." The three-level treatment of political functions—system, process, and policy—was foreshadowed in the first Almond and Powell book (1966) and fully elaborated in the second edition, titled *Comparative Politics: System, Process, and Policy* (1978). Socialization and recruitment shaped and transformed the culture and structure of the political system; the political process consisted of some five distinctive kinds of activities— the articulation of interests and demands, the aggregation of interests into policy alternatives, and the formulation, implementation, and adjudication of policies. The political system interacted with its domestic and international environments through extractive, distributive, regulative, and symbolic outputs. These outputs in turn maintained or transformed the domestic and international structure and culture, producing outcomes feeding back as inputs into the political system and affecting its structure and culture. The communication function seemed to be important at all three levels, between the levels and between the political system and its environments as well.

A typology of political systems (e.g., the varieties of democratic and authoritarian regimes) would be conceived as structural-functional equilibrium states, described in these terms. This, in retrospect, was the theory of comparative statics that emerged out of the theoretical speculation of the 1950s and 1960s. I believe much of it survives in the contemporary political science theoretical vocabulary.

## Crisis, Choice, and Change

Younger colleagues and I organized a workshop at Stanford in 1968 around the theme of "Political Development," to survey and evaluate the various approaches to political change then being pursued. As the work proceeded, Scott Flanagan and Robert Mundt joined me in editing a series of historical developmental studies, which appeared in 1973 under the title *Crisis, Choice, and Change: Historical Studies of Political Development*. Scott Flanagan played an unusually creative role in adapting game theory to political development theory. The book consisted of a theory of political dynamics, presented in the introductory and concluding chapters, and eight historical case studies, done in accordance with our approach: a study of the British Reform Act of 1832, done by Bingham Powell, and one on the British Crisis of 1931, done by Dennis Kavanagh; a study of the formation of the French Third Republic by Robert Mundt; one on the formation of the German Weimar Republic by Volker Rittberger; one on the Cardenas Reforms of Mexico by Wayne Cornelius; a study of the Meiji Restoration in Japan by James White; and one of the Indian crises in the mid-1960s by Thomas Headrick. Scott Flanagan wrote his Ph.D. dissertation on the breakdown of the Japanese Meiji regime.

What our workshop had discovered in the course of our meetings in these turbulent years of the late 1960s through early 1970s was that some four distinct approaches to the explanation of political development had emerged—structural-functionalism, social mobilization, rational choice, and leadership "theory." The approach of *Crisis, Choice, and Change* was based on the recognition that each of these schools had unique strengths as well as distinct weaknesses and liabilities. It seemed logical that a framework of analysis that integrated these separate approaches might be able to combine their separate strengths while at the same time overcoming their individual deficiencies.

In integrating these distinct approaches we tried to bridge two kinds of dichotomies in the comparative field: (1) the static-dynamic or stability versus change perspective; and (2) the determinacy-choice dichotomy, which often assumes the form of a macro versus micro approach. We bridged the first dichotomy by applying different methodologies to different phases of our case studies of historical episodes. System functionalism is appropriate for mapping general system characteristics and explaining system maintenance and stability, and was applied to examining the characteristics of the preexisting political regime, and broader political system, and the new regime and system characteristics that emerged at the end of the historical episode. The differences that these two mapping exercises identified then became our measure of the amount and kind of development and change that had taken place.

By contrast, the process of change was traced successively through social mobilization, rational choice–coalition, and leadership modes of analysis. The analysis of changes in the external environment—the essence of the social mobilization approach—would explain the changing weights and distributions of different resources such as wealth, political incumbency, coercive resources, and the like. Our workshop soon identified the international environment as crucial in the explanation of most of our developmental episodes, rediscovering the insights of historians such as John Robert Seeley (1886) of Cambridge, and Otto Hintze (1975) of the University of Berlin.

The second dichotomy (determinacy-choice) contrasts (1) analysis at the macro, aggregate data level, where most of the independent variables are nonpolitical ones, and the political outcomes that are constrained by these contextual, international security-socioeconomic variables, with (2) an analysis at the micro, actor level (individuals, elites, or masses), where the independent variables are political, and the data ideally are collected at the individual level and focus on the preferences, resources, choices, and actions of individuals and groups, elites and masses.

We presented this as an integrated theory of development, integrated in the sense that each approach is conceptually congruent with the others through a common focus on political resources and utilities. System functionalism, employed to specify the "before and after" of the developmental episode, specifies the distributions of resources among, and the preferences of, the political actors as these are constrained in the more or less stable original political system and in the more or less stable subsequent system. A new resource distribution, and a changed issue agenda, are the end results of the social mobilization process with the emergence of new groups and elites, or of developments in the international environment, which may enhance or decrease the resources of political groups, or change their political preferences. At the micro level, coalition analysis generates the logically possible ruling combinations, again through the analysis of the distribution of resources and utilities among the political actors; and leadership is defined as the capacity to transform utilities or issue orientations through creative ideas, and/or to discover and mobilize new and old political resources. Thus leadership is the creative capacity to broker winning combinations that significantly adapt and transform the politics and public policy of a political system. It is the theoretical integration of these separate methodologies that is the special contribution of the crisis-choice-change approach. It is not simply a more comprehensive checklist of causes of political change.

Our historical case studies showed, for example, how important the strong individual leadership of Cardenas was in the development of the Institutional Revolutionary Party (PRI) in Mexico, and how important the weak leadership of Napoleon III had been in the collapse of the second French Empire. The British Reform Act of 1832, and the Meiji Restoration in mid-nineteenth-century Japan, illustrated the importance of collective leadership. Coalition analysis illuminated the causes of the weakness of the Weimar Republic, and the origins of the *immobilisme* of the French Third Republic. Social mobilization theory, particularly when we recognized the great importance of the international environment in the sense of demonstration effect, flows of capital and trade, and warfare and its threat, were indispensable in explaining our cases: catastrophic military defeat in the cases of the Third Republic and the Weimar Republic, demonstration effect in the case of the Meiji Restoration, the combination of industrialization and the stand-down from the continual warfare of the French Revolution and the Napoleonic era in the case of the British Reform Act of 1832. Finally it became obvious, as we carried on our historical studies, that structural-functional mapping exercises were essential in our efforts to define the "from what to what?" of political development.

## The Appeals of Communism

The system-process-policy approach to comparative analysis and political typology, and the crisis-choice-change approach to political development, represent the culmination of my theoretical efforts, enormously aided by my students and younger associates. You will find their names as coauthors and coeditors on most of my publications. I would not want their creativity in any way undervalued.

Some brief discussion of two other comparative undertakings with which I have been identified may be in point. The first post–World War II decade was an American decade of pride, but also of shame. The Cold War precipitated a paranoid mood—McCarthyism—which resulted in the persecution by congressional and state legislative committees, by the media, as well as by the courts, of thousands of Americans accused of membership of the American Communist Party, or affiliated organizations, or of being subscribers to left-wing journals. The image pressed by the leaders of this persecutory movement was of a far-flung Communist conspiracy, headquartered in Moscow, and with branches throughout the world committed to the support of the Soviet Union in its efforts to overthrow capitalism and imperialism by every and all means, including espionage and violence. The study (1954), which I began in the early 1950s, made the case for a much more complex Communist system cleansed of paranoia, varying from country to country according to the social composition of the membership, and according to rank in the Communist power structure, from rank and file to cadre and the like.

In making this study I was driven equally by the desire to demonstrate the usefulness of social science methodology in confronting problems of public policy, and to make out the case for a more realistic and differentiated public policy to deal with the "Communist threat." We interviewed several hundred former Communists in the United States and England, France and Italy, workers and middle-class members, rank-and-filers and higher-ups. We interviewed American psychiatrists who had had party members among their patients. We made content analyses of the Communist universe of communication—Lenin's and Stalin's writings and the theoretical journals, as well as its mass media—in order to distinguish between the "esoteric" and "exoteric" cultures of the Communist Party.

## The Civic Culture

Sidney Verba, in reflecting on our five-year-long collaboration on *The Civic Culture* (Almond and Verba, 1963), has imputed to us an unusual capacity for chutzpah, the Yiddish expression for "nerve." This expression may be defined on the one hand as "risk-taking," the willingness to take a chance without which important purposes cannot be achieved. Or it may be defined as "foolhardiness," overreaching. In Yiddish much depends on the inflection. In Verba's retrospective in *The Civic Culture Revisited* (Almond and Verba, 1980) he locates our effort somewhere in between the sober risk-taking and foolhardy extremes.

Verba and I might not agree on just at what point the line should be drawn. I had in my memory Merriam's Civic Education series in the 1920s

and the 1930s, which, in a way, was an effort to make a comparative political culture study in that pre–survey research era. Interviewing of citizen-
respondents was the main method Merriam and Gosnell used in their nonvoting studies of the 1920s. I had participated in the survey of German
opinion and attitudes done by the Morale Division of the U.S. Strategic
Bombing Survey in the immediate aftermath of World War II. In my study
of public opinion and foreign policy in the late 1940s, I made substantial
use of public opinion data; and in the *Appeals of Communism* study, I had
employed survey organizations operating in England, France, and Italy. It
was not a big jump to undertake a cross-national study of political attitudes, using probability sampling, open-ended and structured kinds of
questions, and adapting and improving on existing measures and indices
of participation, affiliation, civic competence, and social trust. *The Civic
Culture* ventured into new territory, but it was not very far ahead of the
pack.

　　And by venturing as it did it provided the baseline for the masterful,
carefully researched and analyzed work on political participation done by
Sidney Verba and his associates (with Schlozman and Brady, 1995), as well
as providing the counterpoint for the troubling findings on the decline of
American voluntarism reported by Robert Putnam (1993). Perhaps at least
some of the errors committed in the conduct of the *Civic Culture* study (and
faithfully recorded and acknowledged in *The Civic Culture Revisited*) may
be granted a degree of absolution under Pareto's apothegm, "Give me a
fruitful error, full of seeds, bursting with its own corrections. You can keep
your sterile truth for yourself!"

　　I have been wonderfully fortunate in my coauthors and collaborators—Bernard C. Cohen, Sidney Verba, Lucian Pye, James Coleman,
Bingham Powell, Scott Flanagan, Robert Mundt, and many others. It will
never be possible to separate their ideas from mine. We were an intellectual movement of the second half of the twentieth century, beginning with
great élan in the first decades after World War I and encountering heavy
waters in the politicized and rational choice–economistic later decades.
We cannot measure our impact, but we know that we left marks on the history of comparative politics.

　　I do not neatly fit the "comparative European" category, the boundaries of this "comparative autobiography." I have been a comparativist
from the beginning of my career. My researches of the 1950s—on the
resistance movements of World War II and the Communist parties of the
1950s—were purely European, and European American, in their focus.
The work of my maturity—*The Politics of the Developing Areas, The*

*Civic Culture,* and *Crisis, Choice, and Change*—all sought a broader coverage, the inclusion of the third world, and the recognition of the persistence of the premodern in the modern. More recently, my encounter with the fading of the culture of progress (Almond, Chodorow, and Pearce, 1980), and the emergence of "fundamentalist" religious movements throughout the world (Almond, Sivan, and Appleby, 1995), still finds me an incorrigible comparativist with humanist ambivalence.

# 6

# Area Studies and the Objectivity of the Social Sciences

NOT LONG AGO FRANCIS SUTTON, speaking at his retirement as the Ford Foundation executive in charge of foreign area studies, described the several decades of his service as having witnessed an "expansion of international scholarship that has been one of the academic glories of our time. . . . [A]s a result of these efforts," he said, "the academic world has become a great storehouse of what had been rather scattered pockets of expertise throughout this country, and a great flowering of intellectual effort on far places has resulted" (1982, p. 49).

## The Rise and Significance of Area Studies

Prior to World War II and the national explosion that followed it, the roster of academic foreign area specialists in the Western world was quite short. We can quickly call off the more important names in comparative and area studies in the first decades of the century. Thus British experts on the United States included James Bryce, Harold Laski, and Denis Brogan.

Originally published as "The Political Culture of Foreign Area Research: Methodological Reflections," in *The Political Culture of Foreign Area and International Studies,* edited by Richard J. Samuels and Myron Weiner (Washington, D.C.: Brassey's US, 1992). Reprinted, with minor revisions, with permission of Richard J. Samuels.

American experts on Britain and other European countries included Woodrow Wilson, William B. Munro, British expatriate Herman Finer, and German expatriate Carl Friedrich. For continental European experts on foreign countries we may not overlook Frenchman Alexis de Tocqueville, even though he wrote in the first part of the nineteenth century. At the end of the nineteenth century and in the first decades of the twentieth, there were Andre Siegfried, who wrote on the national character of the French, the Americans, the English, and the Swiss; the Russian Moissaye Ostrogorski, who wrote on the history of politics in England and the United States; the German sociologist Max Weber, who wrote on German, American, British, and Russian politics; and Roberto Michels, who wrote on the Social Democratic Party of Germany.

The Comparative Civic Education series published in the late 1920s and 1930s under the editorship of Charles E. Merriam was a harbinger of the future, more systematic, approach to foreign area studies. That series included studies of civic training (called "political socialization" today) in the United States, Britain, France, the Soviet Union, Italy, and Switzerland, and concluded with a comparative volume that Merriam wrote. I am sure this list is incomplete, but there were not many others. There were very few students of non-European countries, and these were mostly historians. The world was still a rather parochial place.

Area studies in the sense of the interdisciplinary, multimembered programs with which we are familiar in most major universities are strictly modern phenomena, and primarily concentrated in the United States. These foreign area specialists are organized nationally and internationally in learned societies of East, Southeast, and South Asianists, Middle Eastern, East European and Russian, African, and Latin American specialists, having their own learned journals. The database is immense and grows constantly as new generations of scholars go into the field to make increasingly specialized studies. It is still a predominantly American enterprise, although the Europeans and the Japanese share to some extent in the production of this knowledge and have access to much of it. The formerly Marxist-Leninist countries have had foreign area specialists, but they only contributed in limited ways to the scholarly literature of foreign area studies. While there have been Soviet and East European area studies in the United States and other Western countries in the last decades, these countries are now more open to research, and they are entering a new stage. Third-world countries, with the exception of the more advanced among them, are indeed more often objects of this knowledge search than participants in it.

Among the important themes that a survey of the political culture of foreign area studies ought to explore are the causes and the consequences of this uneven distribution of cosmopolitan knowledge—in particular, the relative absence of indigenous, and the relative dominance of American investigators—for developmental prospects in various parts of the world and for international affairs generally. This concentration of foreign area knowledge in the United States, and in the advanced countries generally, and the limited knowledge in third-world areas contributes to the weakness of these countries and to their inability to relate effectively to the forces in the outside world, to develop their own agendas, and to shape and implement their own goals effectively. From this point of view, the diffusion of social science competence and foreign area studies to the third world must have a high priority.

The depth and distribution of detailed and accurate knowledge of foreign countries and cultures around the world is the best single indicator of our capacity to confront and solve our urgent international problems constructively. Knowledge does not guarantee that we will solve them constructively, but lack of it makes it likely that we will not. And it is according to this criterion that we have to examine foreign area studies—the degree to which and the way in which the characteristics of other nations, other cultures, and the international environment are accurately perceived in the nations of the world. Accurate perception is, of course, a limiting concept. And the search for it is an aspect of a particular culture. We might call a political culture that is informed by a rich flow of relatively accurate knowledge of foreign areas and the international environment—through scholarship, journalism, travel, and the like—a "cosmopolitan" political culture (after Robert Merton) characterized by beliefs, values, resource allocations, professions, and the like, sustaining such a flow of relatively accurate knowledge. All historical cultures fall short of this ideal, but those that effectively aspire to it I would call cosmopolitan political cultures, each one having its particular emphases, shortfalls, and parochialisms.

## Area Studies and Political Culture

When we speak of the political culture of foreign area studies, we refer to the values and beliefs of its practitioners as they affect judgments of political characteristics of the countries they study. These values and beliefs derive from the larger national culture as it has been shaped by its historical experience; from its subcultures (e.g., class, ethnic, religious, or regional) as these have been shaped by historical experience; and from its role cultures (i.e., professional and disciplinary values, assumptions, and methods). Each of the disciplines included in area studies—historians, language and literary specialists, anthropologists, sociologists, political scientists, and economists—brings some special perspective and tradition to the study of the area. The characteristics of the area itself, the kinds of issues encountered, and the ideas of leading indigenous scholars similarly enter into the shaping of the political culture of foreign area studies. One of the most powerful shaping experiences of specialists on foreign areas is their doctoral research period in the region and country in which they specialize. Typically they are associated with universities in these foreign countries, where they encounter indigenous scholars in their own disciplines. They tend to be dependent on these scholars for contacts and advice. Thus a young scholar trained in U.S. political science and entering into Latin American area studies in the late 1960s and 1970s could not avoid being demoralized by the Vietnam crisis on the U.S. university campus and be distrustful of U.S. foreign policy. In his fieldwork, he could not avoid exposure to the wave of anti-Americanism among Latin American intellectuals as their countries fell under the control of military dictators and as the United States intervened in their support. He might be headquartered in Santiago, Chile, or in Lima, Peru, where he would be advised and befriended by scholars in his own and related disciplines. He would no doubt read and be influenced by such books as Cardoso's on Latin American dependency. From his U.S. training, he would bring certain ontological and methodological assumptions and particular approaches—such as reliance on historical case studies, aggregate statistical analysis, or survey research—to bear on these issues. A political culture of area studies, an amalgam of assumptions and research priorities, arises out of all these influences.

## The Cold War and Area Studies

Modern area and international studies have arisen in the context of the Cold War. As this menacing confrontation shifted from continent to continent, recruitment to the various area studies waxed and waned. Western Europe dominated the 1950s and 1960s as Britain recovered, France shifted from the Fourth to the Fifth Republic, and Germany took its first steps toward democratization and its *Wirtschaftwunder* (economic miracle). This focus

on Europe was associated with the generous thrust of U.S. foreign policy—
the Marshall Plan and the formation of the North Atlantic Treaty
Organization (NATO). East Asian studies throve in the first decades of the
postwar period, as China turned Communist, Japan worked its way out of
defeat, and the "Newly Industrializing Countries" (NICs) of South Korea,
Taiwan, Hong Kong, and Singapore emerged on the scene. Indian studies
grew as that country emerged as a "democratic Fabian socialist" alternative
to Maoist China. The African national explosion in the 1950s and 1960s,
the exotic countries and cultures that emerged, and U.S.-USSR competition
for control challenged the imaginations and moral commitments of many
young scholars in the 1950s and 1960s. Castro's revolution in Cuba in the
early 1960s, the various coups in South America, and the trends of U.S.
policy in the same decade triggered the rapid growth of Latin American
studies.

This close association of the growth of area studies with the Cold War
raises two questions: What implications does the ending of the Cold
War have for area studies in the quantitative sense and how has the Cold
War affected area studies qualitatively, in substance? To answer the first
question, it may very well be that the waning of the urgency of the Cold War
will result in some attenuation of support for, and some decline in recruitment to, area studies in the United States. Perhaps Western Europe and
Japan will take up the slack and maintain, or even increase, support for area
studies, but this internationalization of area studies will have significant
implications for their growth and development, which areas are fostered,
which neglected, and what kinds of issues will be stressed.

To answer the second question, how the ending of the Cold War is
likely to affect the substance of foreign area studies, we have first to
answer the question of how the Cold War has affected them in the first
place. A crucial factor in the development of the political culture of the
various area studies has been the political tendencies and issues dominant
in the area and the prevailing ideas among the indigenous intellectuals. In
Europe, the pattern on the whole, once the crises of the immediate postwar years were overcome, has been one of a moderate left and moderate
right division, in an atmosphere of growing economic and political
strength. European area studies reflect this relatively temperate political
climate. Some specialists (English, French, German, etc.) have been influenced by such indigenous English socialists as John Goldthorpe, German
neo-Marxists as Klaus Offe, and "critical theorists" as Jurgen Habermas.
But the political debate in Europe has been an increasingly moderate one
as the European economy has flourished. The Communist parties have

declined precipitously, and the revolutionary side of socialism has been toned down. Nevertheless, some of the Europeanists have been persuaded, or partly persuaded, by Marxist and "critical theoretical" views, holding that "ethical neutrality" and "scientific objectivity" are disguised forms of support for the status quo and that scholarship has to be identified with the "progressive"—that is, socialist—forces of history.

Specialists on Japan and East Asia could not avoid the extraordinary growth records of these export-oriented countries, as well as their relatively egalitarian income distribution. An early, strong Marxist orientation among Japanese social scientists attenuated as a result of student extremism in the 1960s and 1970s and Japan's remarkable growth and stable democratization. American specialists on these countries have been preoccupied with the explanation of their growth "miracles" and the patterns of democratic transition in such countries as South Korea and Taiwan.

## Dependency Theory and the Political Culture of Area Studies

The area studies programs most strongly affected by political conditions and by indigenous interpreters of these conditions were the Latin American and the African. In the 1960s and 1970s, Latin American studies took off on university campuses that were agitated by the Vietnam War and stimulated by the Cuban revolution and the rise of "bureaucratic authoritarian" regimes in the major countries of South America. It was a time when governmental legitimacy in the United States, and particularly on university campuses, was at a very low ebb.

Led by a group of Latin American neo-Marxist intellectuals, most U.S. Latin Americanists adopted the "dependency" approach, arguing that the "capitalist center" (North America and Western Europe) penetrated the semi-peripheral and peripheral economies, exploiting and distorting them, and that only socialism could solve these problems. According to the leading dependency theorist, Fernando Henrique Cardoso, only a methodology stressing "the socio-political nature of the economic relations of production—an approach which found its highest expression in Marx," would enable scholars to explain the politico-economic realities of the third world. It is illusory to believe, Cardoso goes on to say, "that capitalist development will solve basic problems for the majority of the population. In the end, what has to be discussed as an alternative is not the consolidation of the state and the fulfillment of 'autonomous capitalism,' but how to supersede them. The important question, then, is how to construct paths toward socialism" (Cardoso and Faletto, 1979, p. xxiv). Or as Richard Fagen put it:

> Real progress in development scholarship has to be associated with a restructuring of asymmetric international power relations and a much more difficult and historically significant assault on capitalist forms of development themselves. . . . Only when this crucial understanding infuses the nascent academic critique of the global capitalist system will we be able to say that the paradigm shift in mainstream U.S. social science is gathering steam and moving scholarship closer to what really matters. (1978, pp. 287–300)

Dependency theorists argued for a principled politicization of scholarship. Andre Gunder-Frank, in a book that appeared several years before the Spanish edition of the Cardoso and Faletto work, put it quite straightforwardly: "I had to free myself from the liberal maxim, according to which only political neutrality permits scientific objectivity, a maxim widely used to defend social irresponsibility, pseudo-scientific scientism, and political reaction. . . . I had to learn that social science must be political science" (1967, p. xviii).

The adoption of views such as this by a substantial part of the community of Latin Americanists is reflected in a volume of papers subsidized by the Joint Committee on Latin American Studies of the Social Science Research Council and the American Council of Learned Societies, authored by American and Latin American scholars and presented at a conference in Lima, Peru, held in November 1972. In the introduction to those papers, coeditors Julio Cotler and Richard Fagen conclude by contrasting the Latin American and American intellectual traditions—the Latin American tradition of historical and macro-sociological studies and the American tradition "of more sharply focused, detailed, empirical studies of events and institutions." Because these empirical and theoretically complex studies are not clearly focused on the hegemonic and exploitative relations between north and south, they may, and are, used to further the exploitation of third-world countries: "The hegemonic machine is a voracious consumer of the *materia prima* produced by the social science community, and it is also a tremendous subverter of talent and independence. How does one continue to practice the craft in ways that diminish or harness the power of that machine rather than contributing to it?" (1974, p. 14). One of the ways of harnessing the craft of Latin American studies in this task of diminishing the power of the hegemonic machine is proposed by Richard Fagen in a later essay in the volume. This is what he calls "documented denunciation":

> essentially muckraking and informational activity, often less than scholarly by conventional definitions, but absolutely vital if the worst excesses of the exercise of North American power, whether perpetrated by the Marines or by the multinationals, are to be held in check. It is an activity for which North Americans with academic and intellectual pretensions are particularly well suited and well situated. (1974, p. 264)

This politicization of area studies, while most marked in Latin American studies, affected third-world studies generally. In Africa, it made more sense to talk in terms of imperialism and neocolonialism. The collapse of the early democratic regimes in the new nations of sub-Saharan Africa, their transformation into neopatrimonial, military, or one-party regimes, and the failure of these countries to make economic progress created this susceptibility to revisionist, anti-neocolonialist thinking. Given the imperialist and exploitative history of the African continent, blaming the great capitalist power centers for the failures of development in the new African nations had a persuasive logic. Scholarship on Africa tended to obscure the more sordid and corrupt aspects of political rule on that continent, and there was a tacit understanding that African scholarship should avoid blaming the victim, a tendency that resulted in protectiveness, evasiveness, and euphemism in the treatment of the domestic politics of the new African nations.

The social sciences more generally experienced demoralization in the cultural revolution of the 1960s–1970s. Marxist ideas and "critical theory" made substantial headway—particularly in history, political science, and sociology—in North America, Western Europe, and elsewhere. Common to Marxism and its offshoots was the rejection of "positivistic" social science on the grounds that it sought to separate the social sciences from the sphere of action and values. This kind of search for objectivity and value neutrality, according to critical theory, tends to "legitimize the existing order" and produce a mood of "resignation to the given." To avoid this sterility and complacency, scholarship had to associate itself with the forces of progress—that is, socialism (Held, 1980, pp. 162 ff.). In a programmatic article surveying the history of development ideas, Tony Smith (1979) reviews and compares the developmental and modernization literature with the dependency literature, casting praise and criticism on both in what appears to be an evenhanded style. But he does not fault the dependency approach for this rejection in principle of scholarly objectivity and neutrality, and this identification of dependency thinking with socialist solutions.

## Area Studies and the End of the Cold War

The Cold War has been brought to an end through an acknowledgment of failure on the part of the Marxist-Leninist countries. The implications of these extraordinary developments for the future of Marxism more generally and for socialism are still unclear. The Marxist-Leninist version of centralized socialism has undoubtedly been discredited. In the capitalist countries there has been a similar discrediting of central planning, nationalization of industry, and similar socialist goals, and a recognition that productivity and equity require some reconciliation of capitalist and socialist practices, some reconciliation of private property and entrepreneurship with distributive equity.

If history can no longer be viewed as moving unambiguously toward socialism, if the future is more open-ended, more uncertain, then it can no longer be argued convincingly that scholarly objectivity and neutrality are inherently static, conservative, and supportive of the status quo and that scholarship must be oriented toward a socialist future. Thus, the end of the Cold War reopens the fundamental methodological questions that Marxism and dependency theory sought to close—that is, the relation of knowledge to politics and public policy. Marxism and its later variants—critical theory, dependency theory, and world system theory—and their followers in foreign area studies not only argued that scholarship had to make a choice between "mindless objectivity" and progress toward socialism, but that the earlier positivist philosophers of a social science of ethical neutrality and objectivity were the pied pipers who had led the social sciences down this garden path of scholarly sterility and worse.

The "dependency" methodological critique of mainstream social science characterized it in classical positivist terms, identifying it with the view that all sciences, including the social ones, "essentially admitted of the same structure and procedure as physics" (Held, 1980, p. 164). This view of social and political science is only one of the meta-methodological views among contemporary social scientists. To suggest, as do the various neo-Marxist schools and the dependency writers, that it is the philosophy of mainstream social science, and of development and modernization theory that are parts of that mainstream, is to create a straw man. It is an egregious error to associate development and modernization theory—the targets of the dependency school—with this hard-nosed "positivistic" methodological position. Talcott Parsons, S. M. Lipset, Samuel Huntington, and other scholars in the development tradition, while staunch adherents of the rules of scholarly evidence and inference, were hardly positivists in this physical science sense.

This is surely not the view of Max Weber, whose early methodological essays, "The Meaning of Ethical Neutrality in Sociology and Economics" and "Objectivity in Social Science and Social Policy" (1949), written in the first decades of the twentieth century, are still the most fully formulated and profound versions of the relationship between social science knowledge and action. Nor is it the view of Karl Mannheim (1949), who along with some of his socialist colleagues of the ill-fated Weimar Republic had worked his way out of the primitive Marxist subordination of the processes of knowledge to socialist politics.

It had, of course, been socialist doctrine that in a capitalist society, objective scholarship was only possible within the framework of Marxist social science—that is, the laws of dialectic materialism and of ultimate proletarian revolution. Since the essence of social reality, as "scientifically proven" by Marx, Engels, and their followers, was this integral social-class confrontation, denial of these assumptions or even neutrality toward them inevitably placed one in the enemy camp, involved bias in favor of the status quo, a procapitalist orientation. To recognize the possibility of objective scholarship as did Karl Mannheim in the 1930s was a courageous step, risking the salvation of one's professional soul.

It is intriguing that the neo-Marxist literature that sets great store on its rejection of positivist views because of their indifference to the human situation and their consequent assent to the injustices of the social order, fails even to refer to these Weberian methodological essays or to the later works of Karl Mannheim, who dealt in great length and depth with these themes. Weber is only cited in these sources for his melancholy observations about the future of capitalism and bureaucracy and the "disenchantment of the world," as a consequence of the spread of science and rationality.

Surely one of the consequences of the termination of the Cold War will be to revisit these basic methodological issues. If socialism is no longer viewed as the unequivocal end of history, and if history, indeed, is viewed as a more open-ended process in which human choices have a great impact, then these themes of ethical neutrality and of objectivity in the social sciences, and their implications for the relationship between social science and public policy, have to be cleaned of the obloquy with which they have been soiled and reexamined. The end of the Cold War then should reopen a meta-methodological debate in area studies, and the first thing that might be done is to reconnect with some of the great documents of social science methodology. The subtlety of these early formulations has been lost sight of, and they are due for a careful rereading.

We in political science and in area studies have not been served well by our methodologists and meta-methodologists. On the one hand, we have been told that we are indistinguishable from the hard sciences, that we are a nomothetic science in search of covering laws, and, on the other hand, that political action and political science are inseparable. Thomas Kuhn's conception of the growth of science (1962) has been bowdlerized by a generation of methodologists who have turned the notion of the scientific paradigm into a justification for theory-bashing and evasion of the scholarly obligation to search the literature, even that part of it with which one disagrees. For many of the scholars of this generation, Max Weber's injunction to seek to separate knowledge from action has been turned into a caricature, a justification for a bloodless objectivity that inevitably supports the status quo. No one familiar with Max Weber and his work would ever characterize him as bloodless. His passionate polemics have left indelible imprints on the scholarly and political debates of the first decades of the twentieth century.

## Revisiting the Methodological Classics:
## Weber and Mannheim

It is indeed true that Max Weber said such things as "it can never be the task of an empirical science to provide binding norms and ideals from which directives for immediate practical activity can be derived" (1949, p. 52), and that "science today is a 'vocation' organized in special disciplines in the service of self-clarification and knowledge of interrelated facts. It is not the gift of grace of seers and prophets dispensing sacred values and revelations, nor does it partake of the contemplation of sages and philosophers about the meaning of the universe" (1958, p. 158).

He spared no feelings in his attacks on those of his generation who refused to draw a clear and unambiguous line around the role of academic intellectuals, that they must keep their values and politics from influencing their scholarship to the extent that they can. But this view of Weber has been caricatured and presented as though this was all that he had to say about the relation between knowledge and action. Quite the contrary, whoever has read the passages in which these views are given such passionate expression will find that after these unambiguous affirmations, Weber goes on to elaborate the important ways in which science can legitimately contribute to value choices and ethical politics.

In this last connection, we may remember that in *Politics as a Vocation* (see *From Max Weber*, 1958) he presents two kinds of ethically oriented political action—the ethics of absolute ends and the ethics of responsibility. Science would have little to contribute to the ethics of absolute ends, only in the selection of means to these given ends. Since the chosen end is sacred or absolute, there can be no opportunity cost analysis of the consequences of pursuing this end for other ends. But the ethics of responsibility calls for the most intimate interpenetration of the two spheres of values and science. It must ask the question of the effect of the choice of particular means for the goals they are supposed to advance. It must ask what the consequences are of selecting one goal or set of goals for other goals. These essentially scientific steps are value-shaping and value-selecting in their implications. More fully in his polemic on "Objectivity in Social Science and Social Policy" (1949, pp. 52 ff.) he elaborates this relationship between knowledge and action, arguing that there are three significant respects in which knowledge can evaluate and ethically enhance action: (1) it can establish whether the means proposed are adequate and appropriate to the end or are likely to overwhelm or subvert it; (2) it can explore the consequences of choosing a particular end for other desired ends; and (3) it can help clarify the value preferences of the acting individual, enabling him to make explicit the basic premises of his value choice (p. 53). In connection with this third point, Weber goes on to say:

> We can also offer the person, who makes a choice, insight into the significance of his goals. We can teach him to think in terms of the context and the meaning of the ends he desires, and among which he chooses. We do this through making explicit and developing in a logically consistent manner the "ideas" which do or which may underlie the concrete end. It is self-evident that one of the most important tasks of every science of cultural life is to arrive at a rational understanding of these "ideas" for which men either really or allegedly struggle. This does not overstep the boundaries of a science which strives for an "analytical ordering of empirical reality," although the methods which are used in this interpretation of cultural values are not "inductions" in the usual sense. . . .
>
> But the scientific treatment of value judgments may not only understand and empathically analyze the desired ends and the ideals which

underlie them; it can also "judge" them critically. This criticism can of course have only a dialectical character, i.e., it can be no more than a formal logical judgment of historically given value judgments and ideas, a testing of the ideal according to the postulate of the internal consistency of the desired end. It can, insofar as it set itself this goal, aid the acting, willing person in attaining self-clarification concerning the final axioms from which his desired ends are derived. It can assist him in becoming aware of the ultimate standards of value . . . which he must presuppose in order to be logical. The elevation of these ultimate standards, which are manifested in concrete value judgments, to the level of explicitness, is the utmost that the scientific treatment of value judgments can do without entering into the realm of speculation.

And here is the punch line: "An empirical science cannot tell anyone what he should do—but rather what he can do—and under certain circumstances—what he wishes to do." (p. 54)

This intimate interaction between knowledge and action, science and political decision, is the real Weberian doctrine of ethical neutrality, often misrepresented in contemporary methodological literature, and more particularly in the literature of area studies. It was written when Weber had just turned forty, when he was assuming the editorship of the *Archiv fur Sozialwissenschaft und Sozialpolitik* in 1903. It stated the philosophy of that perhaps first, genuine social science journal, which survived for three decades until the fall of the Weimar Republic.

Just four years before the Nazi seizure of power and the suppression of the *Archiv*—in 1929—another social philosopher, Karl Mannheim, a Social Democrat, answered the question of the separability of science and politics in the affirmative. He does this in the course of a long chapter in his book *Ideologie und Utopie* (1949), titled "The Prospects of Scientific Politics: The Relationship Between Social Theory and Political Practice." He states midway in this chapter, "The question, whether a science of politics is possible and whether it can be taught, must, if we summarize all that we have said thus far, be answered in the affirmative" (p. 146). In his conclusion to this chapter he accepts Max Weber's view of the relationship between knowledge and politics:

Max Weber has furnished the first acceptable formulation of this conception of politics. His ideas and researches reflect the stage in ethics and politics in which blind fate seems to be at least partially in the course of disappearance in the social process, and the knowledge of everything knowable becomes the obligation of the acting person. It is at this point, if at any, that politics can become a science, since on the one hand the structure of the historical realm, which is to be controlled, has become transparent, and on the other hand out of the new ethics a point of view emerges which regards knowledge not as a passive contemplation but as critical self-examination, and in this sense prepares the road for political action. (p. 171)

Mannheim's own estimate of the sociological constraints on accurate knowledge are very substantial. We end up with a theory of objective knowledge that has strong social-class presuppositions:

[A]n experimental outlook, unceasingly sensitive to the dynamic nature of society and its wholeness, is not likely to be developed by a class occupying a middle position but only by a relatively classless stratum which is not too firmly situated in the social order. . . . This unanchored, relatively classless stratum is, to use Alfred Weber's terminology, the "socially unattached intelligentsia." (p. 137)

It is from this "classless" stratum that the bearers of the new social and political science are recruited, that scholars, publicists, and the like, detached from class interests, can now develop and cultivate the production and accumulation of objective knowledge. Mannheim's advocacy of a sociology of knowledge has unfortunately played into the hands of those who want to reject the very notion of separating political science from social action, since Mannheim places such weight on the social conditioning of political thought. But Mannheim himself fought this battle through to its conclusion with this notion of classless intellectuals and their ability to recognize and mitigate the pressure of class and thereby make objective scholarship possible.

## The Role of Foreign Area Studies and Objective Scholarship

The role of class as limiting the possibility of objectivity in area studies assumed an unusual form in dependency (Cardoso and Faletto, 1979) and "world system" theory (Wallerstein, 1979). Rather than taking as the unit of analysis the national economy divided into a capitalist and a working class, the world became the unit, divided into the capitalist-imperialist core and the penetrated and exploited periphery (with a semi-periphery in the middle). The social sciences and the area studies of the capitalist core were instruments in the exploitation of third-world countries. They produced a "developmentalist" doctrine designed to conceal the exploitative character of the relationship between the core and the periphery and to create the illusion of development. But true development was only possible through a revolutionary break with the core-periphery exploitative relationship and the establishment of socialism in both core and periphery. These theories, which were dominant in Latin American studies in the 1970s and 1980s and very influential in African studies, downplayed the importance of area studies, condemning them to the simple task of confirming the all-important role of the "capitalist core" in explaining the backwardness of third-world economies and the repressiveness of their political institutions.

There is much more to the political sociology of area studies than the analysis of class. There is a well-known propensity for area scholars to become clients of the countries they study or of particular groups within the countries they study. In an earlier era of European studies, for example, it was said of students of British politics that they were Anglophiles, denigrating U.S. separation of powers by comparison with British cabinet government and the "neutral" British civil service, with a kind of "country cousin" eye to pleasing their British colleagues, such as Herman Finer, Ivor Jennings, Harold Laski, W. J. M. MacKenzie, and the like. Contemporary Japanese studies, drawing some financial support from Japanese sources, are said to be influenced by this financial dependence, to convey a view of Japanese culture, society, economics, and politics that is preferred by the Japanese. During the long decades of the Cold War, U.S. scholarship was often accused of being inseparable from U.S. foreign and defense policy, and the financial role of such agencies as the Department of Defense and the Central Intelligence Agency in the support of foreign area research was often cited as evidence of this connection. For the left in U.S. foreign area scholarship, the study of revolutionary regimes, such as the Soviet Union, Maoist China, Castro's Cuba, or the Nicaraguan Sandinistas, might serve as ways of declaring ideological commitments and advocating changes in U.S. foreign and defense policy. In foreign area studies, particularly in the third world, certain subjects—such as the ineptness and/or corruption of indigenous leadership—may be viewed as taboo in light of a long history of imperialism that inhibited and distorted the development of political institutions and practices. Thus, scholarship may be inhibited by protectiveness, a desire to avoid "blaming the victim."

Most recently, "multiculturalism" has entered into the foreign area studies meta-methodological debate. The question being raised has to do with the validity of a corpus of foreign area scholarship produced by foreigners. It may be argued that it takes an indigenous scholarship to understand the issues and patterns of Ghanaian or Indonesian politics and that a scholarly community dominated by foreigners, and particularly by a single national group, as, for example, Americans, is bound to be biased by American cultural and political predispositions. In this connection, we would have to distinguish between a "nativism" that would argue that only the members of a culture can understand it and the appreciation that a foreign area literature without the participation of indigenous scholars presents scholarly and political problems of a serious order. The scholarly problems may be less important than the political ones. If knowledge about one's institutions and practices is produced abroad, in foreign languages and by means of unfamiliar methodologies, indigenous political leaders are disadvantaged in competition with foreigners and in understanding and planning the reform of these institutions. The U.S. semi-monopoly of foreign area studies has this downside aspect, one not likely to be rectified at a time when research and training resources are in short supply, and likely to be further restricted by the termination of the Cold War.

Thus, a political sociology of foreign area studies would have to add to Mannheim's broad category of class interest—xenophilia and xenophobia vis-à-vis one country or another—ideological commitments to socialism, capitalism, and the like; cultural biases of one kind or another; protectiveness toward third-world and new nations; financial inducements; or simple short-term calculations of material interest as causes of bias or lack of objectivity and quality in foreign area studies. And in the place of Mannheim's "classless intellectual" as the safeguard of objectivity, modern scholarship has the norms of professionalism, professional associations with their codes of ethics, and their journals governed by peer review. These institutions and norms are not only concerned with objectivity, but with quantity and quality of scholarship, and with the spread of the profession and its products around the world.

Mannheim wrote at a time when scholarship was largely a labor of individual activity, with books and in libraries. The days of surveys, computerized databases, systematic fieldwork, and statistics had not yet arrived. He could not foresee the enormous growth of scholarship in the post–World War II period, the growth of the social science disciplines, of university departments providing for peer review of scholarly attainment, the formation of disciplinary societies with learned journals also providing for peer review, and similar marks of professionalization—these were just in their beginnings during Mannheim's lifetime. Similarly, the formation of foreign area associations, again with learned journals, and meetings with formal papers, were just in their beginnings when Mannheim was composing his methodological thoughts. Given the present context of foreign area studies, would he have placed such great stress on classlessness and marginality as a basis for political science objectivity? Would not the increasing sophistication of scholarship and peer review by one's colleagues in university departments and in area studies programs, and learned journal editing, approximate the neutralization of which Mannheim speaks?

Foreign area studies represent a special category from the point of view of control of bias through disciplinary norms and processes. The Asianist, Islamicist, the Africanist, or Latin Americanist is a member of an area studies community, as well as of a discipline such as history, literature, anthropology, political science, or economics. Area studies associations and journals do not have a relatively unambiguous disciplinary code to enforce. If anything, area studies organizations and media, because of their multidisciplinary character and their exposure to foreign countries and cultures, encourage departures from disciplinary codes and cultures. Some of these departures may be productive in the sense of interdisciplinary work and collaboration. An economist may learn how to take into account real cultural contexts in place of the formally assumed ones. And sociologists, historians, and political scientists may learn how to handle economic magnitudes and interactions. But this has a downside as well, since area studies associations are probably more open to penetration and domination than are disciplinary societies such as economics, history, and anthropology, where there is a single set of scholarly norms and traditions. This would seem to have been the case with the Latin American Studies Association in the 1970s and 1980s (Packenham, 1992, chap. 11). In this case, we had a relatively new professional community dominated by its younger generations, and a new learned society just in process of developing professional norms and criteria.

Thus, contemporary foreign area scholars are surrounded by institutions and are governed by norms that may provide some insulation from class bias, ethnocentrism, sensationalism, clientelism, and the like. If we assume that post–Cold War foreign area studies will move in the direction of scholarly objectivity, as did Max Weber and Karl Mannheim, what becomes of our theme of the political culture of foreign area studies? The concept of political culture in the area studies field assumes nonrational propensities of one kind or another—social cultural, and moral assumptions—that affect research priorities, interpretations of data, and the drawing of implications for public policy.

Surely there is substantial evidence for the existence of cultural patterning in the conduct of area studies. They make out a case both for the political cultural propensities of foreign area studies and for the variety of such propensities in the different area programs. The search for objectivity in foreign area research, on the other hand, assumes that it is possible for scholarship to control the effects of, or escape from, these nonrational biases.

It is the aim of scholarship in foreign area studies to overcome cultural bias; to ascertain the truth about foreign cultures, social structures, political institutions, and processes; and to disseminate these truths without qualification and restriction. Can one say that to the extent that it succeeds it eliminates these cultural properties? Is the political culture of foreign area studies then to be viewed as a residual, the unavoidable bias, no matter how unequivocal the intent? To the extent that the scholarly program is carried out, is the cultural component of area studies reduced? Are there inherent limits to our capacity for objective knowledge, and hence will area studies always contain cultural biases of one kind or another?

Surely the answers to all of these questions are affirmative. Objective scholarship and cultural biases are in conflict. It is the aim of the first to reduce the second. And yet it can never fully succeed. Our methods, although increasingly precise, never quite capture the whole truth. And even when used judiciously and in combination they are bound to miss much, and particularly to fall short of dealing with the problem of change in the social and historical sense. The reason for this is that, in contrast to the hard sciences, it is in the nature of the data we study to change in significant ways and that what we consider to be important about it is also in a constant process of change. Who predicted the rise of environmentalism and quality of life issues just a decade or two before they became salient? Who predicted the moral collapse of Marxism-Leninism as recently as the first year of the Gorbachev era? Who would be rash enough to predict the demise of socialism from today's prevailing acceptance of the free market? Or the end of authoritarianism from today's democratic trend? Prophecies about the end of ideology or the end of history are appropriately greeted with skepticism.

The inherent instability of the human material, the inescapable creative variety of nations and cultures, despite the homogenizing impact of technology and the media, assures us that there will always be a political culture of area studies—norms and beliefs shaping and distorting our scholarship, however improved philosophically and methodologically. Area studies scholarship, like all scholarship, will see through a glass a bit darkly.

# Part 2

---

# Contributions to Democratic Theory

# 7

# Capitalism and Democracy

JOSEPH SCHUMPETER, A GREAT ECONOMIST and social scientist of the last generation, whose career was almost equally divided between Central European and American universities, and who lived close to the crises of the 1930s and 1940s, published a book in 1942 under the title *Capitalism, Socialism, and Democracy*. The book has had great influence, and can be read today with profit. It was written in the aftergloom of the Great Depression, during the early triumphs of Fascism and Nazism in 1940 and 1941, when the future of capitalism, socialism, and democracy all were in doubt. Schumpeter projected a future of declining capitalism, and rising socialism. He thought that democracy under socialism might be no more impaired and problematic than it was under capitalism.

He wrote a concluding chapter in the second edition, which appeared in 1947 and which took into account the political-economic situation at the end of the war, with the Soviet Union then astride a devastated Europe. In this last chapter he argues that we should not identify the future of socialism with that of the Soviet Union, that what we had observed and were observing in the first three decades of Soviet existence was not a necessary expression of socialism. There was a lot of Czarist Russia in the mix.

If Schumpeter were writing today, I don't believe he would argue that socialism has a brighter future than capitalism. The relationship between

From *PS: Political Science and Politics* (September 1991). Reprinted, with minor revisions, with permission of the American Political Science Association.

the two has turned out to be a good deal more complex and intertwined than Schumpeter anticipated. But I am sure that he would still urge us to separate the future of socialism from that of Soviet and East European Communism.

Unlike Schumpeter I do not include "Socialism" in my title, since its future as a distinct ideology and program of action is unclear at best. Western Marxism and the moderate socialist movements seem to have settled for social democratic solutions, for adaptations of both capitalism and democracy producing acceptable mixes of market competition, political pluralism, participation, and welfare. I deal with these modifications of capitalism, as a consequence of the impact of democracy on capitalism in the last half century.

Economists tend to treat the state and government instrumentally, as a kind of secondary service mechanism. At the time that Adam Smith wrote *The Wealth of Nations,* the world of government, politics, and the state that he knew—pre–Reform Act England, the French government of Louis XV and XVI—were riddled with special privileges, monopolies, interferences with trade. With my tongue only half in my cheek I believe the discipline of economics may have been traumatized by this condition of political life at its birth.

I do not believe that politics can be treated in this purely instrumental and reductive way without losing our analytic grip on the social and historical process. The economy and the polity are the main problem-solving mechanisms of human society. They each have their distinctive means, and they each have their "goods" or ends. They necessarily interact with each other, and transform each other in the process. Democracy in particular generates goals and programs. You cannot give people the suffrage, and let them form organizations, run for office, and the like, without their developing all kinds of ideas as to how to improve things. And sometimes some of these ideas are adopted, implemented, and are productive, and improve our lives, although many economists are reluctant to concede this much to the state.

My lecture deals with this interaction of politics and economics in the Western world in the course of the last couple of centuries, in the era during which capitalism and democracy emerged as the dominant problem-solving institutions of modern civilization. I am going to deal with some of the theoretical and empirical literature dealing with the themes of the positive and negative interaction between capitalism and democracy. There are those who say that capitalism supports democracy, and those who say that capitalism subverts democracy. And there are those who say that democracy subverts capitalism, and those who say that it supports it.

The relation between capitalism and democracy dominates the political theory of the last two centuries. All the logically possible points of view are represented in a rich literature. It is this ambivalence and dialectic, this tension between the two major problem-solving sectors of modern society—the political and the economic—that is the topic of my lecture.

## Capitalism Supports Democracy

Let me begin with the argument that capitalism is positively linked with democracy, shares its values and culture, and facilitates its development. This case has been made in historical, logical, and statistical terms.

Albert Hirschman, in *Rival Views of Market Society* (1986), examines the values, manners, and morals of capitalism, and their effects on the larger society and culture as these have been described by the philosophers of the seventeenth, eighteenth, and nineteenth centuries. He shows how the interpretation of the impact of capitalism has changed from the enlightenment view of Montesquieu, Condorcet, Adam Smith, and others, who stressed the *douceur* of commerce, its "gentling," civilizing effect on behavior and interpersonal relations, to that of the nineteenth- and twentieth-century conservative and radical writers who described the culture of capitalism as crassly materialistic, destructively competitive, corrosive of morality, and hence self-destructive. This sharp, almost 180-degree shift in point of view among political theorists is partly explained by the transformation from the commerce and small-scale industry of early capitalism, to the smoke-blackened industrial districts, the demonic and exploitive entrepreneurs, and exploited laboring classes of the second half of the nineteenth century. Unfortunately for our purposes, Hirschman doesn't deal explicitly with the capitalism-democracy connection, but rather with culture and with manners. His argument, however, implies an early positive connection and a later negative one.

Joseph Schumpeter, in *Capitalism, Socialism, and Democracy* (1947), states flatly, "History clearly confirms [that] modern democracy rose along with capitalism, and in causal connection with it . . . modern democracy is a product of the capitalist process" (p. 296). He has a whole chapter titled "The Civilization of Capitalism," democracy being a part of that civilization. Schumpeter also makes the point that democracy was historically supportive of capitalism. He states: "the bourgeoisie reshaped, and from its own point of view rationalized, the social and political structure that preceded its ascendancy [that is to say, feudalism]. The democratic method was the political tool of that reconstruction" (p. 297). According to Schumpeter, capitalism and democracy were mutually causal historically, mutually supportive parts of a rising modern civilization, although as I shall show below, he also recognized their antagonisms.

Barrington Moore's historical investigation (1966), with its long title, *The Social Origins of Dictatorship and Democracy: Lord and Peasant in the Making of the Modern World,* argues that there have been three historical routes to industrial modernization. The first of these, followed by Britain, France, and the United States, involved the subordination and transformation of the agricultural sector by the rising commercial bourgeoisie, producing the democratic capitalism of the nineteenth and twentieth centuries. The second route, followed by Germany and Japan, where the landed aristocracy was able to contain and dominate the rising commercial classes, produced an authoritarian and fascist version of industrial modernization, a system of capitalism encased in a feudal authoritarian framework, dominated by a military aristocracy and an authoritarian monarchy. The third route, followed in Russia, where the commercial bourgeoisie was too weak to give content and direction to the modernizing process, took the form of a revolutionary process drawing on the frustration and resources of the peasantry, and created a mobilized authoritarian Communist regime along with a state-controlled industrialized economy. Successful capitalism dominating and transforming the rural agricultural sector, according to Barrington Moore, is the creator and sustainer of the emerging democracies of the nineteenth century.

Robert A. Dahl, the leading American democratic theorist, in his book *After the Revolution? Authority in a Good Society* (1990), has included a chapter titled "Democracy and Markets":

> It is an historical fact [he says in the opening paragraph of that chapter] that modern democratic institutions . . . have existed only in countries with predominantly privately owned, market-oriented economies, or capitalism if you prefer that name. It is also a fact that all "socialist" countries with predominantly state-owned centrally directed economic orders—command economies—have not enjoyed democratic governments, but have in fact been ruled by authoritarian dictatorships. It is also an historical fact that some "capitalist" countries have also been— and are—ruled by authoritarian dictatorships.

To put it more formally, it looks to be the case that market-oriented economies are necessary (in the logical sense) to democratic institutions, though they are certainly not sufficient. And it looks to be the case that state-owned centrally directed economic orders are strictly associated with authoritarian regimes, though authoritarianism definitely does not require them. We have something very much like an historical experiment, so it would appear, that leaves these conclusions in no great doubt. (p. 80)

Peter Berger, in his book *The Capitalist Revolution* (1986), presents four propositions on the relations between capitalism and democracy:

Capitalism is a necessary but not sufficient condition of democracy under modern conditions.

If a capitalist economy is subjected to increasing degrees of state control, a point (not precisely specifiable at this time) will be reached at which democratic governance becomes impossible.

If a socialist economy is opened up to increasing degrees of market forces, a point (not precisely specifiable at this time) will be reached at which democratic governance becomes a possibility.

If capitalist development is successful in generating economic growth from which a sizable proportion of the population benefits, pressures toward democracy are likely to appear. (pp. 212–213)

This positive relationship between capitalism and democracy has also been sustained by statistical studies. The "Social Mobilization" theorists of the 1950s and 1960s, who included Daniel Lerner (1958), Karl Deutsch (1961), and S. M. Lipset (1959), among others, demonstrated a strong statistical association between GNP per capita and democratic political institutions. This is more than simple statistical association. There is a logic in the relation between level of economic development and democratic institutions. Level of economic development has been shown to be associated with education and literacy, exposure to mass media, and democratic psychological propensities such as subjective efficacy, participatory aspirations, and skills. In a major investigation of the social psychology of industrialization and modernization, a research team led by the sociologist Alex Inkeles (Inkeles and Smith, 1974a) interviewed several thousand workers in the modern industrial and the traditional economic sectors of six countries of differing culture. Inkeles found empathetic, efficacious, participatory, and activist propensities much more frequently among the modern industrial workers, and to a much lesser extent in the traditional sector in each one of these countries, regardless of cultural differences.

The historical, the logical, and the statistical evidence for this positive relation between capitalism and democracy is quite persuasive.

## Capitalism Subverts Democracy

But the opposite case is also made, that capitalism subverts or undermines democracy. Already in John Stuart Mill (1965) we encounter a view of existing systems of private property as unjust, and of the free market as destructively competitive—aesthetically and morally repugnant. The case he was making was a normative rather than a political one. He wanted a less competitive society, ultimately socialist, that would still respect individuality. He advocated limitations on the inheritance of property, and the improvement of the property system so that everyone shared in its benefits, the limitation of population growth, and the improvement of the quality of the labor force through the provision of high-quality education for all by the state. On the eve of the emergence of the modern democratic capitalist order, John Stuart Mill wanted to control the excesses of both the market economy and the majoritarian polity, by the education of consumers and producers, citizens and politicians, in the interest of producing morally improved free market and democratic orders. But in contrast to Marx, he did not thoroughly discount the possibilities of improving the capitalist and democratic order.

Marx argued that as long as capitalism and private property existed there could be no genuine democracy, that democracy under capitalism was bourgeois democracy, which is to say not democracy at all. While it would be in the interest of the working classes to enter a coalition with the bourgeoisie in supporting this form of democracy in order to eliminate feudalism, this would be a tactical maneuver. Capitalist democracy could only result in the increasing exploitation of the working classes. Only the elimination of capitalism and private property could result in the emancipation of the working classes, and the attainment of true democracy. Once socialism was attained, the basic political problems of humanity would have been solved through the elimination of classes. Under socialism there would be no distinctive democratic organization, no need for institutions to resolve conflicts, since there would be no conflicts. There is not much democratic or political theory to be found in Marx's writings. The basic reality is the mode of economic production and the consequent class structure from which other institutions follow.

For the followers of Marx up to the present day, there continues to be a negative tension between capitalism, however reformed, and democracy. But the integral Marxist and Leninist rejection of the possibility of an autonomous, bourgeois democratic state has been left behind for most Western Marxists. In the thinking of Nicos Poulantzas, Offe, Norberto Bobbio, Habermas, and others, the bourgeois democratic state is now viewed as a class struggle state, rather than an unambiguously bourgeois state. The working class has access to it; it can struggle for its interests, and can attain partial benefits from it. The state is now viewed as autonomous, or as relatively autonomous, and it can be reformed in a progressive direction by working-class and other popular movements. The bourgeois democratic state can be moved in the direction of a socialist state by political action short of violence and institutional destruction.

Schumpeter appreciated the tension between capitalism and democracy. While he saw a causal connection between competition in the economic and the political order, he points out

> that there are some deviations from the principle of democracy which link up with the presence of organized capitalist interests. . . . [T]he statement is true both from the standpoint of the classical and from the standpoint of our own theory of democracy. From the first standpoint, the result reads that the means at the disposal of private interests are often used in order to thwart the will of the people. From the second standpoint, the result reads that those private means are often used in order to interfere with the working of the mechanism of competitive leadership. (1942, p. 298)

He refers to some countries and situations in which "political life all but resolved itself into a struggle of pressure groups and in many cases practices that failed to conform to the spirit of the democratic method" (p. 298). But he rejects the notion that there cannot be political democracy in a capitalist society. For Schumpeter, full democracy in the sense of the informed participation of all adults in the selection of political leaders, and consequently the making of public policy, was an impossibility, because of the number and complexity of the issues confronting modern electorates. The democracy that was realistically possible was one in which people could choose among competing leaders, and consequently exercise some direction over political decisions. This kind of democracy was possible in a capitalist society, though some of its propensities impaired its performance. Writing in the early years of World War II, when the future of democracy and of capitalism were uncertain, Schumpeter leaves unresolved the questions of "Whether or not democracy is one of those products of capitalism which are to die out with it" or "how well or ill capitalist society qualifies for the task of working the democratic method it evolved" (p. 297).

Non-Marxist political theorists have contributed to this questioning of the reconcilability of capitalism and democracy. Robert A. Dahl, who makes the point that capitalism historically has been a necessary precondition of democracy, views contemporary democracy in the United States as seriously compromised, impaired by the inequality in resources among the citizens. But Dahl stresses the variety in distributive patterns, and in politico-economic relations among contemporary democracies:

> The category of capitalist democracies . . . includes an extraordinary variety . . . from nineteenth century, laissez faire, early industrial systems to twentieth century, highly regulated, social welfare, late or post-industrial systems. Even late twentieth century "welfare state" orders vary all the way from the Scandinavian systems, which are redistributive, heavily taxed, comprehensive in their social security, and neocorporatist in their collective bargaining arrangements, to the faintly redistributive, moderately taxed, limited social security, weak collective bargaining systems of the United States and Japan. (1989, pp. 324–325)

In *Democracy and Its Critics* (1989), Dahl argues that the normative growth of democracy to what he calls its "third transformation" (the first being the direct city-state democracy of classic times, and the second, the indirect, representative inegalitarian democracy of the contemporary world) will require democratization of the economic order. In other words, modern corporate capitalism needs to be transformed. Since government control and/or ownership of the economy would be destructive of the pluralism that is an essential requirement of democracy, his preferred solution to the problem of the mega-corporation is employee control of corporate industry. An economy so organized, according to Dahl, would improve the distribution of political resources without at the same time destroying the pluralism that democratic competition requires. To those who question the realism of Dahl's solution to the problem of inequality, he replies that history is full of surprises.

Charles E. Lindblom, in his book *Politics and Markets* (1977), concludes his comparative analysis of the political economy of modern capitalism and socialism with an essentially pessimistic conclusion about contemporary market-oriented democracy. He says:

> We therefore come back to the corporation. It is possible that the rise of the corporation has offset or more than offset the decline of class as an instrument of indoctrination. . . . That it creates a new core of wealth and power for a newly constructed upper class, as well as an overpowering loud voice, is also reasonably clear. The executive of the large corporation is, on many counts, the contemporary counterpart to the landed gentry of an earlier era, his voice amplified by the technology of mass communication. . . . [T]he major institutional barrier to fuller democracy may therefore be the autonomy of the private corporation. [Lindblom concludes:] The large private corporation fits oddly into democratic theory and vision. Indeed it does not fit. (p. 356)

There is then a widely shared agreement, from the Marxists and neo-Marxists, to Schumpeter, Dahl, Lindblom, and other liberal political theorists, that modern capitalism, with the dominance of the large corporation, produces a defective or an impaired form of democracy.

## Democracy Subverts Capitalism

If we change our perspective now and look at the way democracy is said to affect capitalism, one of the dominant traditions of economics from Adam Smith until the present day stresses the importance for productivity and welfare of an economy that is relatively free of intervention by the state. In this doctrine of minimal government there is still a place for a framework of rules and services essential to the productive and efficient performance of the economy. In part the government has to protect the market from itself. Left to their own devices, according to Smith, businessmen were prone to corner the market in order to exact the highest possible price. And also according to Smith, businessmen were prone to bribe public officials in order to gain special privileges, and legal monopolies. For Smith, good capitalism was competitive capitalism, and good government provided just those goods and services that the market needed to flourish, could not itself provide, or would not provide. A good government according to Adam Smith was a minimal government, providing for the national defense and domestic order. Particularly important for the economy were the rules pertaining to commercial life, such as the regulation of weights and measures, setting and enforcing building standards, providing for the protection of persons and property, and the like.

For Milton Friedman (1962, 1981), the leading contemporary advocate of the free market and free government, and of the interdependence of the two, the principal threat to the survival of capitalism and democracy is the assumption of the responsibility for welfare on the part of the modern democratic state. He lays down a set of functions appropriate to government in the positive interplay between economy and polity, and then enumerates many of the ways in which the modern welfare, regulatory state has deviated from these criteria.

A good Friedmanesque, democratic government would be one

> which maintained law and order, defended property rights, served as a means whereby we could modify property rights and other rules of the economic game, adjudicated disputes about the interpretation of the rules, enforced contracts, promoted competition, provided a monetary framework, engaged in activities to counter technical monopolies and to overcome neighborhood effects widely regarded as sufficiently important to justify government intervention, and which supplemented private charity and the private family in protecting the irresponsible, whether madman or child. (1962, pp. 35 ff.)

Against this list of proper activities for a free government, Friedman pinpointed more than a dozen activities of contemporary democratic governments that might better be performed through the private sector, or not at all. These included setting and maintaining price supports, tariffs, import and export quotas and controls, rents, interest rates, wage rates, and the like, regulating industries and banking, radio and television, licensing professions and occupations, providing social security and medical care programs, providing public housing, national parks, guaranteeing mortgages, and much else.

Friedman concludes that this steady encroachment on the private sector has been slowly but surely converting our free government and market system into a collective monster, compromising both freedom and productivity in the outcome. The tax and expenditure revolts and regulatory rebellions of the 1980s have temporarily stemmed this trend, but the threat continues: "It is the internal threat coming from men of good intentions and good will who wish to reform us. Impatient with the slowness of persuasion and example to achieve the great social changes they envision, they are anxious to use the power of the state to achieve their ends, and confident of their own ability to do so" (1962, p. 201). The threat to political and economic freedom, according to Milton Friedman, and others who argue the same position, arises out of democratic politics. It may only be defeated by political action.

In the last decades, a school, or rather several schools, of economists and political scientists have turned the theoretical models of economics to use in analyzing political processes. Variously called "public choice theorists," "rational choice theorists," or "positive political theorists," and employing such models as market exchange and bargaining, rational self-interest, game theory, and the like, these theorists have produced a substantial literature throwing new and often controversial light on democratic political phenomena such as elections, decisions of political party leaders, interest group behavior, legislative and committee decisions, bureaucratic and judicial behavior, lobbying activity, and substantive public policy areas such as constitutional arrangements, health and environment policy, regulatory policy, national security and foreign policy, and the like. Hardly a field of politics and public policy has been left untouched by this inventive and productive group of scholars.

The institutions and names with which this movement is associated in the United States include several universities in the state of Virginia—Virginia State University, the University of Virginia, George Mason University in a Washington, D.C., suburb—the University of Rochester in New York State, the University of Chicago, the California Institute of Technology, and Carnegie Mellon University in Pittsburgh, among others. And the most prominent names are those of the leaders of the two principal schools—James Buchanan, the Nobel laureate leader of the Virginia "public choice" school, and William Riker, the leader of the Rochester "positive theory" school. Other prominent scholars associated with this work are Gary Becker of the University of Chicago, Kenneth Shepsle and Morris Fiorina of Harvard, John Ferejohn of Stanford, Charles Plott of the California Institute of Technology, and many others.

One writer summarizing the ideological bent of much of this work, but by no means all of it, William Mitchell of the University of Washington, describes it as fiscally conservative, sharing a conviction that the "private economy is far more robust, efficient, and perhaps, equitable than other economies, and much more successful than political processes in efficiently allocating resources." Much of what has been produced "by James Buchanan and the leaders of this school can best be described as contributions to a theory of the failure of political processes." These failures of political performance are said to be inherent properties of the democratic political process. "Inequity, inefficiency, and coercion are the most general results of democratic policy formation." In a democracy the demand for publicly provided services seems to be insatiable. It ultimately turns into a special interest, "rent-seeking" society. Their remedies take the form of proposed constitutional limits on spending power and checks and balances to limit legislative majorities (1991).

One of the most visible products of this pessimistic economic analysis of democratic politics is Mancur Olson's book *The Rise and Decline of Nations* (1982). He makes a strong argument for the negative democracy–capitalism connection. His thesis is that the behavior of individuals and firms in stable societies inevitably leads to the formation of dense networks of collusive, cartelistic, and lobbying organizations that make economies less efficient and dynamic and polities less governable. The longer a society goes without an upheaval, the more powerful such organizations become—and the more they slow down economic expansion. Societies in which these narrow interest groups have been destroyed—by war or revolution, for example—enjoy the greatest gains in growth. His prize cases are Britain on the one hand, and Germany and Japan on the other:

> The logic of the argument implies that countries that have had democratic freedom of organization without upheaval or invasion the longest will suffer the most from growth-repressing organizations and combinations. This helps explain why Great Britain, the major nation with the longest immunity from dictatorship, invasion, and revolution, has had in this century a lower rate of growth than other large, developed democracies. Britain has precisely the powerful network of special interest organization that the argument developed here would lead us to expect in a country with its record of military security and democratic stability. The number and power of its trade unions need no description. The venerability and power of its professional associations is also striking. . . . In short, with age British society has acquired so many strong organizations and collusions that it suffers from an institutional sclerosis that slows its adaptation to changing circumstances and technologies.

By contrast, post–World War II Germany and Japan started organizationally from scratch. The organizations that led them to defeat were all dissolved, and under the occupation inclusive organizations like the general trade union movement, and general organizations of the industrial and commercial community, were first formed. These inclusive organizations had more regard for the general national interest and exercised some discipline on the narrower interest organizations. And both countries in the postwar decades experienced "miracles" of economic growth under democratic conditions.

The Olson theory of the subversion of capitalism through the propensities of democratic societies to foster special interest groups has not gone without challenge. There can be little question that there is logic in his argument. But empirical research testing this pressure-group hypothesis thus far has produced mixed findings. Olson has hopes that a public educated to the harmful consequences of special interests to economic growth, full employment, coherent government, equal opportunity, and social mobility will resist special interest behavior, and enact legislation imposing anti-trust and anti-monopoly controls to mitigate and contain these threats. It is somewhat of an irony that the solution to this special interest disease of democracy, according to Olson, is a democratic state with sufficient regulatory authority to control the growth of special interest organization.

## Democracy Fosters Capitalism

My fourth theme—democracy as fostering and sustaining capitalism—is not as straightforward as the first three. Historically there can be little doubt that as the suffrage was extended in the last century, and as mass political parties developed, democratic development impinged significantly on capitalist institutions and practices. Since successful capitalism requires risk-taking entrepreneurs with access to investment capital, the democratic propensity for redistributive and regulative policy tends to reduce the incentives and the resources available for risk-taking and creativity. Thus it can be argued that propensities inevitably resulting from democratic politics, as Friedman, Olson, and many others argue, tend to reduce productivity, and hence welfare.

But precisely the opposite argument can be made on the basis of the historical experience of literally all of the advanced capitalist democracies in existence. All of them without exception are now welfare states with some form and degree of social insurance, health and welfare nets, and regulatory frameworks designed to mitigate the harmful impacts and shortfalls of capitalism. Indeed, the welfare state is accepted all across the political spectrum. Controversy takes place around the edges. One might make the argument that had capitalism not been modified in this welfare direction, it is doubtful that it would have survived.

This history of the interplay between democracy and capitalism is clearly laid out in a major study involving European and American scholars titled *The Development of Welfare States in Western Europe and America* (Flora and Heidenheimer, 1981). The book lays out the relationship between the development and spread of capitalist industry, democratization in the sense of an expanding suffrage and the emergence of trade unions and left-wing political parties, and the gradual introduction of the institutions and practices of the welfare state. The early adoption of the institutions of the welfare state in Bismarck's, Germany, Sweden, and Great Britain were all associated with the rise of trade unions and socialist parties in those countries. The decisions made by the upper- and middle-class leaders and political movements to introduce welfare measures such as accident, old-age, and unemployment insurance were strategic decisions. They were increasingly confronted by trade union movements with the capacity of bringing industrial production to a halt, and by political parties with growing parliamentary representation favoring fundamental modifications in, or the abolition of, capitalism. As the calculations of the upper- and middle-class leaders led them to conclude that the costs of suppression exceeded the costs of concession, the various parts of the welfare state began to be put in place—accident, sickness, unemployment, old-age insurance, and the like. The problem of maintaining the loyalty of the working classes through two world wars resulted in additional concessions to working-class demands—the filling out of the social security system, free public education to higher levels, family allowances, housing benefits, and the like.

Social conditions, historical factors, and political processes and decisions produced different versions of the welfare state. In the United States, manhood suffrage came quite early; the later bargaining process emphasized free land and free education to the secondary level, an equality of opportunity version of the welfare state. The Disraeli bargain in Britain resulted in relatively early manhood suffrage and the full attainment of parliamentary government, while the Lloyd George bargain on the eve of World War I brought the beginnings of a welfare system to Britain. The Bismarck bargain in Germany produced an early welfare state, a postponement of electoral equality, and parliamentary government. While there were all of these differences in historical encounters with democratization and "welfarization," the important outcome was that little more than a century after the process began, all of the advanced capitalist democracies had similar versions of the welfare state, smaller in scale in the case of the United States and Japan, more substantial in Britain and the continental European countries.

We can consequently make out a strong case for the argument that democracy has been supportive of capitalism in this strategic sense. Without this welfare adaptation it is doubtful that capitalism would have survived, or rather, its survival, "unwelfarized," would have required a substantial repressive apparatus. The choice then would seem to have been between democratic welfare capitalism, and repressive undemocratic capitalism. I am inclined to believe that capitalism as such thrives more with the democratic welfare adaptation than with the repressive one. It is in that sense that we can argue that there is a clear positive impact of democracy on capitalism.

\*   \*   \*

We have to recognize, in conclusion, that democracy and capitalism are both positively and negatively related, that they both support and subvert each other. My colleague Moses Abramovitz described this dialectic more surely than most in his presidential address to the American Economic Association in 1980, on the eve of the "Reagan Revolution." Noting the decline in productivity in the U.S. economy during the late 1960s and 1970s, and recognizing that this decline might in part be attributable to the "tax, transfer, and regulatory" tendencies of the welfare state, he observes:

> The rationale supporting the development of our mixed economy sees it as a pragmatic compromise between the competing virtues and defects of decentralized market capitalism and encompassing socialism. Its goal is to obtain a measure of distributive justice, security, and social guidance of economic life without losing too much of the allocative efficiency and dynamism of private enterprise and market organization. And it is a pragmatic compromise in another sense. It seeks to retain for most people that measure of personal protection from the state which private property and a private job market confer, while obtaining for the disadvantaged minority of people through the state that measure of support without which their lack of property or personal endowment would amount to a denial of individual freedom and capacity to function as full members of the community.

Democratic welfare capitalism produces that reconciliation of opposing and complementary elements that makes possible the survival, even enhancement, of both of these sets of institutions. It is not a static accommodation, but rather one that fluctuates over time, with capitalism being compromised by the tax-transfer-regulatory action of the state at one point, and then correcting in the direction of the reduction of the intervention of the state at another point, and with a learning process over time that may reduce the amplitude of the curves.

The case for this resolution of the capitalism-democracy quandary is made quite movingly by Jacob Viner, who is quoted in the concluding paragraph of Abramovitz's paper:

> If . . . I nevertheless conclude that I believe that the welfare state, like old Siwash, is really worth fighting for and even dying for as compared to any rival system, it is because, despite its imperfection in theory and practice, in the aggregate it provides more promise of preserving and enlarging human freedoms, temporal prosperity, the extinction of mass misery, and the dignity of man and his moral improvement than any other social system which has previously prevailed, which prevails elsewhere today or which outside Utopia, the mind of man has been able to provide a blueprint for.

# 8

# The Appeals of
# Communism and Fascism

THIS CHAPTER IS A DELAYED THEORETICAL CONCLUSION to the *Appeals of Communism* project (Almond, 1954). When the field research, analysis, and the first drafts of the substantive chapters of *The Appeals of Communism* were completed, I was confronted with the problem of what kind of conclusion to write. This was in the fall of 1953, when the Korean War dominated our attention abroad, and when McCarthyism was in full sway at home. It then appeared appropriate to emphasize the policy implications of the study. This decision has left me ever since with a feeling of incompleteness about the project, since the theoretical insights that had arisen in the course of the study were left implicit.

The *Appeals of Communism* project was begun when the three volumes of *The Authoritarian Personality* (Adorno et al., 1950) were appearing in print. The theory and methodology of the *Communism* study were influenced by this earlier study, both by its striking accomplishments, as well as by what appeared to be its shortcomings. Much of my criticism has already been anticipated in three of the papers reviewing this project (Christie and Jahoda, 1954). However, it may be useful to place this pioneering project on the psychological aspects of political behavior in its intellectual setting, and compare its research design and findings with those of the *Communism* study.

The philosophical current that dominated the *Authoritarian Personality* study was that amalgam of Marxism and Freudianism that was so influential in "advanced" thinking in the 1930s. Each of these philosophical currents produced its own distortion. The Marxist presuppositions of the study led its authors to associate right-wing extremism with psychological-irrational disorders, while the left tended to come off with a clean bill of mental health. But certainly as crucial a distortion was the one that stemmed from Freud, which led the authors of the study to overstress psychogenetic hypotheses in their efforts to account for fascism.

In overstressing unconscious feelings and attitudes, the scholars of the *Authoritarian Personality* project were continuing the tradition of political interpretation that had begun with Freud and continued by a number of his students and followers. These writings sought to account for political phenomena such as war, pacifism, conservatism, radicalism, fascism, and the like, in terms of Freudian instinct theory. Thus war was reduced to the "death" instinct, and to the peculiar admixture of "death" and "eros" that is involved in sado-masochism (Freud 1913, 1923, 1929). Pacifism became the reaction formation resulting from efforts to cope with sadistic impulses. Conservatism and radicalism were reduced to differing ways of dealing with father-hatred, by seeking to destroy the father, or by a reaction-formative identification with him (Flugel, 1945).

In Harold Lasswell's work, the role of personality factors in political behavior is more systematically formulated. He points out that unconscious patterns, which are the product of special family and childhood experiences, and which are built into the personality, affect choices of political attitudes and roles. Lasswell's writings reflect the development of social-psychological sciences over the decades of the 1920s–1950s, as they became more empirical-experimental, and more multi-causal in explanatory strategy. Thus, his formula to account for the developmental history of political man, "private motives displaced on public objects, rationalized in terms of public interest," was presented in his earlier work (1930). But this view was qualified in his later writings, in his "Triple Appeal Principle" (1932) and in his contribution to Christie and Jahoda's critical volume (1954) on *The Authoritarian Personality*.

This overemphasis on unconscious factors in affecting choices of either attitudes or roles may be understood in its historical and polemical context. No innovation in the social sciences is ever proposed in balanced and qualified terms; it is typically exaggerated in order to gain attention. Lasswell's trail-breaking book *Psychopathology and Politics* (1930) was partly a scientific monograph and partly a tract directed against the naive rationalism of the political science of that generation. In the zeal of affirming the relevance of nonrational factors, there was a tendency to reduce political phenomena to unconscious motivation. Thus in a relatively more recent work Lasswell remarks, "The political type is characterized by an intense and unsatisfied craving for deference. These cravings, both accentuated and unsatisfied in the primary circle, are displaced on public objects" (1948, p. 38). And he goes on to state, "It is not too far fetched to say that everyone is born a politician, and most of us outgrow it. In a society where extreme deprivations are provoked or used by no one, the outgrowing would be complete" (p. 38). This was a conception of politics that treated it as though it was primarily understandable in terms of unconscious tendencies and psychological mechanisms as "compensation for," "projection of," "reaction formation to," or "displacement of" libidinal fixations of one kind or another.

In efforts to reply to this kind of criticism it is not enough to say, as does Else Frenkel-Brunswik:

> Few clinicians, if any, and certainly none of the authors of *The Authoritarian Personality* are inclined to regard psychological factors as the major or exclusive determinants of political or social movements. We have explicitly acknowledged that historical, social, and economic factors are crucial determinants of the rise of political movements. In the introduction to our work we have clearly stated that "Broad changes in social conditions and institutions will have a direct bearing upon the kinds of personalities that develop within a society." (Adorno et al., 1950, p. 1)

What the *Authoritarian Personality* study assumed and what Frenkel-Brunswik reaffirms, is a rather simple pattern of continuity of social process from social structure to personality structure to politics. That political attitudes could have their origin and derive their content predominantly within the political and social process itself (i.e., that the psychological component could be essentially cognitive and adjustive rather than the consequence of basic personality characteristics) is excluded by both the theory and the methodology of the *Authoritarian Personality* study. Thus there is only one kind of "potential fascism" that the study recognizes, and this is a personality-based potential fascism. What is vulnerable in this theory is not the assumption of the importance of personality factors, but the assumption of congruity between personality and political orientation and role. And this assumption of congruity was the consequence of the neglect in the Freudian school of the role of cognition in psychological motivation, a neglect only now being remedied by the newer emphasis on ego psychology.

The general theory that guided the *Authoritarian Personality* study was "that the political, economic, and social convictions of an individual often form a broad and coherent pattern, as if bound together by a 'mentality' or 'spirit,' and that this pattern is an expression of deep-lying trends in the personality" (Adorno et al., 1950, p. 97). Specifically the study proceeds from the hypothesis that anti-Semitism is related to other anti-minority sentiments and to political-economic attitudes of a potentially fascist character. This syndrome of sociopolitical attitudes was alleged to be consistent with basic attitudes toward the self and personal relations, and was the consequence of a particular pattern of early childhood experiences (Christie and Jahoda, 1954, p. 120).

The research method of the study involved the giving of questionnaires to more than 2,000 subjects taken from student groups, members of "service clubs" (e.g., Kiwanis, Elks, etc.), members of civic organizations, members of trade union organizations, psychiatric clinic patients, prison inmates, and the like. Intensive interviews and projective tests were administered to a subsample consisting of those who scored "high" and "low" on the ethnocentrism scales contained in the questionnaires. The "connectedness" between these sociopolitical attitudes was tested by statistical correlation. The relationship of this political-attitude syndrome to "deeper lying personality trends" and to early patterns of child rearing was demonstrated by clinical interviews and the administration of the Thematic Apperception Test.

In their conclusions the authors claim to have proven that

> A basically hierarchical, authoritarian, exploitative parent-child relationship is apt to carry over into a power-oriented, exploitatively dependent attitude toward one's sex partner and one's God and may well culminate in a political philosophy and social outlook which has no room for anything but a desperate clinging to what appears to be strong, and a disdainful rejection of whatever is relegated to the bottom. The inherent dramatization likewise extends from the parent-child dichotomy to the dichotomous handling of social relations as manifested especially in the formation of stereotypes and of ingroup-outgroup cleavages. Conventionality, rigidity, repressive denial, and the ensuing breakthrough of one's weakness, fear and dependence are but other aspects of the same fundamental personality pattern, and they can be observed in personal life as well as in attitudes toward religion and social issues. (Adorno, 1950, p. 97)

The critique of the *Authoritarian Personality* study proceeds along two main lines. Herbert Hyman and Paul Sheatsley attack it on grounds of psychological theory and methodology, and Edward Shils and Harold Lasswell on the grounds of political as well as psychological theory. Hyman and Sheatsley summarize their views as follows:

The authors' propensity for psychodynamic explanations leads them to ignore the widespread distribution of certain sentiments in the American population, their frequent correlation with formal education, and their obvious social determinants and to attribute them instead to psychodynamic processes unique in the ethnocentric individual. Thus the fact that prejudice is "irrational" or highly generalized is assumed to prove that personality factors are responsible, though no objective evidence is provided in support of this contention and other explanations deserve at least equal weight. (Christie and Jahoda, 1954, p. 120)

Although they failed to make explicit the theory of political choice that underlay their critique of the authoritarianism study, Hyman and Sheatsley are arguing that ethnocentrism and political authoritarianism are to be explained not only in terms of psychodynamic factors, but that cognitive and social factors may also explain such phenomena. It is also their conclusion that the psychodynamic theory followed in the *Authoritarian Personality* study led its authors to employ a methodology that obscured the role of these "nonpersonality" factors. To call the theory followed in this study a "monistic" theory would do its authors an injustice. Their error lay in the fact that they failed to provide explicitly for other than psychodynamic factors, even though they often refer to them, and consequently they employed a methodology that tended to overlook if not to suppress them. In other words, what their theory lacked was a psychological typology of fascism, or potential fascism.

Jerome Bruner and Brewster Smith suggest that political as well as other attitudes may be classified into three categories from the perspective of their function for the individual.[1] There are attitudes the function of which is essentially cognitive, "problem solving" where "deeper personality tendencies" are not particularly engaged. In other words the orientation is essentially a response to a political or social situation in terms of the cognitive equipment of the individual and his exposure to communication. Secondly, there are attitudes that have a primarily social adjustive function, where the content of the attitude is secondary to the function of social adjustment or conformity. In this type of attitude similarly deeper personality tendencies may not be particularly engaged. Finally there is the type of attitude that is strongly influenced by unconscious personality tendencies, in which situations are perceived and defined in terms of unconscious patterns and compulsions acquired in earlier life situations. This is the type of potential fascism with which the *Authoritarian Personality* study was concerned, and it is to the great credit of this investigation that this type of political attitude was systematically described and related to other attitudinal components, and to broader psychodynamic tendencies and developmental patterns. But the approach followed by Bruner and Smith as well as others suggests that the collaborators in the *Authoritarian Personality* study would have been better advised if they had proceeded on the basis of a psychological typology of potential fascism. They should have sought for other types of causal sequences than the one they stressed, if they were to satisfy their claims as to the relevance of their findings to the understanding of fascism. If we were to follow the classification of Bruner and Smith, we would conclude that there are "cognitive fascists," "conformity fascists," and "projective fascists." Cognitive fascists would be those whose fascist attitudes were derived from exposure to communication and indoctrination. Conformity fascists would be those whose attitudes were adopted as a way of assimilating to a social milieu in which such attitudes were influential. Projective fascists would be those whose ethnocentric and authoritarian attitudes were related to personality tendencies of the type made familiar in the *Authoritarian Personality* research.

But the errors and simplifications of this study were also caused by a faulty view of politics. Here the critiques of Shils and Lasswell are especially cogent. Shils demonstrates that the personality tendencies described in the *Authoritarian Personality* study are not only supportive of fascist attitudes but of Communist attitudes as well. It may also be argued that the kinds of personality tendencies described may be related to other types of political attitudes, or may have little if any bearing on political attitudes at all. Thus such attitudes as rigidity, lack of spontaneity, repressed hostility, glorification of strength, and contempt for weakness are tendencies commonly met in emotionally disturbed persons, regardless of their politics. They were frequently encountered among "neurotic Communists" in the *Appeals of Communism* project. They are to be observed among members of liberal and conservative movements, where they may be expressed in the intensity rather than the content of attitudes, or may result in "authoritarian" personal relations rather than in authoritarian ideology. If, as appears to be the case, the same basic personality tendencies may be related to fascist attitudes, Communist attitudes, liberal attitudes, and to a nonpolitical orientation as well, the whole theory of the relationship between personality and political attitudes on which the *Authoritarian Personality* study is based needs to be thoroughly restated. It is not only inaccurate to set up personality-based potential fascism as the only significant psychological type of fascism, but it is equally inaccurate to assume that the personality characteristics described are specific to fascism. Careful consideration suggests that personality characteristics affect political choices in a wide variety of ways, and that the assumption of congruity between types of personality and types of political attitudes is an untenable one.

The *Authoritarian Personality* study is lacking in a soundly conceived political phenomenology. Three points may be made in this connection. First, different ideological movements may be characterized by similar affective toning and hence be attractive to similar "basic personality types." What would determine recruitment to the one movement or the other would be such factors as information, exposure to doctrine, and social milieu. Second, it would be an error to assume—as do the authors of this study—that ideological movements are homogeneous. Thus German and Italian Fascism were rather different in their ideological emphases and content; and if one were to include under fascism such phenomena as Japanese militarism, Spanish authoritarianism, and Argentinian Peronism, the differences become even more striking. Even limiting ourselves to a single movement, the assumption of ideological homogeneity is untenable.

Ideological movements are rarely if ever homogeneous in these respects. There are many different political "atmospheres" within the same movement, as I showed in the *Appeals of Communism* study. I distinguished between the different atmospheres of the various national movements, between the images of the party presented at the different levels of assimilation, between the atmospheres characteristic of the working class and the intellectual sectors of the party, and the like. Since I found that the cognitive and affective character of the various sectors of the Communist movement differed—often strikingly—it was impossible to fall into the error of assuming an ideological homogeneity on the one hand and a psychological congruity on the other. And if this is true of a highly integrated international movement such as Communism, with its explicit and self-consciously inculcated doctrine, how much truer would it be of fascism and political authoritarianism, which emerge out of very different political and cultural settings and which are not integrated on an international basis? Indeed for this and other reasons it is arguable as to whether the attitudes described in the *Authoritarian Personality* study can be accurately described as "potentially fascist." Ethnocentrism has entered into U.S. politics for generations and yet it has never produced a native fascist movement with any stability and strength. If there is a political potentiality in the attitudes described in this study, it would be more aptly described as a potentiality for right-wing extremism of the U.S. "nativist" variety—which in most cases can be satisfied by affiliation to such patriotic organizations as the American Legion or the Daughters of the American Revolution, or by the support of right-wing candidates for public office within the two major parties. This is not to deny the many similarities in attitudes between U.S. right-wing extremists and foreign fascists, but only to point out that there are significant differences, and that there is a serious oversimplification in characterizing U.S. potential right-wing extremism as potential fascism (Christie and Jahoda, 1954, pp. 44 ff.).

In still a third respect the lack of a sound theory of politics in the *Authoritarian Personality* study led to oversimplification. There is no recognition of the factors affecting recruitment to political movements, and to particular parts of the role-structure of these movements. The mere presence of certain ideological potentialities in an individual does not imply a readiness to affiliate to an organization advocating such an ideology. Political movements often have a complex division of power and responsibility. There are different levels of leadership and different leadership functions. The requirements of these roles will often set limits as to the kinds of personalities that can perform them. Thus I found in the *Appeals of Communism* project that the incidence of "disturbed personalities" was much higher among the rank-and-file party members, and among the low-echelon party leadership, than among the high-echelon members. The high-echelon leaders tended to come from left-wing political backgrounds, from communities in which Marxism was a common political point of view rather than a deviant one. The responsibilities of leadership roles even in small movements are such as often to rule out recruitment of the more unstable personalities. While high-echelon positions in the *Communism* study were sometimes held by unconsciously hostile persons as long as the hostility was amenable to discipline, they were rarely held by "uncontrollable rage types," or by withdrawn and self-rejective persons.

Whether this would be true of leaders of U.S. "native fascist" movements is another question. Shils argues that the instability of these movements may in some measure be related to the high incidence of unstable personality types among their leaderships (Christie and Jahoda, 1954, p. 46). Lasswell argues the more general hypothesis that large-scale totalitarian movements impose such demands upon top leadership as to exclude highly egocentric and power-oriented personalities from such positions (Christie and Jahoda, 1954, p. 224). While there is undoubtedly something in this hypothesis, it comes into conflict with the known facts about some of the top Nazi leaders. Leadership responsibilities would on the whole appear to be in conflict with extreme forms of psychological disturbance, but "charismatic" leadership often appears to be associated with such disturbance.

It would seem that the *Authoritarian Personality* study failed to put its basic question properly. The proper question was not "What kinds of personality characteristics are related to the potential choice of fascism as a political ideology?" but rather, "What kinds of characteristics—psychological, social, and political—are related to what kinds of fascist attitudes?" By virtue of the way in which the authors of the study put their question, they did succeed in describing one kind of potential right-wing fascism, but they did not come to grips with the broader question of potential fascism in the United States.

The *Appeals of Communism* study began with the assumption that there are many types of Communists and susceptibility to Communism. It first distinguished between "esoteric" and "exoteric" Communism through an analysis of the Communist communication system as reflected in its literature (for a description of the methodology of the *Appeals of Communism* study, see pp. ix ff.). This analysis showed that there were striking differences between the internal "upper-level" atmosphere of the Communist movement and the "mass" atmosphere. There were many different exoteric atmospheres in the Communist movement; the party takes on a different content in different cultures and countries—"worker" Communism differs from "peasant" Communism, and from "intellectual" Communism. The task of the study was not to describe the "psychology" of communism, but the various kinds of "psychology" that might create susceptibility to Communism.

Thus we found that Communism in France and Italy was essentially cognitive and adjustive in its psychological function, rather than projective according to the Smith-Bruner functional typology. In France and Italy, joining the Communist Party was consistent with the political tradition of certain groups, was a cognitive response to the system of communication to which they were exposed, and was adjustive to a particular social and political structure. In England and the United States, and particularly among the middle-class "rank-and-filers" of the party, psychological problems were typically, though by no means always, involved. Interesting enough, the high-echelon American and British Communists were similar to the continental European variety in their social and political backgrounds; that is, they were recruited from American and British communities where there was already a revolutionary, proletarian, even sometimes a Marxist tradition. In other words, high-level American and

British Communists were also frequently "cognitive" and "adjustive" Communists rather than "projective" Communists.

Comparison between the two studies confronts the difficulty that the two studies defined their "indicators" differently. Though both were interested in the motivations of political "extremists," the *Authoritarian Personality* study called a certain kind of attitude syndrome "susceptibility to fascism," while the *Appeals of Communism* study used former Communists as subjects and hence was unavoidably open to the criticism that its sample was biased. Thus the one study in its search for susceptibility to fascism took individuals who had never adhered to fascist movements, the other in its search for susceptibility to Communism took individuals who had been Communists but had rejected it. These decisions were the consequences of research conditions beyond the control of the researchers, but they nevertheless raise serious questions as to the validity of the findings.

Despite these basic differences in theory and research design and these quite genuine questions as to validity, there are certain respects in which some of the findings of the two studies may be compared. The *Authoritarian Personality* study did describe the characteristics of a certain type of American personality-based right-wing extremist; and the *Appeals of Communism* study did describe the characteristics of a comparable personality-based left-wing extremist. A comparison of these two groups will enable us to provide a tentative answer to the question of whether or not the personality characteristics of these two groups are different or similar as Shils maintains. If they are similar, we will then have to face the question of what characteristics are responsible for these two contrasting political choices.

The description of the emotional characteristics of the ethnocentric and prejudiced personalities in the *Authoritarian Personality* study is based on a number of collections of material, two of which will be summarized here: the intensive interviews and projective tests of "high-scorers" on the studies of psychoanalytic patients and psychiatric casework clients who had expressed anti-Semitic and prejudiced views in the course of their treatment. Stimulated by the Ackerman and Jahoda device of using psychoanalytic case material, the *Appeals of Communism* study collected thirty-five psychoanalytic case histories of persons who were Communist Party members at the time of their treatment, or who had been members of the party sometime before their treatment (Almond, 1954, pp. 259 ff.).

In their summary of their cases, Ackerman and Jahoda observed that "the complaints concerned a feeling of insecurity, loneliness, unhappiness, confusion, difficulty in finding friends or establishing a satisfactory sex life, absence or vagueness of life goals, inability to maintain interest, etc." (Ackerman and Jahoda, 1950, pp. 27 ff.). They also reported that there was no correlation between anti-Semitism and specific symptoms or psychological patterns. In other words, almost any kind of emotional disturbance might lead to prejudiced attitudes and behavior. Specifically they enumerated the following emotional predispositions to anti-Semitism:

1. Almost all of their cases manifested anxiety: "Socially, economically, emotionally, and sexually, they are plagued by this exaggerated sense of vulnerability. . . . Often these fears are not apparent on the surface, but analysis reveals their existence under a facade of superficial self-confidence. The general picture is one of weakness and incompleteness in total personality organization, and fear of injury in a vast variety of contexts. Because of their inner weakness and negligible insight, these patients view the outer world as hostile, evil, and inexplicably hard" (p. 29).

2. They reflected confusion about themselves: "So confused and vague is their self image that they do not seem to know who or what they are, what they desire, and what they can forego . . . they waver between feelings of inferiority and superiority" (p. 32).

3. Their interpersonal relations were inadequate and disturbed: "continually endangered by attitudes of overaggressiveness or overdependence . . . often there is not even the capacity for such tentative, incomplete relationships, since fear and mistrust of other people make some of these patients uneasy, shy and awkward in company" (p. 34).

4. Another characteristic is the fear of the different, and strong impulses toward conformity: "The fear of the different is not in proportion to the extent of the objective, measurable difference. Rather it is in proportion to the emotional deficiency which produces the need for conformity and belonging. . . . His striving for acceptance is governed by the desire to appear like everyone else rather than to achieve genuine identification, and frequently he shifts from one group to another, overprotesting the strength of his allegiance to this or that cause according to the immediate situation" (p. 37).

5. The sense of reality of these individuals is "vague, dull, and indefinitely formed. . . . It is not surprising that no evidence of clearly defined life goals can be found in these persons. Unaware of what

they want, they seem vaguely concerned with impotent desires to establish their relationship to the outside world" (pp. 43 ff.).

Ackerman and Jahoda conclude as to the childhood background of these "prejudiced personalities":

> Common to every case of anti-Semitism collected for this study is the strikingly similar psychological atmosphere into which the patient is born. There is not a single example of a permanently well-adjusted marital relationship between the parents. In almost half the cases, their superficial respectability was violated by open quarrels, physical violence, divorce, or desertion. At best, only the semblance of a respectable family union was preserved through conformity to conventional standards. Basically there was no warmth, affection or sympathy between the parents; and what little evidence of the sexual adaptation between the parents is available indicates that sexual relations were unsatisfactory. (p. 55)

It is to the credit of Ackerman and Jahoda that they do not consider these characteristics unique in the anti-Semite. They state: "there is no reason to believe that all who share such characteristics will necessarily manifest anti-Semitic attitudes. But the fact still remains that where anti-Semitism is demonstrated in the cultural environment, individuals with this specific syndrome will utilize this handy prejudice for their irrational purposes" (p. 55). What Ackerman and Jahoda do not point out is the fact that ethnocentrism and anti-Semitism may also not be associated with such emotional tendencies at all, but may be simply learned attitudes in communities where prejudice is common.

The clinical cases of Communists shared these same emotional characteristics with the fascists and anti-Semites with one exception. But the method and theory of the *Communism* study never made it possible to lose sight of the fact that persons could become Communists without such deep-lying disturbed personality trends, that the decision to join the party could be (and in most cases was) situational. Thus the study concluded:

> In the case of persons joining the party outside of the Communist orbit itself, alienative feelings are typically involved—that is, feelings of rejection and resentment, impulses to attack and withdraw, or some combination of these and other feelings. Such negative impulses may be partly unconscious, chronic, a consequence of the maladjustive way in which the individual seeks to relate to others, or they may be the result

of some situational impairment or damage—the consequence in other words of some event or development which might influence the decision to join the party. In a normal person, resentment of a situation in which he was unemployed through no fault of his own might also lead to joining the party. In a neurotic person, withdrawal from interpersonal relations and feelings of isolation and loneliness resulting from this tendency may contribute to susceptibility. In a normal individual, experiencing a society or social situation which rejects him, which disqualifies him from certain kinds of roles, may create a readiness to join the party. In a neurotic person, feelings of confusion, of conflict, and of uncertainty may contribute to the attraction of the party; and confusions and uncertainties which are the consequence of the objective situation in which the normal person finds himself may have the same effect. But the neurotic person will join the party in response to the pressure of internal needs, and often in defiance of the modal patterns of his social grouping. The normal person who has suffered some situational damage will join the party in response to the situation, and often (but by no means always) in conformity with patterns prevailing in his social grouping. (Almond, 1954, pp. 235 ff.)

The study also concluded that where the party is a small, deviant movement as in the United States and England, it is likely to be a haven for disturbed personalities and marginal social types. Where, however, the party takes on mass proportions as in France and Italy, such deviants are the exceptions, and the appeal of Communism has to be understood in terms of deep-seated social and political problems, political tradition, and historical experiences.

That the emotionally maladjusted American Communist has on the whole similar characteristics to the emotionally maladjusted American ethnocentric is borne out by an examination of the tendencies manifested among the "high-scorers" on the various scales employed in the master study of the *Authoritarian Personality* project. Thus Else Frenkel-Brunswik points out that these "high-scorers" typically try to keep in repression

fear, weakness, passivity, sex impulses and aggressive feeling against authoritative figures. Among the rigid defenses against these tendencies there is, above all, the mechanism of projection by which much of what cannot be accepted as part of one's ego is externalized. Thus it is not one's self but others that are seen as hostile and threatening. Or else one's own weakness leads to an exaggerated condemnation of everything that is weak; one's own weakness is thus fought outside instead of inside. At the same time there is a compensating—and therefore often compulsive—drive for power, strength, success, and self-determination. (Adorno et al., 1950, p. 474)

Frenkel-Brunswik goes on to enumerate other characteristics of the "high-scorer," such as excessive conventionality or conformism, worship of power and contempt for weakness, as well as emotional rigidity (p. 476). She also portrays a childhood similar to that described in the Ackerman and Jahoda study.

An examination of the relevant sections of the *Appeals of Communism* study clearly makes out the case that the personality tendencies and family background related to neurotic ethnocentrism and authoritarianism are substantially the same as those related to the neurotic appeal of Communism. In other words, we are dealing with personality problems that may be resolved either by right-wing or left-wing extremism (or that may not affect politics at all). There is, however, one significant exception, and this is the dimension of conformity. On the surface the neurotic ethnocentric is a conformist, while the neurotic Communist is an anti-conformist, an iconoclast, often a Bohemian. But even this is a surface difference, for it would appear that both types are badly adjusted to authority and convention, but they solve the problem differently. Thus the "high-scorer" ethnocentric solves his basic feelings of isolation, vulnerability, and antagonism by overconforming (the "200 percent American") and by expressing antagonism toward outgroups such as Jews, blacks, Catholics, and the like. The neurotic Communist, on the other hand, solves his problems by underconforming or by anti-conforming. But the interesting thing about the neurotic Communist is that, Bohemian and emancipated though he may be, he is affiliated with an organization which within its own community is far more conformist than the outside society.

The differences would seem to be the following: The neurotic ethno-centric represses his anti-authoritarianism and unconventional impulses and projects these impulses on outgroups, which are pictured as immoral, unclean, and generally threatening. The neurotic Communist expresses his anti-conventional impulses, projects his own antagonistic and hostile impulses on dominant groups in his own society (e.g., capitalism, the FBI, and the like), and expresses his deep-lying needs for order, authority, and submissiveness by affiliating himself with a rigidly authoritarian Communist Party.

This essential difference, however, is not at the level of basic personality tendencies, but rather the consequence of psychological mechanisms and cognitive patterns. Thus most of the neurotic Communists were members of minority groups who were not accepted on a fully equal basis by the dominant society. They were also individuals who had been exposed to higher education, and who consequently had more complex intellectual requirements for their political views. They had found in Communism a way of solving their emotional and social adjustment problems in a political movement that appealed not only to their underlying antagonistic needs, but also to their relatively complex moral and intellectual requirements. Thus it is in these social and intellectual traits that the neurotic Communists and neurotic ethnocentrics differ, and not in their basic personality tendencies.

It is not within the scope of this chapter to describe in detail the social and other differences between right- and left-wing extremists in the United States, since adequate data are not available for this purpose. But certain hypotheses based upon these and other studies may be proposed:

1. It is probably correct that both right- and left-wing extremists in the United States tend to have some emotional axe to grind. They are not "normal, adjusted" personalities, but have the personality maladjustments commonly found among neurotics. There is no such thing as "political neurosis," just as there is no such thing as "fascist neurosis" or "Communist neurosis." Deviant, extremist, outlaw movements attract deviant, extremist, and outlaw personalities. What factors lead some neurotic individuals to seek in politics some solution of their inner conflicts, while others take to drink, marital conflict, sexual promiscuity, inordinate professional ambition, and the like, are the accidents of experience, learning, and social milieu.

2. In the United States, right-wing extremists are more likely to be of native stock, while left-wing extremists are more likely to be foreign-born and first-generation native-born.

3. On the score of social mobility there does not appear to be a clear pattern. The middle-class intellectuals in the *Appeals of Communism* study appeared to be upwardly mobile individuals of foreign background whose problems of adjustment appeared to be the consequence of acculturative problems. The ethnocentric war veterans described in one of the volumes of the *Authoritarian Personality* study appeared to be downwardly mobile.

4. As far as social class in the general sense is concerned, there appear to be no significant differences between the two types of extremists. Both right-wing and left-wing extremists are recruited

among the middle classes and the working classes. However, there do appear to be occupational differences. Left-wing extremists tend to be recruited frequently from intellectual occupations such as journalism, the teaching profession, and social work, while this is rarely the case for the right-wing extremists.

5. There appears to be a significant difference in the intellectual characteristics of the right- and left-wing extremists. The right-wing extremist is rarely an intellectual. Indeed, he is typically an anti-intellectual. The left-wing extremist on the other hand has more exacting intellectual requirements. His political rationalizations are more elaborate. There appear to be significant differences in the educational attributes of the two groups, with the right-wing extremists being less well educated. There are also differences in the religious characteristics of the two groups. The left-wing extremist has typically broken from religious tradition, while the right-wing extremist is more likely to be affiliated with a religious community.

Thus, the left-wing extremist in American society often tends to be both psychologically and socioethnically alienated. Hence the direction of his antagonism is against the dominant society. The right-wing extremist on the other hand more typically tends to be psychologically alienated, though socioethnically integrated. Hence the direction of his antagonism is against deviants, minority groups, foreign countries, and the like.

These criticisms of the *Authoritarian Personality* study should not diminish the importance of this major investigation into the psychological determinants of political attitudes. If one views this study in the context of intellectual history, it represents a major scientific turning point. It represents the first major effort to test the hypotheses of psychoanalytical psychology with the empirical and statistical methods of social psychology. All future research in the psychology of political and social attitudes, even though it proceeds on the basis of more adequate theories, will be affected by its methodology and its substantive findings (Adorno et al., 1950, p. 476).

Coming out of its particular intellectual tradition it is difficult to see how the overstress on certain significant determinants of political behavior could have been avoided. If the *Appeals of Communism* study avoided some of these simplifications and overemphases, it was in considerable measure due to the fact that the *Authoritarian Personality* study had preceded it, and set up its problem and reported its results in such a way as to facilitate the learning process.

Since the *Appeals of Communism* study came out of the political science tradition, there were certain errors into which it could not have fallen. Thus it could not have made the assumption that ideological movements are homogeneous, nor could it have overlooked the structural and historical aspects of political movements. Thus it could not fail to reject monistic, psychological explanations of political phenomena, since its historical, comparative, and institutional methods are by their very nature designed to bring out the complexity and variety of political phenomena. In these days when some political scientists seem to be turning in desperation to the other social sciences for an unattainable salvation, it may be useful to call to mind the fact that they have a rather more secure grasp on certain aspects of social and political reality than do their colleagues in the other social science disciplines.

One of the characteristics of a mature science is the existence of a common stockpile of theory and substantive knowledge. As new research disproves or substantiates old hypotheses, or suggests new ones for testing, the results are rapidly communicated within the discipline, and an effective learning process is thereby attained. From the standpoint of this criterion we can hardly view the study of politics as a mature science. It is rather in a stage of schools and sects in which idealists and realists, legalists and functionalists, empiricists and theorists, confront and confute one another. Each school and approach has its own stockpile of knowledge, theory, and clichés. It is therefore all the more important when such an opportunity as the present one arises to make a genuine effort at scientific cumulation even at the cost of saying things that may be obvious to some of us.

From this point of view it would appear to be clear that certain of the theories of the school of "political personality" must be set aside. There is no type of personality that is specific to any kind of politics. The same personality tendencies may be related to revolutionary and reactionary ideologies, and may indeed coexist with a moderate democratic ideology. All that one can say in this connection is that there is a certain tendency for deviant personalities to select deviant political ideologies, while normal or modal personalities tend to select normal or modal ideologies. The factors that influence these specific political choices are the social and intellectual characteristics of the individual, and the objective political exposures with which he is confronted.

If we appear to reject the concept of political personality, we are by no means rejecting political psychology as one of the constituent fields of interest in the study of political behavior. On the contrary, we reject the theory of political personality and turn to political psychology precisely because its theory and methodology are open to all of the factors that affect political choices, and are more likely to produce an adequate political behavior typology. This approach does not reject the influence of personality factors on political behavior but attempts to place them in a system of variables that will take into account the complexity of political choice.

## Note

1. The Bruner and Smith classification of types of attitudes has been developed in lectures and unpublished papers that have been made available to me in the last year. I have also had correspondence with Jerome Bruner in the course of the *Appeals of Communism* study.

# 9

# The Cultural Revolution in the United States

IN THE QUIET OF CONTEMPORARY UNIVERSITY LIFE, it is difficult to believe that just a few short years ago our campuses were the scenes of bullhorn confrontations, bombings, police charges, window crashing, and even killings. The copious literature on the student rebellion and the counter-culture was produced in the heat of the events themselves, and principal-ly by the participants or scholars directly affected by them. So great has been the relief over the subsidence of the rebellion that even curiosity about its causation and significance has dwindled to almost nothing. A few years ago it was impossible to discuss anything else at academic dinner tables; today the student rebellion has practically become a non-subject. What caused it? And does it have any long-run significance?

Social scientists were poorly prepared to deal with the campus phe-nomena of the 1960s. The prevailing theories of political socialization and political culture had no place for such tidal waves of youth rebellion. These theories had risen out of an interaction of three developments in the social sciences. The first of these developments was psycho-anthropology, which brought the clinical insights of psychoanalysis to bear on the study of child-rearing practices, and their relationship to cultural patterns and

Originally published as "Youth Character and Changing Political Culture in America," in *We the People: American Character and Social Change,* edited by Gordon J. DiRenzo (Westport, Conn.: Greenwood Press, 1977). Reprinted, with minor revisions, with permission of Gordon DiRenzo.

values. The second was Weberian sociological theory, which, elaborated in the work of Parsons, stressed the importance of the subjective side of culture for the processes of social change and introduced a theory of historical modernization. The third development was the invention of modern social science research methodology—sample surveys, sophisticated interviewing, rigorous data analysis, statistical techniques, and the like.

The psycho-anthropological part of this heritage led to conceptual models stressing childhood and adolescent socialization as an explanation for the persistence of cultural patterns. The Weberian-Parsonian part of the heritage stressed the interrelationship of the social and political structural tendencies of industrialization, urbanization, bureaucratization, mass political organization, and mass education and communications, with the cultural tendencies of secularization, achievement motivation, and participant propensities. These two intellectual traditions suggested the research designs that were employed in the empirical studies of political socialization and political culture that began to proliferate in the 1960s.

The socialization literature tended to view youth as an adaptive and assimilative phase in the life cycle in which the young acquire the skills, attitudes, and expectations appropriate to their roles in society. Associated with this process during the immediately pre-adult or adolescent years, there is a certain amount of experimental, resistant, and disruptive behavior, a conflict-filled period of "coming of age." To come of age implies giving things up, "settling down," taking on disciplines and responsibilities, all of which tend to produce uncertainty, anxiety, and rebellion. The political aspect of youth in this model of the socialization process is a tendency toward hypo- and hyperactivity. Studies of political participation (Nie, Verba, and Kim, 1974) show that the rates of voting and the like among young people tend to be low compared to those of the older generations. But youth is also a time of openness to political novelty. Young people tend to be more liberal and idealistic in their political views (see Lane, 1959; Milbrath, 1965).

Studies of political culture change did not attribute any particular innovative role to youth. Surveys of attitudes and statistical studies of social change emphasized broader trends of modernization contributing to the emergence of an increasingly secular, worldwide political culture based upon industrialization, urbanization, the spread of mass media, and modern education, and producing a more participant, pragmatic, and pluralistic political culture. The flower of this literature was the "end of ideology" hypothesis, which predicted a gradual trend toward incrementalism and peaceful bargaining processes in the solution of political conflicts. The ink was hardly dry on this "end of ideology" hypothesis before events began to challenge it. The younger age groups throughout the advanced industrial world, particularly in the United States, pitted themselves against the dominant political culture and challenged the adult world and behaved in ways that confounded the social and political theorists. It seemed for a while that youth was creating the political culture and that the adult society was adapting to it.

Three different kinds of literature were produced in partial response to these events: (1) a romantic, prophetic current typified in the work of Theodore Roszak (1969) and Charles Reich (1970); (2) a revisionist social science critique attacking the prevailing notions of political culture and socialization as well as the model of a stable society, functionalism, pluralism, incrementalism, pragmatism, and the like, typified in the work of Alvin Gouldner (1970), Dell Hymes (1969), Theodore Lowi (1969), and others; and (3) a speculative-historical-empirical polemic regarding the prospects of advanced industrial society and the significance of the "great disturbances" of the 1960s. The conflicting points of view engaged in this polemic sought to interpret these youth phenomena by varying combinations of three explanatory principles. Roszak, Reich, and others come close to a pure cultural revolution explanation, viewing the youth mobilization and counterculture as a dialectical rejection of the establishment culture, and as moving man to a higher cultural plane. Ronald Inglehart (1971) and Daniel Yankelovich (1972), reporting results from attitude surveys during the events of the late 1960s, offered some support for this generational-discontinuity, cultural revolution interpretation. I shall present and discuss their evidence at a later point.

The third explanatory principle stressed life-cycle phenomena as the major cause of the student rebellions of the 1960s. Lewis Feuer (1969) comes close to this opinion, though he does include some specific "period effects" that may impart explosiveness to these life-cycle phenomena. Feuer finds in a historical study of student movements, including the rebellions of the 1960s, a general tendency toward "elitism, suicidalism, populism, filiarchy, and juvenocracy," which intermittently combined with a "deauthoritization" of the older generation to produce explosive and violent youth politicization. He rejects an out-and-out "oedipal determinism," offering instead the hypothesis of an endemic generational conflict that may be mitigated, if not dispelled, by understanding. The student revolts of the 1960s are thus explained by reference to these inherent generational conflict impulses, multiplied and accentuated by the loss of confidence in adult authority resulting from the black rebellion and the Vietnam War.

Seymour M. Lipset offers a combination of life-cycle, period, and generational effects to illuminate the dimensions of the youth rebellion, particularly its impingement on university campuses in the 1960s. In Lipset's review of the history of student movements and youth politicization, historical events such as the Revolution of 1848, World War I, and the Great Depression intermittently combine with life-cycle propensities to produce student movements of an explosive sort, though he argues that the scale, extent, and duration of the recent rebellion were greater than for any of the earlier manifestations. In arguing the case for generational change, he points out that in the last decade, the size of the youth cohort relative to the population as a whole has increased substantially, and that the proportion of that age cohort moving into higher education has similarly increased substantially. The historical experiences and memories of these student generations may affect their attitudes for a long time to come, but he points to evidence suggesting a tendency toward the accentuation of liberal-activist impulses as these age cohorts mature (Lipset and Schaflander, 1971, p. 236).

Now that we have the advantage of a time perspective, and now that passions have cooled, perhaps we can assemble the pieces of the puzzle in a more orderly and satisfying way than the earlier interpreters could. An eclectic explanatory strategy is followed here. First, we examine demographic, sociological, and cultural trends affecting the life situations and contexts of choice of young people, and then we review the salient events and issues impinging on them. Taken together, these sociological trends and political experiences enable us to view value and attitude changes among young people as being constrained and conditioned by the structural and cultural developments. The evidence on value and attitude change can be evaluated as transitory and responsive to immediate historical stimuli, or as having possible long-run implications based on enduring social changes or lasting political issues.

## Demographic, Sociological, and Cultural Trends Affecting Youth

A demographic and sociological profile of those Americans fifteen to twenty-four years of age as of the 1970 census is given in Table 9.1. These 35 million young people were born during the years 1946–1955. The oldest cohort would have been of college age in 1964, at the beginning of the Berkeley rebellion. The median age groups born in 1950–1951 would have been of college age in 1968 and 1969 during the peak of the college disorders.

One of the most important characteristics of this youth cohort in the late 1960s was its rapid growth, both absolutely and as a proportion of the population. In 1960, it constituted 13 percent of the total, while in 1970 it had risen to 17 percent, an increase of almost one-third. The ratio of these youth cohorts to the older, active population (ages twenty-five to sixty-four) was sharply rising during this decade. While in 1950 and 1960 for every individual between the ages of fifteen and twenty-four there were 3.5 individuals in the age cohorts twenty-five to sixty-four, the ratio of youth to active adults had increased to 1:2.6 by 1970.

This demographic evidence suggests that for this generation there was a significant shortage of experienced older persons and an oversupply of peers. For this generation the objective opportunities for interaction and communication with older, more experienced persons had seriously declined, while the opportunities for peer group interaction and communication had sharply increased. Based on this evidence, it is safe to assume that peer group socialization would acquire greater importance and that adult-youth socialization would attenuate. Peer group socialization tends to accentuate the life-cycle propensities of the particular age cohort involved. For adolescents this would mean the accentuation and proliferation of rebellious tendencies, enthusiasm, idealism, and experimentalism.

The unusually rebellious nature of this generation is shown in Table 9.2, which reports statistics of arrests among various age groups in 1960

Table 9.1    Size of the Youth Cohort in the American Population, 1950–1970

| Age Cohort | 1950 | 1960 | 1970 |
|---|---|---|---|
| Number of persons aged 15–24 | 23,000,000 | 24,000,000 | 35,500,000 |
| Percentage of persons aged 15–24 in total population | 15 | 13 | 17 |
| Ratio of persons aged 15–24 to persons aged 25–64 | 1:3.5 | 1:3.5 | 1:2.6 |

*Source:* Adapted from U.S. Department of Commerce, Bureau of Census, *General Population Characteristics, U.S. Summary,* January 1972, pp. 1–259, and U.S. Department of Commerce, Bureau of Census, *Statistical Abstracts of the United States, 1952,* p. 134.

**Table 9.2　Percentage of Arrests by Age Cohort Compared with Percentage of Age Cohort in Total Population**

| | 1960 | | 1970 | |
|---|---|---|---|---|
| Age Cohort | Population | Arrests | Population | Arrests |
| Under 14 | 29 | 6[a] | 26 | 9 |
| 14–17 | 6 | 9 | 8 | 16 |
| 18–24 | 9 | 16 | 12 | 27 |
| 25–34 | 13 | 21 | 12 | 17 |
| 35 and over | 43 | 48 | 42 | 31 |
| Total | 100 | 100 | 100 | 100 |

*Source:* Adapted from U.S. Department of Commerce, Bureau of Census, *Statistical Abstracts of the United States, 1974* (Washington, D.C.: U.S. Government Printing Office, 1974); and from Department of Justice, FBI, *Uniform Crime Reports for the U.S., 1960, 1970* (Washington, D.C.: U.S. Government Printing Office, 1961, 1971).

a. Arrests for 1960 are reported for under 15 years of age.

and 1970. The age cohort eighteen to twenty-four constituted 9 percent of the population in 1960 and contributed 16 percent of the arrests; in 1970, it had grown to 12 percent of the total population but was involved in 27 percent of the arrests. Its percentage of the population had increased by a third, while its percentage of arrests had increased by more than two-thirds. A similarly sharp disproportionate increase in arrests occurred among those between the ages of fourteen and seventeen. These increases are only partly attributable to changing patterns of law enforcement and the reporting of enforcement statistics.

These findings lend support to the view that the baby bulge of the 1950s, which became the youth bulge of the 1960s, had not only produced a higher proportionate incidence of adolescent clashes with authority, but had also accentuated these tendencies through peer group socialization, a kind of swarming effect. This big, disorderly generation had grown into adolescence during a period of declining ethical and normative indoctrination and attenuating authority structures. By virtue of its size alone, it would have strained the socializing institutions of family, school, church, and community. But during these decades, families, particularly middle-class families, were democratizing, schools were becoming more participant-oriented, and church influence was declining.

That families and schools were becoming less authoritarian and more participant is suggested in Table 9.3. These trends were reported for all five countries included in the *Civic Culture* study (Great Britain, Germany, Italy, Mexico, and the United States), but the highest percentages

**Table 9.3    Percentage Reporting Participation in Family and School in the United States, by Selected Age Groups, 1959–1960**

|  | 18–25 | 36–40 | 61 and over |
|---|---|---|---|
| Participated in family decisions at age 16 | 85 | 72 | 48 |
| Ever protested teacher treatment while in school | 66 | 48 | 29 |

*Source:* Adapted from Almond and Verba (1963, p. 339). See also Glen H. Elder Jr., "Democratic Parent-Youth Relations in Cross-National Perspective," *Social Science Quarterly* (September 1968), pp. 216 ff.

were reported by the young American respondents (Almond and Verba, 1963). The younger respondents in this survey were recalling family and school atmospheres during the 1940s and 1950s. There is reason to believe that this trend continued for the age cohort that was adolescent and attending school during the 1960s.

Similarly, the impact of organized religion was attenuating. Thus, Gallup surveys show that, in 1954, 46 percent of a cross-section sample of Americans reported having attended church within the preceding week. While this proportion had only declined to 42 percent in 1970, the drop was most marked among the younger age groups and those receiving higher education. While 45 percent of the respondents aged fifty and over reported attending church in the preceding week, this was true of only 32 percent of the twenty-one- to twenty-nine-year-olds. A survey in 1972 showed a strong relationship between amount of higher education and rate of church attendance. Thus, 45 percent of the freshmen respondents in 1972 reported having attended church within the preceding week, compared to only 27 percent of the seniors and 20 percent of the graduate students.

Thus, the childhood and early adolescence of this bulging age cohort had been marked by a loosening up of the socializing agencies. While the scale and difficulty of the process of socialization of the young had sharply increased, the institutions normally performing these functions were losing some of their authority and indoctrinative capacity.

In addition, there was little disciplinary impact from the economy. From the perspective of this generation, as it entered the high schools, colleges, and graduate schools during the 1960s, their material futures were ensured. Access to higher education was open. Per capita income (in constant 1958 dollars) in the United States rose from $1,810 in 1950 to $2,157

Table 9.4    Per Capita GNP and Personal Income in the United States, 1950–1970
(Constant 1958 Dollars)

|                   | 1950  | 1960  | 1970  |
|-------------------|-------|-------|-------|
| Per capita GNP    | 2,342 | 2,699 | 3,524 |
| Per capita income | 1,810 | 2,157 | 3,043 |

*Source:* U.S. Department of Commerce, Bureau of the Census, *Statistical Abstracts of the United States, 1973*, p. 322.

in 1960, to $3,043 in 1970 (see Table 9.4). The discipline of the market was lacking; it was a job-hunter's economy. The childhood of these young people had been spent amid rising affluence and consumerism. Nothing in their own experience suggested an adult day of reckoning.

## The Changing Structure and Culture of Higher Education

This raw aggregative account of the sharply increased difficulty and scale of the problem of socialization of youth into American culture, along with the suggested declining effectiveness of the major socializing institutions and experiences, applies to this age cohort as a whole. Of particular interest here is that part of the youth population that attended colleges and universities, since they have been the presumed bearers of cultural innovation. The number of undergraduate students registered for degree credit in institutions of higher education rose from a little over 2.5 million in 1950 to over 3 million in 1960, to over 7 million in 1970 (see Table 9.5). The number of faculty members increased from 247,000 in 1950 to 381,000 in 1960, to 551,000 in 1970.

By 1970, more than 40 percent of those aged eighteen to twenty-one were enrolled for degree credit higher education. The absolute numbers tell the story more impressively than do the percentages. A more than doubling of student enrollment in a single decade could not be accommodated without a large increase in educational facilities and faculties. Thus, the number of colleges and universities increased from 1,851 in 1950 to 2,525 in 1970; college and university faculties jumped from a little over a quarter of a million in 1950 to over 550,000 in 1970.

At the same time that the physical dimensions of higher education were rapidly increasing, the culture and social structure of these education insti-

**Table 9.5   Growth in Higher Education in the United States, 1950–1970**

|                                                                    | 1950      | 1960      | 1970      |
| ------------------------------------------------------------------ | --------- | --------- | --------- |
| Undergraduate degree credit students in institutions of higher education | 2,659,000 | 3,216,000 | 7,136,000 |
| Students per hundred persons aged 18–21                            | 28.58     | 34.86     | 44.43     |
| Graduate students                                                  | 237,000   | 342,000   | 828,000   |
| Colleges and universities                                          | 1,851     | 2,008     | 2,525     |
| Faculty members                                                    | 247,000   | 381,000   | 551,000   |

*Source:* U.S. Department of Commerce, Bureau of Census, *Statistical Abstracts of the United States, 1973*, p. 131.

tutions were undergoing significant changes. The triumph of the scientific revolution brought with it a rapid increase in the research and graduate training activities of faculties, a rapid proliferation of specialized and technical courses, as well as a growth of para-faculties in the form of research and teaching assistants (Smelser and Almond, 1974). In this context, the exposure of a large proportion of students to senior and experienced faculty, and to ideal-setting, synthesizing, and evaluative education experiences, was declining.

Along with the shift in the curriculum in the direction of specialization and technical virtuosity, the social structure of student bodies was undergoing change. The dominance of fraternities and sororities in social life, and of athletics as the arena for the creation of campus heroes, became increasingly suspect as American campuses filled with returning GIs, first from World War II and then from the Korean War, and finally from disadvantaged ethnic groups as they were increasingly recruited into student bodies during this period. The ethos of campus life no longer tolerated the older forms of snobbery, and a new set of campus heroes emerged from the leaders of marches and the veterans of "Mississippi summers." The important point here is that there were no new primary structures to take the place of the discredited older ones, so that these new and more socially heterogeneous student bodies tended to become relatively unorganized masses, volatile and susceptible to sudden mobilization and politicization in response to the events of this period.

These social trends pointing to a substantial overloading of the agencies of socialization, at a time when the principal socializing agencies of family, church, and school were losing their socializing capacity, suggest a volatile generation, a value-searching generation, a generation less likely to comply with authority. They also suggest some themes of cultural innovation growing out of the conditions just described. But these "pronenesses" do not add up to the "counterculture" or to the great youth disorders of 1965–1970. The salient events of the period created the issues of the rebellion and triggered some of the cultural innovations.

## The Youth Rebellion as Problem-Solving Behavior: Issues and Events of the Period

The campus disorders cannot simply be explained in these sociological and psychological terms. They also have to be examined as coping and problem-solving behavior, often primitive, but intended to attain ends and relieve stress. Alongside these sociological and cultural changes in the condition of youth in America is placed a chronology of salient events, beginning with the Eisenhower "Silent Generation" period (see Box 9.1). As we glance at the "big stories" of the Eisenhower era, it is evident that the Cold War set the issues of the times, even though Stalin died in March 1953, just two months after Eisenhower's inauguration. In June 1953, the Rosenbergs were executed for espionage.

But the McCarthy period of security paranoia and domestic American Communism was coming to an end, as the Senate censured Senator Joseph McCarthy in December 1954. Conflict with and anxiety over the Soviet Union during this period fluctuated. In August 1953, the Russians exploded their first H-bomb, not long after the first successful H-bomb explosion by the United States.

De-Stalinization in the Soviet Union began in February 1956 with Khrushchev's "Secret Speech on the Crimes of the Stalin Era," but the thaw in the Communist orbit was arrested when the Polish and Hungarian revolts occurred in July and November 1956. Détente with the Soviet Union had its ups and downs as Soviet and U.S. competition in the development of satellites intensified in 1957 and 1958. Khrushchev visited the United States in September 1959, but in May 1960, the U-2 incident resulted in the cancellation of a summit conference intended to allay East-West tensions. The seizure of power by Castro in Cuba in January 1959 introduced a new element of potential contention between the Soviet Union and the United States.

Two other events in the 1950s suggest tendencies that were to surface in the 1960s and give that decade its style and character. In May 1954, the Supreme Court issued its school desegregation decision, and in December

---

**Box 9.1  First Chronology: The Eisenhower Years**

| | | |
|---|---|---|
| 1953 | January | Eisenhower inaugurated |
| | March | Death of Stalin |
| | June | Rosenbergs executed for espionage |
| | July | Korean Armistice |
| | August | Russians explode H-bomb |
| 1954 | May | *Brown v. Board of Education* school desegregation decision |
| | December | Senator McCarthy censured by the Senate |
| 1955 | December | Bus boycott in Montgomery, Alabama (Martin Luther King Jr.) |
| 1956 | February | Khrushchev's "Secret Speech on the Crimes of the Stalin Era" |
| | July | Polish revolt crushed |
| | November | Hungarian revolt crushed |
| 1957 | October | Soviets launch *Sputnik* |
| 1958 | January | U.S. launches earth satellite |
| 1959 | January | Castro takes power in Cuba |
| | September | Khrushchev visits United States |
| 1960 | May | U-2 incident—summit conference canceled |

---

1955, Martin Luther King Jr. led his first boycott in Montgomery, Alabama. Nevertheless, this decade was dominated by foreign policy and Cold War issues; it was a period of bipartisan foreign policy and broad consensus on other issues.

The Kennedy years (see Box 9.2) were also dominated by security and Cold War issues. The year 1961 was marked by the Bay of Pigs, the Laotian crisis, and the building of the Berlin Wall by the East German regime; in 1962, the Cold War reached a high level of crisis in the Cuban missile confrontation. In the last years of the Kennedy administration, the black rebellion was acquiring momentum with riots at the University of Mississippi over the admission of James Meredith in September 1962, and in the 200,000-strong march on Washington led by Martin Luther King Jr. in July 1963.

In the first year of the Johnson administration (see Box 9.3), the three themes of the great disturbances of the 1960s were struck. In June 1964,

---

**Box 9.2  Second Chronology: The Kennedy Years**

| | | |
|---|---|---|
| 1960 | January | Kennedy inaugurated |
| 1961 | April | Bay of Pigs |
| | | Laotian crisis |
| | August | Berlin Wall |
| | October | Soviet 60-megaton blast |
| 1962 | September | Riot at University of Mississippi over admission of James Meredith |
| | October | Cuban Missile Crisis |
| 1963 | July | Largest-ever D.C. demonstration, led by Martin Luther King Jr. |
| | November | John F. Kennedy assassinated |

---

student volunteers streamed into Mississippi in the first stages of a major voter registration campaign. Three of these "freedom fighters" were murdered and their bodies were discovered in August. In July, the first of the "hot summers" occurred with race riots in Harlem, the Bedford-Stuyvesant section of Brooklyn, and Rochester. In August 1964, the destroyer *Maddox* incident and the Gulf of Tonkin Resolution opened the overt phase of the Vietnam War. And in December 1964, the Berkeley campus of the University of California exploded with the free speech sit-in and demonstrations. By 1965, the black rebellion and the Vietnam War began to impinge directly on university campuses, just when the baby bulge was moving into colleges.

The black rebellion had trained a generation of student activists who had participated in the nonviolent movement and in registration campaigns. The number of blacks admitted to higher education also began to increase rapidly during this period, as many universities actively recruited in efforts to equalize opportunity. The Vietnam War touched university campuses through the increasing demands of the draft and through the granting of draft exemptions to students enrolled in higher education. Troop commitments rapidly increased during this period, with the total exceeding half a million men by the end of 1967.

The peak of student protest and activism was reached in early 1968 with the Tet offensive in January and Senator Eugene McCarthy's remarkable showing in the New Hampshire primary in March. In April, the assas-

## Box 9.3　Third Chronology: The Johnson Years

| | | |
|---|---|---|
| 1964 | June | Voter registration campaign in Mississippi |
| | July | First "hot summer"—Harlem, Brooklyn, and Rochester |
| | August | Destroyer *Maddox* incident and Gulf of Tonkin Resolution |
| | December | Free speech sit-in at Berkeley |
| 1965 | July | U.S. troops in Vietnam exceed 100,000; draft doubled |
| | August | Second "hot summer"—Watts riot |
| 1966 | May | Protests at University of Chicago and Community College of New York against use of class standing for draft deferment |
| | | U.S. casualties in Vietnam reach 1,000 per week |
| | July | Third "hot summer"—Chicago West Side and Hough section of Cleveland |
| 1967 | August | Johnson announces Vietnam commitment to exceed 500,000 |
| | | Fourth "hot summer"—Newark |
| 1968 | January | Tet offensive |
| | March | New Hampshire primary and Johnson's withdrawal |
| | April | Martin Luther King Jr. assassinated |
| | | Columbia University sit-in |
| | May | Preliminary Vietnam peace talks begin |
| | June | Robert Kennedy assassinated |

sination of Martin Luther King Jr. mobilized American campuses and, as an aftermath, produced a major influx of blacks and other ethnic groups into university communities. In June, the assassination of Robert Kennedy, and in August, the riots at the Chicago Democratic Convention, brought the student rebellion to a fever pitch. It was during 1968 and 1969 that strikes, sit-ins, violence, and "trashings" struck American campuses one after the other—Columbia, Cornell, Harvard, the University of Wisconsin, San Francisco State, Stanford, Boston University, and many others. War issues, ethnic issues, and student power issues all combined to produce these years of extraordinary mobilization and politicization.

The signing of the Vietnam peace agreement in January 1973 (see Box 9.4) and the withdrawal of the last U.S. troops in Vietnam eliminated Vietnam as a cause of campus disorders. The racial issue declined in salience with the liberalization of admissions policies and the development of the "Black Power" movement. The cessation of the rapid growth

---

### Box 9.4  Fourth Chronology: The Nixon Years

| | | |
|---|---|---|
| 1969 | January | Nixon inaugurated |
| | April | Harvard University sit-in |
| | | Cornell University sit-in |
| | July | First moon landing |
| | October | Vietnam moratorium |
| | November | Vietnam total casualty figure of over 300,000 announced |
| 1970 | April | U.S. attack on Cambodia |
| | | Millions celebrate Earth Day |
| | | Yale student strike over Bobby Seale trial |
| | May | Kent and Jackson State killings |
| | August | Fatal bombing at University of Wisconsin |
| 1971 | May | 12,000 arrested in Washington demonstration |
| | July | 26th Amendment (18-year-old vote) ratified |
| | September | Riot and occupation at Attica prison |
| 1972 | February | Nixon visit to China |
| | March | Watergate break-in |
| | May | Nixon visit to Russia |
| | August | McGovern nominated |
| | November | Nixon reelected |
| 1973 | January | Vietnam peace agreement signed |
| | April | Watergate hearings begin |
| | July | Double-digit inflation begins |
| | October | Arab oil embargo and energy crisis begin |
| 1974 | July | Impeachment hearings begin |
| | | Supreme Court decision on subpoena of tapes |
| | August | Nixon resigns |

of higher education, the declining support of fellowship and research programs, the declining rate of growth in the national economy, and the consequent increasing difficulties in finding suitable employment changed the campus mood. Finally, in 1973, the Yom Kippur war, the Arab oil embargo, and the energy crisis brought a new set of issues to the fore in the United States.

Only by combining an account of changing social trends affecting young people with an account of the salient issues affecting their lives and concerns can we begin to suggest some plausible explanations of both the level of protest and its content. The demographic youth bulge, the declining effectiveness of socializing agencies, the increasing concentration of this numerous generation in university campuses, which themselves were undergoing significant changes, tell us something about the overloading of institutions of higher education, the fragility of their authority, and the declining vitality of their solidaristic institutions and norms. As the sparks of the ethnic rebellion and the Vietnam War were thrown into these volatile populations, it is not surprising that they went up in flames. The challenge to university authority and the issue of "student power" can be explained by this generation's earlier experience in participatory families and schools, by a general decline in its faith in the legitimacy of a social order that produced Vietnam and segregation, and also by the changing culture and structure of the institutions of higher education themselves.

## Evidence of Value and Attitude Change

It almost seems that we have more explanations for the violence in the 1960s than we need, that the explosion was "overdetermined." But the youth rebellion and the counterculture were complex and multidimensional. Hence, all of the explanatory components reviewed here are needed to illuminate its various dimensions and to separate the lasting from the transitory trends.

Before turning to these problems, the evidence on value and attitude trends during the periods that concern us will be reviewed. Two major surveys of youth attitudes were carried out during the 1960s: one covering European countries and the United States by Ronald Inglehart, a political scientist at the University of Michigan; and the second by the Yankelovich Survey organization, which was limited to U.S. data. Both studies have the advantage of time perspective, since the same questions have been asked several times in recent years. Thus, they report data gathered during the heat of the rebellion, as well as during calmer times.

Inglehart's first findings were reported in a striking article published in 1971. The article aroused great interest and has produced at least two polemical-empirical responses (see Ike, 1973; Marsh, 1975). Since his first report, Inglehart has administered two other surveys, which include a number of additional European countries and the United States. The results of all these investigations are reported in Inglehart's *The Silent Revolution* (1976).

In his first study based on surveys in France, Germany, Great Britain, Italy, Belgium, and Holland, Inglehart concluded:

> A transformation may be taking place in the political cultures of advanced industrial societies. This transformation seems to be altering the basic value priorities of given generations, as a result of changing conditions influencing their basic socialization. The changes seem to affect the stand one takes on current political issues and may have a long-term tendency to alter existing patterns of political partisanship. (1971, p. 991)

Inglehart links his hypotheses to Maslow's "need hierarchy" concept and the theory of socialization. Maslow (1954) argues that there are five basic need areas: (1) physiological-subsistence, (2) safety and security, (3) affection and belonging, (4) esteem, and (5) self-actualization. The needs are sequential or occur in a hierarchy, the basic level being physiological, the second level safety, the third level affection and belongingness, and so on. As you satisfy the one, you go on to the next.

Inglehart argues that the generation born after 1945 in Western Europe had experienced a period of peace, uninterrupted economic growth, and rising living standards. Hence, for this post-1945 generation, physiological and safety needs have been met, and their value priorities ex hypothesi should be of the affection-belongingness, esteem, and self-actualization order. From socialization theory, which argues that value orientations formed in childhood persist into adulthood, Inglehart predicts that the newer values would be more frequently encountered among the young, while the older generation would continue to give greater weight to scarcity and security values that were salient in their childhood and youth.

In testing his hypothesis in Western Europe, Inglehart used a forced choice question in which respondents were required to pick two out of four sociopolitical goals. Two of these four were security and economic goals, and two were libertarian and participatory. His findings were sub-

Table 9.6    "Postbourgeois" and "Acquisitive" Value Choices by Age Cohorts in Four
European Countries

| Ages | Germany | | France | | Italy | | Great Britain | |
|---|---|---|---|---|---|---|---|---|
| | PB | Acq | PB | Acq | PB | Acq | PB | Acq |
| 16–24 | 23 | 21 | 20 | 21 | 28 | 18 | 14 | 25 |
| 25–34 | 15 | 35 | 11 | 35 | 15 | 30 | 9 | 29 |
| 55–64 | 4 | 60 | 6 | 48 | 7 | 42 | 8 | 41 |
| Total spread across cohorts | 56 | | 47 | | 60 | | 34 | |

*Source:* Adapted from Inglehart (1971, p. 1000).
*Note:* PB = postbourgeois; Acq = acquisitive.

stantial. Table 9.6 shows a clear pattern from country to country of greater preference for what he calls "postbourgeois" value patterns among the younger age cohort born after 1945, and a declining preference for these values as we go on to the older age groups.

Table 9.7, controlling age by socioeconomic status, shows an even more striking pattern of difference. Thus, the more educated, affluent stratum of the post-1945 generation opts for Inglehart's postbourgeois values to an even more striking degree and in sharp contrast to the older, less educated stratum, the percentages being 49 to 3 for Germany, 31 to 5 for France, 40 to 7 for Italy, and 16 to 8 for Britain. The fact that Britain, though manifesting the same trends, had a smaller postbourgeois sector and smaller differences according to age and socioeconomic status, Inglehart

Table 9.7    "Postbourgeois" Value Preference by Age and Socioeconomic Status,
in Percentages

| Ages | Germany | | France | | Italy | | Great Britain | |
|---|---|---|---|---|---|---|---|---|
| | Upper | Lower | Upper | Lower | Upper | Lower | Upper | Lower |
| 16–24 | 49 | 15 | 31 | 8 | 40 | 23 | 16 | 10 |
| 25–34 | 35 | 10 | 23 | 2 | 37 | 11 | 8 | 10 |
| 55–64 | 16 | 3 | 8 | 5 | 5 | 7 | 14 | 8 |

*Source:* Adapted from Inglehart (1971, pp. 1002 ff., table 7).
*Note:* Inglehart bases socioeconomic status (SES) on a combination of educational and occupational criteria. The "upper" SES category would include those respondents who have had secondary education or higher and are employed in nonmanual occupations in the modern sector of the economy; the "lower" SES category would include persons with primary school education or less, and employed in manual work.

attributes to the relatively low rate of economic growth in Britain in the postwar years, and to postbourgeois attitudes in the six countries surveyed.

One of the main difficulties with Inglehart's first study was the discrepancy between his theoretical variables and his operational indicators. He identifies participationism and libertarianism as postbourgeois, and concern with economic stability and security as bourgeois or acquisitive values. Since liberty and participation were central beliefs of the bourgeois revolution of the eighteenth and nineteenth centuries, his first formulation left many students intrigued by the magnitude of the generational differences he uncovered, but unconvinced by his interpretation of their significance.

In his second report, Inglehart confronts this and other problems. Not wanting to lose the advantage of comparison over time, he repeats his four-item forced choice question, but calls the libertarian-participatory pair "postmaterialistic." He adds additional items, tapping other issue areas such as the environment, economic democracy, and the impersonality of modern society. Although he offers interesting evidence from his data to support Maslow's "need hierarchy" hypothesis, he does not insist on it. He offers a less complicated hypothesis—the marginal utility notion that "people tend to place a high priority on whatever needs are in short supply" (Inglehart, 1976, p. 2). Thus, in an age of affluence and peace with material and safety needs satisfied, people turn to nonmaterial attitudes and values.

The data from the later surveys as they relate to age, and now including the United States, confirm the earlier finding of a higher incidence of postmaterial options among the youth cohort and materialist options among the older groups (see Table 9.8). Inglehart attributes the smaller spread in youth and older-age attitudes in the United States and Britain to the fact that, while experiencing an age of affluence in the postwar period, these two countries did not experience the remarkable rates of growth enjoyed by France, Germany, Italy, and other continental European countries.

His findings on changes in the distribution of value types from the first survey in 1970 to the second series in 1973 show some slight tendency to decline in postmaterialist orientations (Inglehart, 1976, tab. 14). But by and large the pattern persists. He also demonstrates that the postmaterialist-materialist scoring device genuinely taps these dimensions. Thus, those picking the postmaterialist pair are much more likely to prefer the human interaction and creativity aspects of their work than the security and moneymaking aspects, to favor helping the developing nations, to be internationalist and cosmopolitan rather than nationalist and

Table 9.8    Value Types by Age Cohorts in Advanced Industrial Societies, 1972–1973

| Ages | United States PM | United States M | Great Britain PM | Great Britain M | France PM | France M | Germany PM | Germany M | Italy PM | Italy M |
|---|---|---|---|---|---|---|---|---|---|---|
| 19–28 | 17 | 24 | 11 | 27 | 20 | 22 | 19 | 24 | 16 | 26 |
| 59–68 | 6 | 37 | 5 | 36 | 3 | 50 | 7 | 52 | 4 | 49 |
| Total spread across cohorts | 26 | | 17 | | 51 | | 56 | | 42 | |

*Source:* Adapted from Inglehart (1976, chap. 3, tab. 4).
*Note:* PM = postmaterialist, M = materialist.

parochial in their orientations, to favor women's rights, to be open to new things, to prefer a less impersonal society, and to view themselves as "liberal" or "left" in their political inclinations. The percentage differences in all these respects among the materialists and postmaterialists are quite large. They do indeed suggest that Inglehart has identified a significant new value trend among the young, particularly the educated young, in advanced industrial societies. However, he leaves unresolved the question of whether these changes are of the "period-bound" sort, or whether they are the harbingers of genuine, persistent culture change. The explanatory workhorses upon which Inglehart relies are economic growth and associated affluence and peace.

Inglehart acknowledges that, in contrast to the 1960s, the decade of the 1970s is one of actual and impending scarcities as population and technology press on limited resources and as rising levels of demand produce inflation. Unanswered is the question as to whether this postmaterialist cluster of new cultural values is likely to be generalized over time as advanced industrial societies move into a "no-growth" or "slow-growth" phase and encounter the uncertainties of inflation and of critical shortages. Inglehart's work was primarily focused on Europe. He only included the United States in one of his most recent surveys, and did not administer his full instrument to the American sample. It is still of interest that the generation gap in the United States, according to his findings, was not as large as it was among the continental European countries. A more recent survey exploring these hypotheses is still unreported.

Daniel Yankelovich's work is solely concerned with the United States and centers on the university and college student population, though general and working-class youth samples are included as well. Overall, Yankelovich has carried out five surveys of American youth attitudes—in

1968, 1969, 1970, 1971, and 1973. Two of the studies (1969 and 1973) include a noncollege youth sample.

In his first major report on the culture of the American college student population based on his surveys through 1971, Yankelovich claimed to have discovered a new "culture" among college youth in the United States, which he called "The New Naturalism." Among its principal features were a turning off toward the achievement ethic, competition, science, technology, and bureaucracy, and a turning on toward direct sensory experience, adapting to nature rather than seeking to master it, cultivating deep and honest relationships in small groups, and seeking self-knowledge through introspection. In his analysis of trends during the four years covered in his first report, Yankelovich (1972) argued that, while political radicalism was beginning to subside by 1971, specifically cultural value innovations were persisting. In his 1974 report, he pointed out that much of this cultural innovation was surviving, and even spreading to noncollege youth in the United States.

In the second report, he dropped the concept of a "New Naturalism" culture in favor of "New Values" (1974). He divides them into three categories: (1) new moral norms, (2) new social values, and (3) a self-fulfillment ethic. The new moral norms include the adoption of liberal attitudes toward sexuality; a skepticism toward the legitimacy of such institutions as the legal system, government, political parties, business corporations, and religious institutions; and a dilution of national feeling and patriotism. The new social values include changing attitudes toward work and success, and toward marriage and the family—a kind of general reevaluation of adult roles and expectations. The new ethic of self-fulfillment is closely related to the first two categories of value change. It implies establishing a place for self-gratification and creativity beyond "making a living" and fulfilling role obligations to others.

Yankelovich's evidence is reported in Tables 9.9 and 9.10. The first table shows that in the period 1969–1973 the proportion of college students favoring more sexual freedom, more privacy, and less emphasis on money increased, while the population stressing the importance of religion and patriotism decreased, despite the dramatic subsidence of student radicalism and activism in this period. Table 9.10, on the other hand, demonstrates a return to the work and achievement ethic, with stress on the advancement, security, and money aspects of jobs increasing among college students; but at the same time, the preference for self-expressive values on the job also increased.

**Table 9.9    Trends in College Student Values, Yankelovich Surveys, 1969–1973, in Percentages**

| Values | 1969 | 1973 |
|---|---|---|
| More sexual freedom | 43 | 61 |
| Importance of religion | 38 | 28 |
| Importance of patriotism | 35 | 19 |
| Importance of privacy | 61 | 71 |
| Less emphasis on money | 65 | 80 |

*Source:* Adapted from Yankelovich (1974, pp. 12 ff.).

**Table 9.10    What College Students Want on the Job, Yankelovich Surveys, 1969–1973, in Percentages**

| Job Goals | 1969–1971 | 1973 |
|---|---|---|
| Self-expression | 56 | 68 |
| Challenge | 64 | 77 |
| Opportunities for advancement | 35 | 51 |
| Security | 33 | 58 |
| Money | 36 | 61 |
| Prestige | 15 | 28 |

*Source:* Adapted from Yankelovich (1974, pp. 17 ff.).

A particularly interesting finding of the Yankelovich surveys is that noncollege youth seem to have assimilated these new values in recent years and that there has been a diffusion of "new" cultural values from lower to higher socioeconomic status. Table 9.11 shows that the new morality has been adopted by almost half the noncollege youth, that the authority of the church and nation has attenuated among these groups, and that work and money motives have lost some of their glamour.

Inglehart and Yankelovich are emphasized here because they have been directly concerned with the problem confronted in this essay. Inglehart's work, having already involved three surveys, is now in its fourth and major phase. Since this current phase includes the United States, trend data for the United States will soon be available. Two studies—one of Japan and one of Britain—challenge some of Inglehart's conclusions. Nobutake Ike, in a secondary analysis of Japanese survey data for the period 1953–1968, finds some evidence supportive of the Inglehart thesis: "Japanese youth, when

Table 9.11    **Noncollege Student Values and Attitudes, Yankelovich Surveys, 1969–1973, in Percentages**

| Values and Attitudes | 1969 | 1973 |
|---|---|---|
| More sexual freedom | 22 | 47 |
| Importance of religion | 64 | 42 |
| Importance of clean moral life | 77 | 57 |
| Importance of patriotism | 60 | 40 |
| Less emphasis on money | 54 | 74 |
| Belief that hard work pays off | 79 | 56 |

*Source:* Adapted from Yankelovich (1974, pp. 24 ff.).

compared to their elders, appear to be less acquisitive, more democratic, and somewhat more inclined to value freedom; in short they show signs of preferring the kind of values defined by Inglehart as Post-Bourgeois" (1973, p. 1200). Ike argues, however, that the pattern of political culture change in Japan is more complex than that presented by Inglehart for Europe. Thus the older age groups over time have been moving toward democratic and participant values, and the trend has been toward a convergence in attitude among the young and old rather than a divergence as in Europe. He also points to a marked tendency among Japanese young people toward privatization and individuation rather than in the direction of "belongingness," consistent with the Maslowian "need hierarchy" hypothesis. Inglehart's more recent work seems to be more concerned with differences in historical experience and cultural characteristics as they may explain differences in the political attitudes between generations.

Alan Marsh's analysis of satisfaction with various aspects of life produced mixed findings. On the one hand, he found that the postbourgeois respondents were younger, better off, and better educated than the "acquisitives." On the other hand, he discovered that the postbourgeois respondents, while dissatisfied with their social surroundings and the political and qualitative aspects of their lives, were also "more prone to material dissatisfactions and security anxieties than are the acquisitive group" (1975, p. 9). Marsh's findings for Britain would appear to be more consistent with those of the most recent Yankelovich survey, which noted a return to "materialistic" job values and concerns among American college students.

Other studies tend to confirm Inglehart's and Yankelovich's findings, particularly those that suggest a decline in the legitimacy and stability of the political and social institutions of advanced industrial society. Arthur

H. Miller (1974), in a study of "trust in government" in the United States, based on five University of Michigan Survey Research Center election studies over the period 1964–1970, found a strong trend toward decline in trust in government and political alienation among American respondents, particularly among the younger age groups. The younger, educated respondents tended to manifest a left-oriented distrust in government that was associated with support of student demonstrations, dealing constructively with problems of poverty and discrimination, and bringing the Vietnam War to an end. Gallup surveys in the 1970s have shown a similar decline in confidence in U.S. governmental, economic, and social institutions; this decline was most marked among the young and the more educated.

The literature pointing to increased volatility in partisan voting in advanced industrial society, and particularly the decline of class as a predictor of party affiliation, is so substantial as not to merit citation here. This tendency is most evident among the educated young. Some evidence already cited shows that the attenuation of party commitment and confidence in government, church, and other social institutions among the educated young seems to be associated with support for unorthodox and relatively violent political practices. Inglehart's work showed this to be the case for support of student demonstrations in his European studies. Alan Marsh (1975), in a more focused study in England involving fifty each of university students, young workers (ages sixteen to twenty-four), older working-class people (forty-eight to fifty-four), and older middle-class people (forty-five to fifty-four), found a strikingly unorthodox "protest potential" among the university students and an almost equal protest potential among young workers. In sharp contrast, the older middle- and working-class respondents tended to prefer more moderate and orthodox methods.

Further evidence suggesting greater alienation from American institutions and greater liberalism and unorthodoxy among the younger generation is reported in the University of California (Berkeley) Survey Research Center study of political alienation. Although the study is limited to the San Francisco Bay area, it has the great virtue of depth and discrimination in testing satisfaction-dissatisfaction with a variety of American institutions and values. Its preliminary findings support the view that Americans in the younger age groups (eighteen to twenty-six) are somewhat less trustful of their national government, less confident of its honesty, responsiveness, efficiency, and the like, than the older age groups. They also support the view that young Americans tend to be more liberal in welfare, environmental, racial, and foreign policy attitudes than older groups, more distrustful of the business community and of organized religion, and somewhat more turned off by materialism and the work and achievement ethic. The differences in satisfaction-dissatisfaction and trust-distrust in this study are reported on a five-point scale; the distance between the younger and older age groups tends to be on the order of one scalar point, which is not a very large contrast but tends to be consistent. The findings also suggest that the educated young manifest these tendencies of alienation, liberalism, and antimaterialism to a larger extent than the youth cohort as a whole.

## Conclusion

Any satisfying interpretation of the late 1960s requires an explanation of the remarkable combination of large-scale political rebellion and cultural experimentalism among young people, particularly among college students. An extraordinary set of causes is needed to convert the normal pattern of political apathy, liberal impulses, and experimental behavior characteristic of young people into the massive and violent political mobilizations and cultural explosions of the period.

Table 9.12 cites a series of mental experiments showing how different combinations of causes might have affected youth behavior during this period. This step-by-step analysis may help us speculate about the future directions of culture change. The table suggests that a life-cycle interpretation has no explanatory power at all. Even Lewis Feuer's combination of life-cycle tendencies with political period effects producing a loss of legitimacy on the part of adult authority cannot explain the explosiveness of the youth rebellion and the lush cultural innovations of the period. Item 2 in the table suggests that the Feuer combination would have produced politicization on the campuses, but there is no logic to suggest that the Vietnam War and the black rebellion would have produced the counterculture with its rejection of the work and achievement ethic, its communalism, its primitive and instant ideologism, and the like.

Similarly, the socioeconomic period effects—the youth bulge, the quantum jump in higher education, the increasing technicization of the curriculum, and the rising trend of economic growth and material affluence—can be seen to have a causal connection to the various cultural innovations and to the crisis of university authority. However, they cannot account for the political mobilizations of the period. Rising affluence and

**Table 9.12    Explanation of the Great Disturbances of the 1960s**

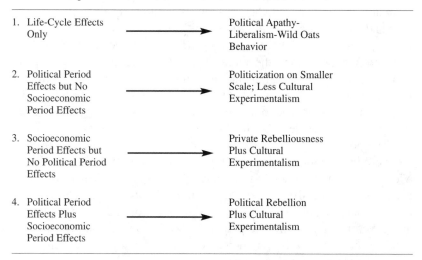

1. Life-Cycle Effects Only ⟶ Political Apathy-Liberalism-Wild Oats Behavior

2. Political Period Effects but No Socioeconomic Period Effects ⟶ Politicization on Smaller Scale; Less Cultural Experimentalism

3. Socioeconomic Period Effects but No Political Period Effects ⟶ Private Rebelliousness Plus Cultural Experimentalism

4. Political Period Effects Plus Socioeconomic Period Effects ⟶ Political Rebellion Plus Cultural Experimentalism

opportunity made the rejection of materialism and the work ethic possible. The rapid growth of student bodies and the decay of the traditional social structure of university life may have contributed to the commune movement and to the emphasis in the youth culture on "meaningful" personal relationships. The size of the youth cohort and the consequent enhancement of the role of peer group socialization at the expense of cultural transmission through adults and authority figures help explain the "generation gap," the lack of a sense of history in the "now generation," and the primitive quality of its ideological, political, and aesthetic formulations. These socioeconomic period effects can help us understand Woodstock, the commune movements, and the "countercurriculum," but not the massive political demonstrations and confrontations of the period.

When we combine these socioeconomic and political period effects, we begin to get a set of independent variables capable of explaining the complex set of dependent variables that made up the great disturbances of the late 1960s. They suggest that the political and cultural rebellions were essentially period-bound, being tied to the political issues, the state of the economy, the age distribution of the population, and the educational developments of the time. Both the socioeconomic and political sets of period-bound developments had a distinctive relation to each of the two components of the disturbances—the socioeconomic ones with the cultural manifestations, and the political issues with the political rebellion. In addition, the two sets of period-related causes interacted one with the other and fed upon one another, making the political rebellion more explosive and the cultural rebellion more bizarre. The loss of legitimacy of political and social authority resulting from the ethnic rebellion and the Vietnam War weakened the moral and cultural order and made it fair game, justifying the experimentation with new values and social arrangements. On the other hand, the youth bulge, the rapid growth of higher education, and the boom economy created volatile masses, responding quickly and on a large scale to political stimuli.

The political rebellion began to subside after the turn of the decade. As the ethnic mobilization lost its intensity and as the U.S. role in the Vietnam War drew to a close, the political stimuli lost their force. What seems to have persisted in the population as a whole, but particularly among young people, is an increased skepticism of and distrust in nation and government, an increased partisan volatility, and, among the younger generations particularly, an increased acceptance of "unconventional" forms of political participation and protest.

The fate of the counterculture is intriguing and offers an interesting case history for the ruminations of social theorists. A sharp change in the age structure of the population and an accentuation of peer group socialization seem to have conspired with a sudden increase in investment in higher education to turn the educated young into a cultural-innovating generation. The hedonism, the sexual libertarianism, and in some respects the communitarianism of the counterculture have been co-opted by the dominant culture, affecting legislation, sex roles and behavior, clothing styles and fashions, residential patterns, and the like. These innovations were consistent with, but sharply discontinuous in degree from, the longer-run processes of cultural secularization affecting these patterns.

In the 1970s a new set of political issues and problems has begun to dominate our politics. These issues have arisen from the slowdown of economic growth and actual or impending scarcities resulting from population growth and increasing pressure on resources. While the more pessimistic forecasts of the future are undoubtedly exaggerated, the basic assumption of limitless material progress and an ever-improving standard of living that has dominated the political ideologies (both left and right) of the West for the past two centuries can no longer be seriously entertained. If our basic economic realities and expectations undergo this fundamental shift, our politics and culture cannot help being transformed in similarly important ways.

The difficulty in projecting these tendencies into the future is that we have no sure way of predicting the rate and pattern of this slowdown, or of forecasting the technological inventions that might mitigate and postpone its consequences. It seems clear, however, that the material optimism that lies at the basis of Western culture and politics will begin to abate. A slowdown in the rate of growth is bound to produce a domestic and foreign politics dominated by the issues of conservation and redistribution. These are conflictual policies, and they suggest an increasing power in governmental agencies, and an increasing creation of supranational authority and institutions.

The kind of political culture that fits this set of emerging problems, issues, and institutions is one that is less rigidly committed to the enhancement and defense of material interests, and to the full sovereignty of the nation-state. Table 9.13 suggests a kind of race between the politico-economic issues and problems growing out of the slowdown of economic growth on the one hand, and political-cultural adaptations on the other. The slowdown of economic growth brings with it sharpened political antagonisms over the distribution of the material product both within and between countries, particularly the rich and the poor ones. Increased political tension and antagonism contribute to governmental instability and are particularly threatening to liberal democratic systems. If we press the known relationship between economic stagnation and decline and intensity of partisan antagonism and group conflict into the future, it is realistic to expect political culture change in the direction of ideological confrontation and a domestic and international politics of protest.

Table 9.13   Long-Term Developments in National Problem Solving

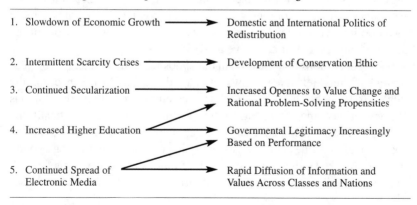

1. Slowdown of Economic Growth  ——▶  Domestic and International Politics of Redistribution

2. Intermittent Scarcity Crises  ——▶  Development of Conservation Ethic

3. Continued Secularization  ——▶  Increased Openness to Value Change and Rational Problem-Solving Propensities

4. Increased Higher Education  ——▶  Governmental Legitimacy Increasingly Based on Performance

5. Continued Spread of Electronic Media  ——▶  Rapid Diffusion of Information and Values Across Classes and Nations

As the remaining natural space contracts and precious materials begin to reach the point of exhaustion, we may expect an increasing spread of a conservation and recycling ethic and a reverence for nature, particularly in the advanced industrial countries and among the materially advantaged strata in these countries. But the development of this conservation ethic and reverence for nature among the privileged will sharpen the politics of redistribution, for if benefits for the poor are not to come from a high rate of growth, then they have to come from the benefits going to the privileged.

The long-run tendencies toward more rational problem-solving propensities listed in Table 9.13 conceivably may mitigate the sharpness of this class antagonism and rich nation/poor nation confrontation. I have already referred to the waning indoctrinative powers of the modern family and church. This process of secularization, decreasing dogmatism, and greater ecumenism and cultivation of individual responsibility in the making of choices contributes to a greater openness to value change. While these tendencies are already far advanced in the area of sexual morality, they have yet to be tested in the area of political ideology.

Contributing to an openness to value change and rational problem-solving capacity is the increase in the proportion of the population in advanced industrial societies experiencing higher education. As the indoctrinative power of family and church has declined in the last decades, the impact of formal education and the mass media has increased. During the 1960s, this growth was a special period effect. Students in higher education in the United States doubled from around 20 percent to 40 percent, and in Western Europe and Japan they increased from roughly 10 percent to 20 percent. Whereas the elite members of advanced societies have for some time been predominantly college- or university-educated, the middle echelons of society are increasingly obtaining a higher-educational experience. However one may fault it, higher education creates a more cosmopolitan world-view, an increased capacity to assimilate information, and the development of cognitive analytic skills.

The generations that matured in the 1960s were the first television generations. Surely television contributed to the great disturbances of the 1960s. It brought the Vietnam War, the ethnic rebellion, the campus demonstrations, and the counterculture to the attention of practically the entire population of the advanced industrial societies. It helps explain the swift spread of values and styles from college youth to noncollege youth, noted in the Yankelovich studies. In the future, the electronic media will continue to facilitate the diffusion of information and values across classes and nations. It seems to be playing a role similar to that of higher education, widening horizons and facilitating the flow of information.

The decline of dogmatism and the spread of rational analytic skills and information attributable to these long-run social changes will not only increase the human problem-solving capacity, but will also transform the bases of political and governmental legitimacy. The evidence for this trend is already impressive. Class position and party identification have long been losing their capacity to predict voting behavior during this period, and implicit trust and faith in governmental institutions have been declining. The test for governmental support is increasingly based on performance; political elites are held on a shorter tether than was true in the past.

In these continued processes of culture change, young people are unlikely to play the special role characteristic of the 1960s. The accidental concatenation of demographic, educational, and economic trends, and political issues especially impinging on them, is unlikely to be repeated. The youth cohorts who made and supported the rebellion are now passing into full adulthood, carrying with them the special memories of those extraordinary days. Similarly, the political and social elites who sought to cope with the problems they posed carry memories that continue to affect the structure of social authority.

Each passing year in the advanced societies will see an influx of new members carrying with them this greater value openness and analytical capacity, and replacing older cohorts who are more parochial and more rigid in orientation. We can therefore say of the politics and political culture of the future that on the one hand the problems are more threatening and more divisive, while on the other hand our problem-solving capacity is being enhanced. To say more would be yielding to wishful thinking or to despair.

# 10

# The Civic Culture:
# Retrospect and Prospect

AMONG THE SCHOLARLY EVENTS during the decade of my residence at the University of Chicago (1928–1938) were the publication of the volumes of Charles Merriam's Civic Education series, called *The Making of Citizens*. This study was inspired, in part, by the differing performance of the various countries involved in World War I. Merriam served as head of U.S. information efforts in Italy in 1917, where he dealt with the lagging morale of that country in its conduct of the war. Newly embarked in the war, with new resources and ideas, the United States took on the assignment of trying to prevent Italy from going the way of Russia in its 1917 revolution. The collapse of the Austro-Hungarian Empire and the redrawing of the boundaries of Central Europe and the Balkans after the end of World War I dramatically illustrated the power of nationalism and the ethnic, linguistic, and religious characteristics on which it was based.

The *Making of Citizens* study, begun in the early 1920s, included volumes describing these processes in Great Britain, the Soviet Union, the Austro-Hungarian Empire, Germany, France, Italy, Switzerland, and, to represent the simpler societies, the Duk Duks of Melanesia. Merriam's contribution consisted of a concluding volume on comparative civic training (1931), and a later volume, *Civic Training in the United States* (1934). Today we would call what Merriam was studying "comparative political culture and socialization." Merriam called it "civic training" and "civic education," reflecting the more rational-voluntarist conceptual terminology of the social sciences as of that time.

The exploration of the psychological and sociological aspects of political behavior was just in its beginnings. Merriam had sent Harold Lasswell off to Europe to study Freud and psychoanalysis in the mid-1920s, and his book *Psychopathology and Politics* (1930) came out a year before Merriam's *The Making of Citizens*. And Harold Gosnell was experimenting with the use of statistical and survey methods in the study of political behavior. It seems as though Merriam was working at two different levels: the experimental and innovative level of his young departmental colleagues, and the older generation of colleagues whom he invited to cooperate in his Civic Training study.

The scholars who wrote the country studies for the Civic Training series were reputable but conventional American and European historians and political scientists who knew little about the emerging social sciences that Merriam was then fostering in his political science department at the University of Chicago. While in the talents and skills of his younger colleagues in the department he had the makings of a modern comparative political socialization study, such area specialists as Merriam was able to draw upon—Samuel Harper (USSR), Herbert Schneider (Italy), Carleton J. H. Hayes (France), Paul Kosok (Germany), Oskar Jaszi (Austria-Hungary), John Gaus (Great Britain), and Robert Brooks (Switzerland)—were good historians and political scientists, but not up to the challenges of Merriam's imaginative and innovative mind. The Civic Training project was fated to be disappointing, given the discrepancies between the training, capacities, and interests of its participants, and Merriam's ambitions. Highly visible when the study was begun, it faded from memory quite soon. As I and my graduate cohort moved off into our own careers, we carried away the feeling that the Civic Training project hadn't come off. But some of us felt that it could be done, and that it ought to be done with sharper theories and better methods.

One of Merriam's lost bets in the Civic Training project was his effort to recruit Robert Michels, the German sociologist and author of the "Iron Law of Oligarchy," to do the study of Italian Fascism (Karl, 1974). Michels actually agreed to do the Italian study, but unable to make an academic career in Germany because of his socialist and pacifist record, and in general disillusioned both with socialism and democracy, he sought employment in Italian universities, ultimately ending up with a chair at Perugia. He also joined the Fascist Party around this time, and decided that doing a book on fascism and political socialization was too risky. Instead he wrote a tame book on the history of Italian nationalism. Merriam tried to get Michels to revise his manuscript, but without avail, and nothing came of what might have been one of the more interesting monographs of the Civic Training series.

This was not the last time that politics disrupted international scientific collaboration. One that I recall with anguish occurred decades later, long after *The Civic Culture* (1963) had been published, when Sidney Verba, then become a colleague at Stanford, was embarked on the seven-nation study (Verba, Nie, and Kim, 1977), a follow-up of the *Civic Culture* study emphasizing political participation that might be viewed as the grandchild of Merriam's Civic Training project. Verba was having problems with Pablo Gonzalez Casanova, the head of the Mexican team, who had compunctions about collaborating with "gringos." We thought that I might be able to reassure him. I spent three days wandering around Mexico City, engaged in heart-to-heart talks with my Mexican colleague. I finally seemed to convince him that our purposes were not political, that we could be trusted, and that it would be good for the development of the social sciences in Mexico if he joined the project and led a Mexican team. We solemnified the occasion by a toast and a drink of Tequila, preceded by pouring salt on my hand, licking it, and then downing the Tequila in one gulp. We gave him a substantial grant, including funds for the purchase of a jeep in order to facilitate interviewing in the more remote areas of Mexico, where a four-wheel-drive vehicle was essential. A few months later the Mexican scholar withdrew from the project, on the grounds that we were agents of the CIA and worse. We felt betrayed, particularly when he held on to the jeep.

To come back to the Civic Training series, I carried away from my graduate years at Chicago feelings of frustration and unfinished business. During the next two decades several experiences prepared me for the venture into the study of comparative political culture. During World War II, I served in the U.S. Strategic Bombing Survey, trying to learn about the effects of bombing on the German war effort in order to apply these lessons to the Japanese phase of the war. The Morale Division of which I was a member did a sample survey of German attitudes, immediately after the Nazi capitulation. I learned a bit about sampling, and question construction from this exercise.

During the late 1940s and early 1950s in connection with my studies for *The American People and Foreign Policy* (1950) and *The Appeals of Communism* (1954), I did secondary analysis of public opinion surveys, and actually used British, French, and Italian survey research groups to carry out my foreign interviewing. By the middle and late 1950s (and particularly after *Sputnik*—the Soviet aerospace triumph of 1957), research funds became plentiful, and the Princeton Center of International Studies and I became the recipients of a substantial research grant from the Carnegie Corporation to carry out a cross-national study of political attitudes.

I cite this history going back to graduate student days to make the case that the *Civic Culture* study, though an innovating one, was not a jump into the blue. The theories and hypotheses that it tested were well discussed in the historical and social science literature. Just as the fact of differences in national behavior and morale had been dramatized in World War I, and had led Merriam and his colleagues to the question of how to explain these differences, even more so in the aftermath of World War II, scholars and intellectuals were both troubled and challenged by the collapse of Weimar Germany and the rise of Nazism, and the fall of the French Third Republic and the Vichy regime, contrasted with the stability of British and U.S. politics. The political cultural implications of these differences were unmistakable. Rather than acknowledge any excess of chutzpah in undertaking the *Civic Culture* study, from my perspective in the late 1950s when the *Civic Culture* study was launched it was a study whose time had come. Just a little bit ahead of the game, but not too much. Its timeliness was reflected in its early reception. We had an argument with the Princeton University Press. Verba and I wanted a paperback as soon as possible. The press people didn't think it would sell enough to justify a paperback. We asked them if they would allow us to contract for a paperback with Little, Brown (1965) of Boston. They agreed, and the paperback version went into more than a dozen printings.

For its hypotheses the *Civic Culture* study drew heavily for its core ideas on the thoughts of colleagues. Harry Eckstein contributed in important ways. In the later phases of analysis of the *Civic Culture* data, Sidney Verba had the benefit of colleagueship with Eckstein at a time when Eckstein was deep in writing and lecturing on his theory of democratic stability. Verba and Eckstein had become colleagues at Princeton at a time when Eckstein was writing his memorandum on democratic stability, and it appears in full in his book on Norway (1966). It is cited in the concluding chapter of *The Civic Culture* as the source of our hypothesis that more stable democracies have "mixed political cultures." We got from Harry Eckstein the idea that a democratic political system requires a blending of apparent contradictions, "balanced disparities" as he called them, if it is to function effectively. On the one hand a democratic government must govern; it must have power and leadership and make decisions. On the other hand it must be responsible to its citizens. For if democracy means anything, it means that in some way governmental elites must respond to the desires and demands of citizens. The need to maintain this balance between governmental power and governmental responsiveness, as well as the need to maintain other balances that derive from the power-responsivness balance—balances between consensus and cleavage, between affectivity and affective neutrality—explain the way in which the more mixed patterns of political attitudes associated with civic culture theory are appropriate for a democratic system. Verba and I found confirmation of Eckstein's "balanced disparity" theory in our analysis of British and American attitudes, contrasted with those of Germany, Italy, and Mexico.

We were also influenced by Harry Eckstein's congruence theory of political authority, the argument that political stability was enhanced if nonpolitical authority patterns—particularly in groups and institutions closest to the state—were similar or congruent. Thus we had found in our data that there was a stronger relationship between civic competence and adult participation in workplace decisions, than civic competence and earlier participation by the child in family decisionmaking.

There was a thirtieth-anniversary "retrospective" on the *Civic Culture* study at the 1994 meetings of the American Political Science Association. Among the commentators was Robert Putnam of Harvard, who concluded his remarks with the observation that civic culture theory reminded him of "Goldilocks." In the story *Goldilocks and the Three Bears,* the young heroine, possessed of even more than ordinary feminine curiosity, ventures into the house of the three bears and proceeds to explore its furnishings and contents. In sequence she tries out the three chairs at the dining table, the three plates of porridge, and the three beds, in each case finding the Papa and the Mama versions not to her liking, and settling on the baby bear's chair, plate of porridge, and bed as being more appropriate for her, as being "just right." As you may recall, she is ultimately discovered fast asleep in his bed by the baby bear. Not to leave the reader in suspense, Goldilocks escapes from the bears by leaping through a window.

At the time I didn't fully grasp what Putnam meant by the Goldilocks metaphor. Was it his way of putting a common criticism of the *Civic Culture* study that it was conservative, smugly Anglo-American, and morally indifferent? That while its "balanced disparity" theory of political stability enabled a democracy to run cool, and avoid intense and sustained conflict and breakdown, it also meant the postponement and moderation of political action intended to achieve social justice? Or was Putnam speaking from his current preoccupation with what he calls "declining American social capital," the attrition of the American propensity for forming voluntary associations, and in general the evidence of decline in the vibrancy of American civil society (1995)? Was it this that made the celebration of political coolness in the *Civic Culture* study seem particularly smug to Bob Putnam?

As a Goldilocks theory, the *Civic Culture* study was saying that to run well a democratic polity had to avoid becoming overheated on the one hand or apathetic or indifferent on the other—that it had to combine obedience and respect for authority with initiative and participation, and not too much of the one or of the other; that not all groups, interests, and issues would ignite simultaneously, but that different groups, issues, and sectors of the electorate would become mobilized at different times, thus regulating the pressure on the political system. Putnam's Goldilocks metaphor is really an equilibrium theory, comparable to the economic theory of the market, a situation in which sellers and buyers reach a price at which the market is "cleared." We were specifying in civic culture theory a set of conditions under which political markets would clear when the price of responsive public policy was "just right."

The model of effective democratization that has come out of what Samuel Huntington has called the "third wave" of democratization has much in common with Putnam's Goldilocks model and tends to confirm civic culture theory. Students of contemporary democratization have discovered, in Nancy Bermeo's words, that effective democratization rests on "the patience of the poor" (1990, p. 360). In the same sense more than half a century ago the German Jewish exile Adolf Lowe, reflecting on British and German political experience, commented that we pay the price of liberty by foregoing integral political demands and final resolutions, settling for half or a quarter of a loaf, or simply keeping options open in hope of some future improvement (1936). I would argue that the theories of democratic transition of the last decade, with their step-by-step, hard-line, soft-line, gradualist-maximalist bargaining process, were foreshadowed in the *Civic Culture* study and in Harry Eckstein's theories more than three decades ago.

Civic culture theory is a democratic equilibrium theory, a theory that democratic stability tends to be sustained when processes and propensities are in balance—when the heat of political conflict does not exceed or fall below a given temperature range. I am prepared to accept Putnam's characterization of civic culture theory as a Goldilocks theory. And I share his concern about the survival of the civic culture.

*      *      *

The five years of our lives that Sid Verba and I spent in doing the *Civic Culture* study, 1957–1962, were the last years of the Eisenhower presidency, and the Camelot years of the Kennedy administration. They were a high point in American pride and glory. Our GIs had come back from victory, educated themselves, raised families, bought and built homes in newly forming suburbs, bought cars, dishwashers, washing machines, and power mowers that disturbed the quiet of Sunday mornings. Their wives—mothers of the baby boom and mostly homemakers—joined the PTAs and Leagues of Women Voters. We were still basking in the afterglow of the victory in Europe; the Korean War was fading from memory. We had an immensely productive economy; Europe and Asia had recovered from the war's devastation, and our foreign policy and aid had much to do with this recovery. We had wrestled our worst paranoid and persecutory impulses in the form of McCarthyism to the ground, and were beginning to express our finer political impulses toward coming to grips with our ethnic inequalities and injustices. The welfare state—an impulse toward a broader social justice come late to the United States—was beginning to be put in place.

It was this America that the *Civic Culture* study captured—just as it captured the re-Europeanized, low-keyed Germany of late Adenauer; the "I'm all right Jack" Great Britain of McMillan; the culturally fragmented Italy of Gasperi; and Mexico during the prime of the Institutional Revolutionary Party (PRI). We could not have known at that time that we were capturing civic culture at its peak, when what we found in England and the United States did indeed look a bit like Goldilocks in her search for things that were "just right." But when we took a second sounding two decades later, in *The Civic Culture Revisited* (1980), it was already apparent that the bloom was off the United States and Britain, that Germany seemed to be moving into civic culture territory, that Italy had not changed much, and that the PRI was no longer an inclusive coalition.

What we learned from *The Civic Culture Revisited* was that political culture is a plastic, many-dimensioned variable, that it responds quickly to structural change. It was not that Verba and I failed to appreciate structural variables. Somewhere in *The Civic Culture* (in the chapter on methodology) there is the observation that our study had to be viewed as a dated "snapshot." But we surely did not appreciate how quickly the change would come, how steep its curves would be.

The play of structural change and of history on the attitudes making up the *Civic Culture* study since we measured them in the late 1950s has been enormous and complex. For the political culture of the United States, Britain, Germany, and other advanced democracies to have remained unchanged would have been inconceivable. An impressive literature charting these changes has emerged in the more than three decades that have elapsed since *The Civic Culture* appeared. Ronald Inglehart quite early (1971) forecast an emerging participatory populism and self-involvement—which might undermine the "balanced disparities" of Harry Eckstein—among the generations born after World War II, suggesting how these cultural changes might destabilize and disarticulate political parties and electoral processes. He and his colleagues have charted these changes over time in three publications (1977, 1990, 1994) for what by 1994 had become forty countries, broadly distributed culturally and economically. His explanatory variables are economic development and increasing physical security. As the post–World War II generations experienced economic growth and military security, the values of self-realization and creative participation replaced the primacy of concern for material welfare and physical safety, as though by a process of marginal utilitarian calculation.

Samuel Barnes and others (1979), and Russell Dalton, Scott Flanagan, and Paul Allen Beck (1984, 1990, 1994), in an impressive series of studies of the transformation of the democratic infrastructure in the industrial democracies, explored a new world of unconventional political action, of the rise of new movements, and of dealigned and realigned voters. This growing political spontaneity and disrespect for political convention, tradition, and authority, this complication of "political space," surely was straining the norms of *The Civic Culture.*

While the work of Inglehart, Barnes, Dalton, and others raised serious questions about the survival of crucial components of *The Civic Culture,* the appearance of Robert Putnam's *Making Democracy Work* (1993), his longitudinal study of regional differences in Italian political culture, was a strong argument in support of the validity of political socialization theory, and of the importance of voluntary associations based on widespread social trust passed on from generation to generation, as a necessary condition of civic voluntarism, and economic entrepreneurship. However, any optimism conveyed by Putnam's work had to be questioned after the publication of his "Bowling Alone" (1995), which demonstrated a decline in social trust and "civic engagement" in the United States. He comments:

> In the established democracies, ironically, growing numbers of citizens are questioning the effectiveness of their public institutions at the very moment when liberal democracy has swept the battlefield, both ideologically and geopolitically. In America, at least, there is reason to suspect that this democratic disarray may be linked to a broad and continuing erosion of civic engagement that began a quarter century ago. High on our scholarly agenda should be the question of whether a comparable erosion of social capital may be under way in other advanced democra-

cies, perhaps in different institutional and behavioral guises. High on America's agenda should be the question of how to reverse these adverse trends in social connectedness, thus restoring civic engagement and civic trust. (pp. 76–77)

As causes of this decline in civic engagement, Putnam cites the weakening of the family resulting from the movement of women into the labor force, as well as cultural changes such as the legitimation of birth control, abortion, and divorce. The family has become less effective in political socialization and the transmission of norms. A second major factor that he cites is the transformation of leisure by the electronic media. Television preempts going outside in the interest of entertainment and edification: "We are now provided with 'virtual reality' helmets in order to be entertained and edified in isolation" (p. 77).

The "two-step flow" of communication, discovered almost half a century ago by Elihu Katz and Paul Lazarsfeld (1955), in which the impacts of the mass media are seen to be filtered and moderated through discriminating and trusted "opinion leaders" (face-to-face contacts with older, more experienced, "wiser" relatives, friends, local politicians, interest group leaders, and the like), has given way to the power of electronic journalism, primarily of the populist variety. Brilliantly celebrated by Tocqueville almost a century and a half ago, and become a cliché of political science, the America of "voluntary associations" and of social trust seems to be disappearing under our very eyes.

Surely the equilibrium assumptions of civic culture theory have been challenged by the decline of broad aggregating partisanship, by disaffiliation and privatization, issue fragmentation and polarization, electronic populism, and the attenuation of legitimacy accorded to governmental agencies. Electoral turnout, partisan affiliation, interest group membership—all have significantly declined, transforming the participant component of civic culture. Confidence in government and in public officials has declined even to a greater extent, reflecting the spread of an alienated subject mentality. *The Civic Culture* rested on an "allegiant" subject mentality, and a constrained and filtered "participant mentality."

In the substantial literature describing the ups and downs of political culture in the last several decades, there has been a tendency to emphasize the explanatory power of domestic social change—demographic change, economic growth and development, the spread of education and the media, and changing social structure—as transforming political attitudes and processes. In our characterization of civic culture as a mixed political culture, we emphasized the importance of the subject role, the willingness of citizens to be governed, to accord discretion to political leaders, to accept power and authority as well as to participate in power and decisions. Effective political decision is a mix of command and obedience. The literature describing changes in the political culture of the advanced industrial societies in the decades since the 1960s has emphasized domestic social change and its effects on participant patterns. There has been a tendency to neglect changes in the international environment and their effects on governmental authority and subject patterns.

The three decades that have transpired since the publication of *The Civic Culture* have witnessed significant change in every aspect of social and international structure. To begin with, demography—the age and sex distribution of population, the rate of growth in population, its regional distribution, urban concentration, and the like. The "baby bulge," the oversize cohorts born in the 1946–1955 decade, and reaching adolescence in the early 1960s and 1970s, were one-third again as large as the cohorts of the preceding decade, and were raised, mentored, and role-modeled by the relatively thinner older cohorts. The younger males between the ages of fifteen and twenty-five are by far the more frequent committers of crime, agents of innovation, disorder, dissent. The rapid increase in the size of these cohorts helps explain the magnitude and violence of the anti-Vietnam, pro–Civil Rights political protest of the later 1960s and 1970s, and the excesses of the so-called cultural revolution, which have had a lasting impact on morals and values (Almond, 1977). The cultural revolution of the 1960s and 1970s set in motion a political polarization—a mobilization of the "social right" in response to the civil rights, feminist, and sexual mobilization on the left—a rising level of political antagonism threatening the balances and equilibria of civic culture.

A second change in social demography—this time in relation to gender—has produced a weakening of family ties as a consequence of the entry of women into higher education and into the labor force, the increase in the divorce rate, and the number of one-parent and broken families. This in turn has had serious consequences for the role of the family in political socialization—the transmission of political affiliations, norms and ideologies, and skills.

Economic changes have also been of great significance in the transformation of political culture. The postindustrial society of Daniel Bell (1973)—the rise of the tertiary sector, the decline of the smokestack, hard-hat industry—has transformed class structure, weakening the power of trade unions and left-wing political parties and moving the center of political gravity to the right. The impact of industry on environment—air, water, land, forest, animal species—has raised doubts about economic growth as unambiguous progress, and has divided politics by a new set of political issues and movements (Dalton, Flanagan, and Beck, 1994).

A third set of structural changes results from the communication revolution. Television and radio have largely preempted the print media, and the primary opinion leaders, as I have suggested above. Domestic and international events are brought into the living room with powerful visual and emotional impact—a telepopulism that constrains and distorts public policy. The deliberative processes of politics are diluted and heated by this populism, and by "instant" public opinion polls based on telephone samples. The media elites have acquired great and problematic powers as demonstrated by Verba in his studies of elite attitudes. He shows that American and other elites (including the media elites themselves) believe that the media elites have "too much power" (1987).

We can distinguish some four sets of political changes resulting from these structural changes. Two of these—partisan realignment and partisan dealignment—have to do with the transformation of the party systems of advanced industrial societies, in response to changes in social structure and culture. A third is the rise of new social movements—both of the left and of the right—resulting in partisan polarization and consequent difficulties in the making of coalitions and policy. The fourth is a set of antigovernmental tendencies—movements toward decentralization of authority, debureaucratization, deregulation, privatization, tax rebellion.

All of the processes of social change of the last half century that are called upon to explain these political transformations are internal, domestic. And they are indeed important parts of the explanation. But the international system as such does not enter into this explanation of changing political structure and culture, though the changes that have occurred are very substantial in the sense of cost in blood, treasure, and anguish. In the fifty years since the end of World War II, we have moved into the increasingly tense bipolarity of the world of the Truman Doctrine, the Marshall Plan, the Berlin Blockade, the North Atlantic Treaty Organization (NATO), the Korean War; then into the tense confrontations of the 1960s and 1970s—the Bay of Pigs, the Cuban Missile Crisis, the Vietnam War; then into the diplomacy of arms control and disarmament of the 1970s and early 1980s, the glasnost and perestroika of Gorbachev, the coup attempt, the collapse of the Soviet Union, and the end of the Cold War at the end of the 1980s and the turn of the 1990s. We have moved from a World War II U.S.-USSR alliance to a sustained tense bipolarity—to a sustained relatively stable bipolarity—and after the collapse of the Soviet Union to a kind of reluctant unipolarity.

Inglehart includes physical "security" as one of the two changes (the other is material prosperity) bringing about his postmaterial, postmodern political culture. But he operationalizes physical security as the absence of "total war" during the lifetimes of respondents (1977, p. 22). His physical security variable is dichotomous—total war or no total war. In actual fact the structure of the international system is a continuous variable. For about thirty-five years the bipolar balance of the Cold War, while creating a sense of uneasy safety, also conveyed a justification for a vigilant state, armed to the teeth, militarily deployed and engaged with a powerful and cunning enemy around the world. Bipolarity took shape in the first decades; then stabilized; then in the 1980s a disengagement began. The large tax revenues and budget expenditures of the "Cold War" state could provide a "piggyback" for the American "welfare state," just as it had done in Britain, France, and Germany in earlier decades. In the sustained crisis of the Cold War, a welfare net, and civil rights for the poor and for ethnic minorities, could be justified on the grounds of national security as well as justice. The Cold War sustained and legitimized the subject role in the political cultures of the advanced democracies. We needed government in order to be secure, and politics had to be kept under control to avoid division, and in order not to risk the loss of vigilance.

What happens when this bipolarity and delicate balance collapses through the resignation of one of the parties? Let me spell out the possible implications for political culture of the collapse of the Soviet Union, and the disappearance of the Cold War as the organizing principle of international relations. Theories have been around for quite some time as to how international politics affects domestic politics in general terms. At the end of the nineteenth century, after a number of decades of accumulating historical information, sophisticated historians began to derive hypotheses from comparative historical analysis. Sir John Seeley (1886) of Cambridge, and Otto Hintze (1975) of the University of Berlin, produced what I have referred to as the Seeley-Hintze law (Almond, 1991a, pp. 286 ff.) of the interaction of international conflict and internal authoritarian centralization. Seeley put it elegantly: "It is reasonable therefore to conjecture that the degree of government will be directly proportional, and that means that the degree of liberty will be inversely proportional, to the degree of pressure. . . . [I]ntense government is a reaction to intense pressure, or relaxed government is the effect of relaxed pressure" (1886, p.

286). Hintze took this theory and tested it against European history of the eighteenth and nineteenth centuries.

With this theory it is possible to get from the powerful, centralized U.S. government (the "imperial presidency") of the Cold War era to the post–Cold War era of the apologetic reinvention of government of the Clinton administration, and the demonization of government of the Gingrich Contract with America. The relaxation of the U.S.-Soviet confrontation is slowly working its way through transformations of the international political system—a mix of relatively weak multipolarity and reluctant unipolarity. A state no longer defending against a powerful, centralized, nuclearized foe begins to lose some of its "necessity." There is an open season on vilifying a welfare state that had piggybacked on the security state. Government becomes a cuss word, bureaucracy an unmitigated evil.

What this suggests is that we can work causally from the international environment to domestic institutions and attitudes, and observe how they combine with, filter, or magnify these international tendencies. Or we can begin with technological change and observe how the rise of the tertiary sector, the information and communication revolutions, have interacted with international structural changes to transform political culture. What I am stressing is that in our efforts to explain political cultural change, we need to be monitoring both the international and the domestic structure and the ways in which these several processes interact. We have tended to take the international structure for granted, and the "subject part" of political culture as a given. It has taken the Gingrich revolution to show that there are tendencies in American political culture that, in the absence of a clear-cut international threat, are prepared to go quite far in disassembling the national state. The collapse of Communism, and the discrediting of macrosocialism, have shifted the center of political gravity to the right, thus weakening support for a welfare net no longer justified by national security.

Thus the balanced mix of the civic culture of loyal subject and consensual participatory elements celebrated in our book of 1963 begins to give way to an alienated subject culture combined with a form of participation weakened and demoralized by populism, extremism, and apathy. Students of the emerging political cultures of the modern democracies are going to have to ask anew what democratic equilibria are possible given these structural changes, now that *The Civic Culture* has had its day.

# 11

# Civic Culture as Theory

CIVIC CULTURE THEORY ASSERTS THAT DEMOCRACY is stable or consolidated when specifically democratic attitudes and practices combine and function in equilibrium with certain nondemocratic ones. It is a literature that reconciles role theory with citizenship theory, recognizing that civic participation and activity is one of the many roles performed by most individuals and that effective and good citizenship requires a certain harmonization of these roles. "Strong democracy," "participatory politics," various kinds of "populism"—these tend to deny respect to, and to invade, subject, parental, matrimonial, professional, recreational, and other roles. The concept of civic culture as an equilibrium is a dynamic one; that is to say, changes in demography, economy, literacy and education, media exposure and impact, culture, lifestyle, and the like may transform this equilibrium.

The theory was formulated in a social science literature written during the early post–World War II decades, and was deeply influenced by the interwar history of the stalemated French Third Republic, deeply flawed Weimar Germany, and the Austrian and Spanish civil wars. It drew from the long tradition in political theory of "mixed government," from Plato and Aristotle through to Montesquieu, which supported this antipopulism and prudentialism. Among the post–World War II social science influences

From *International Encyclopedia of the Social and Behavioral Sciences,* edited by Neil J. Smelser and Paul B. Baltes (Amsterdam and New York: Elsevier, 2001). Reprinted, with minor revisions, with permission of Elsevier Science.

were works of Joseph Schumpeter, Bernard Berelson and Paul Lazarsfeld, Edward Shils, Robert A. Dahl, and Harry Eckstein, among others.

Joseph Schumpeter (1947, chaps. 21–22) rejected the "classic democratic" assumption of the necessity of an informed, activist, rational public for a genuine democracy, and proposed in its place an "elites competing for votes" theory. This minimalist theory could be reconciled with more realistic assumptions of a relatively ignorant and indifferent demos.

Paul Lazarsfeld and Bernard Berelson (with William McPhee, 1954, chap. 14), theorizing from their "panel" voting studies of the 1940s, similarly saw democracy as associated with a set of cultural and social conditions having the effect of limiting the intensity of conflict. These included relative economic and social stability, a pluralistic social organization, a basic value consensus, and what we would now call a "civil society." They described a democratic equilibrium as involving mixes of involvement and indifference, stability and flexibility, consensus and cleavage.

Edward Shils (1960, pp. 387 ff.), writing on the democratic prospects of the new nations, emphasized the importance of a "widely dispersed civility." By this he meant a moderate sense of nationality, a degree of interest in public affairs, a consensus on values, institutions, and practices, and a recognition of individual rights and obligations. He wrote: "These qualities should not be intense, and they need not be either equally or universally shared."

Robert Dahl's theory of polyarchy, elaborated in 1956 in a full-length contrast with populistic and Madisonian democracy, belongs among these social science influences on the idea of a civic culture. His early characterization of the American political system as providing "a high probability that any active and legitimate group will make itself heard effectively at some stage in the process of decision" (p. 145) reflected the minimalist mood that Dahl shared with the generation that emerged out of the Great Depression and World War II. Dahl's theory of polyarchy introduced an empirically grounded and quantitative set of concepts into democratic theorizing. Democracy was not an essence. In its full sense it did not exist, and probably could not exist. Hence the concept polyarchy to refer to real political entities that attained measured performance levels on specified empirical dimensions.

Harry Eckstein was the first to emphasize the "mixed" or paradoxical side of democracy, recognizing the necessity for a democracy not only to represent and formulate the will of the public, but to govern it authoritatively. In "A Theory of Stable Democracy" (1966, pp. 225 ff.), he describes some of the qualities that enable democracies to reconcile responsible authority and democratic responsiveness. This is facilitated by balances among contrasting qualities: participant behavior is balanced by deference to authority, dogmatism by pragmatism, and the like. Institutionally he attributes democratic stability to the degree to which social authority patterns coincide or are "congruent" with political ones.

Civic culture theory was codified, and given its name, in the context of a major empirical investigation informed by this historical experience and benefiting from this prior research and scholarship. Its results were reported in book form in 1963 (Almond and Verba, 1963), in paperback form in 1965, and were reprinted in 1989 and remain in print. The book was widely reviewed in social science periodicals and in 1980 a retrospective volume was published with critiques of the theory and the findings. The data were made available in the Interuniversity Consortium for Political and Social Research at the University of Michigan, and have been utilized in many secondary studies.

Four of the five countries that it investigated were chosen because they exemplified democratic stability and instability in the first half of the twentieth century—the United Kingdom and the United States exemplifying stability on the one hand—Germany and Italy exemplifying democratic instability and breakdown on the other. The fifth, Mexico, was a target of opportunity selected with the thought that it might provide some insight into problems of democratization outside the North American–European area. The method used in the study of combining structured and open-ended questions administered to probability samples of national populations provided us with a richer set of data specifically responsive to questions arising out of this historical experience and body of speculative theory.

The conception of stable democratic political culture as a "mixed" political culture received a fuller elaboration than it had been given in the earlier work of Berelson and Lazarsfeld, and Eckstein. The mix of democratic political culture was based on political role theory. People in stable democracies were both citizens and subjects, and they needed to accommodate their nonpolitical, private, and parochial roles. A thriving, stable democracy consists not only of voters, demonstrators, petition signers, and politician button-holers, but also of taxpayers, jurors, and military conscripts; all of its members have been children, most of its members are parents themselves, may be mates, siblings, workers, voluntary-association members, vacationers, as well as private, self-involved individuals.

It is this incredible mix of roles—participant as well as subject, non-political as well as political—that democratic citizens of a stable democracy must balance and accommodate, and that institutions must choreograph in a process of converting demands and supports into outputs and outcomes. Hence civic culture theory is an equilibrium theory in which political buyers and sellers reach prices at which the political market is cleared. We were specifying in civic culture theory what conditions had to be present in order to clear these markets.

We were able to locate these mixes and balances empirically in the British and American cases in the late 1950s and early 1960s—this combination of political activism and deferentialism, involvement and indifference, conflictual and consensual attitudes, principled and instrumental ones. And we noted the relative absence of these balances in the German and Italian cases. There was more deference and less participation in the British case than in the American. We also located a "reserve of influence" in the American and British cases based on the finding that Americans and Britishers acknowledged the obligation to participate far more frequently than they reported actually participating. This discrepancy between performance and obligation could be viewed as a kind of "default" mode, a reserve supply of participatory energy available for crises. The civic culture would run cool normally and at a moderate speed, but it had a reserve of influence to draw upon in the twists and turns of democratic politics, as the concerns and interests of different groups of voters were engaged.

By the time the retrospective volume *The Civic Culture Revisited* was published in 1980, it was evident that British and American civic culture were in trouble (Almond and Verba, 1980, chaps. 5–6). The balance of consensus and conflict had moved toward conflict. Pride in nation and confidence in government were down. Participation had declined. In contrast, Germany (chap. 7) showed dramatic gains in social trustfulness, confidence in government, and civic competence. In Italy (chap. 8), political alienation and extreme partisan antagonism continued largely unchanged. In Mexico (chap. 9), the political culture of ambivalent belief in the legitimacy of the democratic revolution, and the corruption of politicians and office-holders, also still survived.

That patterns of political culture would change in response to changes in economy, demography, politics and public policy, communications technology, and popular education should not have occasioned surprise. That the exemplars of the civic culture of the 1950s—Britain and the United States—should be showing signs of wear and tear in the 1970s and 1980s, and that the problem child of democracy—Germany—was showing strong signs of an emerging civic culture, were not causes for rejecting civic culture theory. The question was whether the changes observed in the two decades after the *Civic Culture* study were in a direction that sustained or disproved the theory. The evidence was moderately supportive of the theory. Thus, for example, the withdrawal of Johnson from the 1968 presidential race, despite the fact that political tradition would have legitimized another term of office, and the resignation of Nixon from the presidency in the 1970s were clear evidences of U.S. instability; and the political disorders of the 1960s and 1970s were clear evidences of cultural disequilibria of one kind or another—conflict had undermined consensus, the legitimacy of government had declined, the modes of participation had radicalized. In contrast, Germany had had several decades of experience of effective political leadership and remarkable economic growth appearing to produce a moderating *koalitions-fahig* partisanship, growing popular trust in government, civic obligation, and the like.

The place of civic culture theory in the contemporary theory of democracy is in some doubt. In the continuing theoretic polemic about the nature of democracy, anything settling for less than perfection partakes of sin. It was precisely to avoid this commingling of the sacred and the secular that led Robert Dahl to invent the concept of polyarchy and to place the concept of democracy somewhat but not quite off-limits. However, Dahl's "Polyarchy III" (which is the closest to ultimate democracy that he gets) is achieved through increasing the depth and extent of attentive publics within the larger mass public, corresponding to the significant issues confronting the polity, and policy elites. Modern communication and information technology make it possible that this gap between policy elites and the mass public might be significantly reduced (Dahl, 1989, p. 338).

The state of the polemic regarding the competence, rationality, and potential effectiveness of mass publics in contemporary polyarchies is well argued in a recent symposium. The merits of the several options—elitism, inventive utilization of information technology, or reducing the scope of politics—are among the issues debated (Friedman, 2000). Civic culture theory might have enriched this discussion somewhat by affirming the legitimacy of other than political claims upon humankind. If one views the full range of role demands on the time and resources of humans, how do we choose among them? How do these choices interact? What are the tradeoffs, synergies, and opportunity costs? How do we weight the claims of the civic world against the demands of profession, family, edification, and pleasure?

# References

Abramovitz, Moses (1981) "Welfare Quandaries and Productivity Concerns." *American Economic Review* (March).

Ackerman, Nathan, and Marie Jahoda (1950) *Anti-Semitism and Emotional Disorder.* New York: Harper.

Adorno, Theodor, Else Frenkel-Brunswik, Sanford Levinson, and Nevitt Sanford (1950) *The Authoritarian Personality.* New York: Harper.

Almond, Gabriel A. (1947) "The Resistance and the Political Parties of Western Europe." *Political Science Quarterly* 62.

——— (1948a) "The Christian Parties of Western Europe." *World Politics* 1, no. 1.

——— (1948b) "The Political Ideas of Christian Democracy." *Journal of Politics* 10.

———, ed. (1949) *The Struggle for Democracy in Germany.* Chapel Hill: University of North Carolina Press.

——— (1950) *The American People and Foreign Policy.* New York: Harcourt Brace.

——— (1954) *The Appeals of Communism.* Princeton: Princeton University Press.

——— (1956) "Comparative Political Systems." *Journal of Politics* (August).

———, ed. (1974) *Comparative Politics Today.* Boston: Little, Brown.

——— (1977) "Youth Character and Changing Political Culture in America." In Gordon DiRenzo, ed., *We the People: American Character and Social Change.* Westport, Conn., Greenwood Press.

——— (1991a) *A Discipline Divided.* Newbury Park, Calif.: Sage.

——— (1991b) "Rational Choice Theory and the Social Sciences." In Kristi Monroe, ed., *The Economic Approach to Politics.* New York: HarperCollins.

——— (1998) *Plutocracy and Politics in New York City.* Boulder: Westview Press.

Almond, Gabriel A., Marvin Chodorow, and Roy Harvey Pearce, eds. (1980) *Progress and Its Discontents.* Berkeley: University of California Press.

Almond, Gabriel A., and James Coleman, eds. (1960) *The Politics of the Developing Areas.* Princeton: Princeton University Press.

Almond, Gabriel A., Scott Flanagan, and Robert Mundt (1973) *Crisis, Choice, and Change: Historical Studies of Political Development.* Boston: Little, Brown.

Almond, Gabriel A., with Wolfgang Krauss (1999) "The Size and Composition of the Anti-Nazi Opposition in Germany." *PS: Political Science and Politics* 32, no. 3: 563 ff.

Almond, Gabriel A., and G. Bingham Powell (1966) *Comparative Politics: A Developmental Approach.* Boston: Little, Brown.

——— (1978) *Comparative Politics: System, Process, and Policy.* Boston: Little, Brown.

Almond, Gabriel A., Emmanuel Sivan, and Scott Appleby (1995) "Fundamentalism Comprehended." In Martin Marty and Scott Appleby, eds., *The Fundamentalism Project.* Chicago: University of Chicago Press.

Almond, Gabriel A., and Sidney Verba (1963) *The Civic Culture: Political Attitudes and Democracy in Five Nations.* Princeton: Princeton University Press.

——— (1965) *The Civic Culture: Political Attitudes and Democracy in Five Nations.* Boston: Little, Brown.

——— (1980) *The Civic Culture Revisited.* Boston: Little, Brown.

——— (1989) *The Civic Culture: Political Attitudes and Democracy in Five Nations.* Newbury Park, Calif.: Sage.

Alt, James, and Alec Chrystal (1983) *Political Economics.* Berkeley: University of California Press.

American Political Science Association (1994) *Directory of Members.* Washington, D.C.: APSA.

Anderson, William (1962) *Man's Quest for Political Knowledge.* Minneapolis: University of Minnesota Press.

Arrow, Kenneth (1951) *Social Choice and Individual Values.* New Haven: Yale University Press.

Banfield, Edward (1958) *The Moral Basis of a Backward Society.* Glencoe, Ill.: Free Press.

Barker, Ernest, ed. and trans. (1958) *The Politics of Aristotle.* Oxford: Oxford University Press.

Barnes, Samuel H., et al. (1979) *Political Action: Mass Participation in Five Western Democracies.* Beverly Hills, Calif.: Sage.

Barry, Brian (1970) *Sociologists, Economists, and Democracy.* London: Routledge and Kegan Paul.

Bates, Robert (1988) "Macro-Political Economy in the Field of Development." Duke University Program in International Political Economy, Working Paper no. 40 (June).

——— (1990) Alt and Shepsle, eds., *Perspectives on Positive Political Economy.* Cambridge: Cambridge University Press.

————— (1996) *Newsletter of the Organized Section in Comparative Politics.* Washington, D.C.: American Political Science Association.

Beer, Samuel (1965) *British Politics in the Collectivist Age.* New York: Knopf.

Bell, Daniel (1960) *The End of Ideology.* New York: Free Press.

————— (1973) *The Coming of Post Industrial Society.* New York: Basic Books.

Benz, Wolfgang (1994) "Deutscher Widerstand, 1933–1945." *Informationen Zur Politischen Bildung* (2d quarter).

Berelson, Bernard, Paul Lazarsfeld, and William McPhee (1954) *Voting: A Study of Opinion Formation in a Political Campaign.* Chicago: University of Chicago Press.

Berger, Peter (1986) *The Capitalist Revolution.* New York: Basic Books.

Berger, Suzanne (1981) *Organizing Interests in Western Europe.* Cambridge: Cambridge University Press.

Bermeo, Nancy (1990) "Rethinking Regime Change." *Comparative Politics* 22, no. 3 (April): 359–377.

Bettelheim, Bruno, and Irving Janowitz (1950) *The Dynamics of Prejudice.* New York: Harper.

Binder, Leonard, et al. (1971) *Crises and Sequences in Political Development.* Princeton: Princeton University Press.

Black, Duncan (1958) *The Theory of Committees and Elections.* Cambridge: Cambridge University Press.

Blythe, James M. (1992) *Ideal Government and the Mixed Constitution.* Princeton: Princeton University Press.

Brodie, Bernard, ed. (1946) *The Absolute Weapon.* New York: Harcourt Brace.

Bryce, James (1908) *The American Commonwealth.* New York: Commonwealth.

Brzezinski, Zbigniev, and Samuel Huntington (1963) *Political Power: U.S.-USSR.* New York: Viking Press.

Buchanan, James, and Gordon Tullock (1962) *The Calculus of Consent.* Ann Arbor: University of Michigan Press.

Cameron, David (1978) "Social Democracy, Corporatism, and Labor Quiescence." In John Goldthorpe, ed., *Order and Conflict in Contemporary Capitalism.* Oxford: Oxford University Press.

Cardoso, Fernando, and Enzo Faletto (1979) *Dependency and Development in Latin America.* Berkeley: University of California Press.

Castles, Francis G., ed. (1989) *The History of Public Policy.* Cambridge: Polity Press.

Catlin, George E. G. (1964) *The Science and Method of Political Science.* Hamden, Conn.: Archon Books.

Christie, Richard, and Marie Jahoda, eds. (1954) *Studies in the Scope and Method of the Authoritarian Personality.* Glencoe, Ill.: Free Press.

Coleman, James, ed. (1965) *Education and Political Development.* Princeton: Princeton University Press.

Collier, David (1993) "The Comparative Method." In Ada Finifter, ed., *Political Science: The State of the Discipline.* Washington, D.C.: American Political Science Association.

Committee on Comparative Politics, SSRC (1971) *Report on Activities, 1970–71.* New York: SSRC.

Converse, Jean M. (1987) *Survey Research in the United States: Roots and Emergence, 1890–1960.* Berkeley: University of California Press.

Cotler, Julio, and Richard Fagen, eds. (1974) *Latin America and the United States.* Stanford: Stanford University Press.

Crick, Bernard (1959) *The American Science of Politics.* Berkeley: University of California Press.

Daalder, Hans, ed. (1997) *Comparative European Politics: The Story of a Profession.* London and New York: Pinter, 1997.

Dahl, Robert A. (1956) *A Preface to Democratic Theory.* Chicago: University of Chicago Press.

——— (1961) *Who Governs?* New Haven: Yale University Press.

———, ed. (1966) *Political Oppositions in Western Democracies.* New Haven: Yale University Press.

——— (1970) *After the Revolution: Authority in a Good Society.* New Haven: Yale University Press.

——— (1971) *Polyarchy: Participation and Opposition.* New Haven: Yale University Press.

——— (1973) *Regimes and Oppositions.* New Haven: Yale University Press.

——— (1982) *Dilemmas of Pluralist Democracy.* New Haven: Yale University Press.

——— (1985) *A Preface to Economic Democracy.* Berkeley: University of California Press.

——— (1989) *Democracy and Its Critics.* New Haven: Yale University Press.

——— (1990) *After the Revolution? Authority in a Good Society.* Rev. ed. New Haven: Yale University Press.

Dalton, Russell, Scott Flanagan, and Paul Allen Beck (1984) *Electoral Change in Advanced Industrial Democracies.* Princeton: Princeton University Press.

——— (1990) *Challenging the Political Order: New Social and Political Movements in Western Democracies.* New York: Oxford University Press.

——— (1994) *The Green Rainbow: Environmental Groups in Western Europe.* New Haven: Yale University Press.

Deutsch, Karl (1961) "Social Mobilization and Political Development." *American Political Science Review* 51, no. 3 (September): 494–514.

Diamond, Larry (1992) "Economic Development and Democracy Reconsidered." In Gary Marks and Larry Diamond, eds., *Reexamining Democracy.* Newbury Park, Calif.: Sage.

Diamond, Larry, and Marc Plattner, eds. (1993) *The Global Resurgence of Democracy.* Baltimore: Johns Hopkins University Press.

Dogan, Mattei, and Dominique Pelassy (1990) *How to Compare Nations.* Chatham, N.J.: Chatham House.

Downs, Anthony (1957) *The Economic Theory of Democracy.* New York: Harper and Row.

————— (1991) "Social Values and Democracy." In K. R. Monroe, ed., *The Economic Approach to Democracy.* New York: HarperCollins.

Dryzek, John, and Stephen Leonard (1988) "History and Discipline in Political Science." *American Political Science Review* 82, no. 4 (December): 1245–1260.

Dryzek, John, Stephen Leonard, James Farr, John Gunnell, and Raymond Seidelman (1990) "Can Political Science Be Neutral?" *American Political Science Review* 84, no. 2 (June): 587–607.

Duguit, Leon (1917) *The Law and the State.* Cambridge: Harvard University Press.

Durkheim, Emile (1960) *The Division of Labor in Society.* Glencoe, Ill.: Free Press.

Duverger, Maurice (1965) *Political Parties.* 2d ed. New York: Wiley.

Easton, David (1953) *The Political System.* New York: Knopf.

————— (1965) *A Systems Analysis of Political Life.* New York: Wiley.

————— (1990) *The Analysis of Political Structure.* New York: Routledge.

Eckstein, Harry (1966) "A Theory of Democratic Stability." In *Division and Cohesion in Democracy: A Study of Norway.* Princeton: Princeton University Press.

————— (1975) "Case Study and Theory in Political Science." In Fred Greenstein and Nelson Polsby, eds., *Handbook of Political Science,* vol. 3. Reading, Mass.: Addison Wesley.

Ehrmann, Henry (1957) *Organized Business in France.* Princeton: Princeton University Press.

————— (1958) *Interest Groups on Four Continents.* Pittsburgh: University of Pittsburgh Press.

Eulau, Heinz, and Kenneth Prewitt (1973) *Labyrinths of Democracy.* Indianapolis: Bobbs Merrill.

————— (1976) "Understanding Political Life in America." *Social Science Quarterly* 57, no. 1 (June): 112 ff.

————— (1993) "The Congress as Research Arena: An Uneasy Partnership Between History and Political Science." *Legislative Studies Quarterly* 18 (November): 570 ff.

Fagen, Richard (1978) "A Funny Thing Happened on the Way to the Market: Thoughts on Extending Dependency Ideas." *International Organization* 32 (November): 287–300.

Farr, Raymond, and Raymond Seidelman (1993) *Discipline and History: Political Science in the U.S.* Ann Arbor: University of Michigan Press.

Farr, Raymond, John Dryzek, and Stephen Leonard (1995) *Political Science in History.* Cambridge: Cambridge University Press.

Ferejohn, John, and Debra Satz (1995) "Unification, Universalism, and Rational Choice Theory." *Critical Review* 9, nos. 1–2 (Winter–Spring).

Feuer, Lewis (1969) *Conflict of Generations.* New York: Basic Books.

Figgis, John Neville (1896) *The Divine Right of Kings.* Cambridge: Cambridge University Press.

Finer, Herman (1932, 1949) *The Theory and Practice of Modern Government.* New York: Henry Holt.

Finifter, Ada (1983, 1993) *Political Science: The State of the Discipline.* Washington, D.C.: American Political Science Association.

Fiorina, Morris (1995) "Rational Choice, Empirical Contributions, and the Scientific Enterprise." *Critical Review* 9, nos. 1–2 (Winter–Spring).

Fishkin, James (1992) *The Dialogue of Justice.* New Haven: Yale University Press.

Flora, Peter, and Arnold Heidenheimer (1981) *The Development of Welfare States in Europe and America.* New Brunswick, N.J.: Transaction Books.

Flugel, J. C. (1945) *Man, Morals, and Society.* New York: International Universities Press.

Fox, William T. R. (1944) *The Superpowers.* New York: Harcourt Brace.

Freud, Sigmund (1913 [1918]) *Totem and Taboo.* New York: Moffat, Yard.

——— (1923) *Group Psychology and the Analysis of the Ego.* New York: Boni and Liveright.

——— (1929 [1958]) *Civilization and Its Discontents.* New York: Garden City.

Friedman, Jeffrey, ed. (2000) "Special Issue: Public Ignorance and Democratic Theory." *Critical Review* 12, no. 4.

Friedman, Milton (1953) *Essays in Positive Economics.* Chicago: University of Chicago Press.

——— (1981) *Capitalism and Freedom.* Chicago: University of Chicago Press.

Friedrich, Carl J. (1937) *Constitutional Government and Politics.* New York: Harper.

Galston, William (1993) "Political Theory in the 1980s: Perplexity amid Diversity." In Ada Finifter, ed., *Political Science: The State of the Discipline.* Washington, D.C.: American Political Science Association.

Garceau, Oliver (1941) *The Political Life of the American Medical Association.* Cambridge: Harvard University Press.

Geertz, Clifford (1973) *The Interpretation of Culture.* New York: Basic Books.

George, Alexander (1980) *Presidential Decision-Making.* Boulder: Westview Press.

George, Alexander, with Andrew Bennett (1997) "An Alliance of Statistical and Case Study Methods: Research on the Interdemocratic Peace." *Newsletter of the APSA Organized Section on the Interdemocratic Peace* 9, no. 1: 6.

George, Alexander, and Timothy McKeown (1982) "Case Studies and Theories of Organizational Decision-Making." *Advances in Information Processing in Organizations* 2:21–58.

George, Alexander, and William E. Simons (1994) *The Limits to Coercive Diplomacy.* 2d ed. Boulder: Westview Press.

George, Alexander, and Richard Smoke (1974) *Deterrence in American Foreign Policy.* New York: Columbia University Press.

Gierke, Otto (1868) *Die Deutsche Genossenschaftsrecht.* Berlin: Weidman.

Goldhagen, Daniel (1995) *Hitler's Willing Executioners: Ordinary Germans and the Holocaust.* New York: Knopf.

Goldthorpe, John H., ed. (1984) *Order and Conflict in Contemporary Capitalism.* Oxford: Oxford University Press.

Goodin, Robert E., and Hans-Dieter Klingemann, eds. (1996) *A New Handbook of Political Science.* Oxford and New York: Oxford University Press.

Goodnow, Frank (1900) *Politics and Administration.* New York: Macmillan.

Gouldner, Alvin (1970) *The Coming Crisis of Western Sociology.* New York: Basic Books.

Gosnell, Harold (1927) *Getting Out the Vote.* Chicago: University of Chicago Press.

Green, Donald, and Ian Shapiro (1994) *Pathologies of Rational Choice Theory.* New Haven: Yale University Press.

Grew, Raymond, et al. (1978) *Crises of Political Development in Europe and the United States.* Princeton: Princeton University Press.

Gunder-Frank, Andre (1967) *Capitalism and Underdevelopment.* New York: Monthly Review Press.

Habermas, Jurgen (1992) Craig Calhoun, ed., *Habermas and the Public Sphere.* Cambridge: MIT Press.

Hamilton, Alexander, et al. (1937) *The Federalist.* Washington, D.C.: National Home Library.

Heidenheimer, Arnold, Hugh Heclo, and Carolyn Adams (1990) *Comparing Public Policy.* New York: St. Martin's Press.

Held, David (1980) *Introduction to Critical Theory.* Berkeley: University of California Press.

Herodotus (1910) *The History of Herodotus.* Bk. 3. Trans. George Rawlinson. London: J. M. Dent.

Herring, Pendleton (1929) *Group Representation Before Congress.* Washington, D.C.: Brookings Institution.

Hibbs, Douglas (1978) "On the Political Economy of Long Run Trends in Strike Activity." *British Journal of Political Science* 8 (April): 165 ff.

Hill, Christopher (1982) *The Century of Revolution.* New York: W. W. Norton.

Hilton, Rodney (1990) *Class Conflict and the Crisis of Feudalism.* London: Verso.

Hintze, Otto (1975) *The Historical Essays of Otto Hintze.* Trans. Felix Gilbert. New York: Oxford University Press.

Hirschman, Albert (1970) "The Search for Paradigms as a Hindrance to Understanding." *World Politics* 22, no. 3:329–343.

——— (1986) *Rival Views of Market Society.* New York: Viking.

Hobbes, Thomas (1914) *The Leviathan.* New York: J. P. Dutton.

Hobsbawm, Eric (1962) *The Age of Revolution.* New York: New American Library.

——— (1987) *The Age of Empire.* New York: Pantheon Books.

——— (1994) *The Age of Extremes: A History of the World, 1914–1991.* New York: Pantheon.

Huntington, Samuel, ed. (1957) *Changing Patterns of Military Politics.* New York: Free Press.

——— (1967) *Political Order in Changing Societies.* New Haven: Yale University Press.

——— (1991) *The Third Wave: Democratization in the Twentieth Century.* Norman: University of Oklahoma Press.

Hyman, Herbert, and Paul Sheatsley (1954) "The Authoritarian Personality: A Methodological Critique." In Richard Christie and Marie Jahoda, eds., *Studies in the Scope and Method of the Authoritarian Personality.* Glencoe, Ill.: Free Press.

Hymes, Dell, ed. (1969) *Reinventing Anthropology.* New York: Random House.

Ike, Nobutake (1973) "Economic Growth and Intergenerational Change in Japan." *American Political Science Review* (December): 1194 ff.

Inglehart, Ronald (1971) "The Silent Revolution in Europe: Intergenerational Change in Post-Industrial Societies." *American Political Science Review* 65, no. 4 (December): 991–1017.

——— (1976) *The Silent Revolution.* Princeton: Princeton University Press.

——— (1977) *The Silent Revolution: Changing Values and Styles Among Western Publics.* Princeton: Princeton University Press.

——— (1990) *Culture Shift in Advanced Industrial Societies.* Princeton: Princeton University Press.

——— (1994) *Modernization and Post-Modernization: Cultural, Economic, and Political Change in Forty-three Societies.* Manuscript draft.

Inkeles, Alex (1950) *Public Opinion in Soviet Russia.* Cambridge: Harvard University Press.

——— (1959) *The Soviet Citizen.* Cambridge: Harvard University Press.

Inkeles, Alex, and David Smith (1974a) *Becoming Modern: Individual Change in Six Developing Countries.* Cambridge: Harvard University Press.

——— (1974b) *Becoming Modern: Individual Change in Seven Countries.* Cambridge: Harvard University Press.

Judt, Tony (1995) "Downhill All the Way." *New York Review of Books* 42, no. 9 (May 25): 22–25.

Karl, Barry (1970) Foreword to Charles E. Merriam, *New Aspects of Politics.* Chicago: University of Chicago Press.

——— (1974) *Charles E. Merriam and the Study of Politics.* Chicago: University of Chicago Press.

Katz, Elihu, and Paul Lazarsfeld (1955) *Personal Influence.* New York: Free Press.

Keniston, Kenneth (1968) *Young Radicals.* New York: Harcourt Brace.

King, Gary, Robert Keohane, and Sidney Verba (1993) *Scientific Inference in Qualitative Research.* Cambridge: Cambridge University Press.

Konig, Rene (1968) "Auguste Comte." In *International Encyclopedia of the Social Sciences.* New York: Crowell-Collier and Macmillan.

Kuhn, Thomas (1962) *The Structure of Scientific Revolutions.* Chicago: University of Chicago Press.

Lalman, David, Joe Oppenheimer, and Piotr Swistak (1993) "Formal Rational Choice Theory: A Cumulative Science of Politics." In Ada Finifter, ed., *Polit-*

*ical Science: The State of the Discipline.* Washington, D.C.: American Political Science Association.

Lane, Robert E. (1959) *Political Life.* Glencoe, Ill.: Free Press.

LaPalombara, Joseph, ed. (1963) *Bureaucracy and Political Development.* Princeton: Princeton University Press.

——— (1964) *Interest Groups in Italian Politics.* Princeton: Princeton University Press.

LaPalombara, Joseph, and Myron Weiner, eds. (1966) *Political Parties and Political Development.* Princeton: Princeton University Press.

Laski, Harold (1919) *Authority in the Modern State.* New Haven: Yale University Press.

Lasswell, Harold D. (1923) "Chicago's Old First Ward." *National Municipal Review* 12:127–131.

——— (1925) "Prussian Schoolbooks and International Amity." *Journal of Social Forces* 3:718–722.

——— (1927) *Propaganda Technique in the First World War.* London: Kegan Paul.

——— (1929a) "Problem of Adequate Personality Records: A Proposal." *American Journal of Psychiatry* 7:1057–1066.

——— (1929b) "The Study of the Mentally Ill as a Method of Research into Political Personalities." *American Political Science Review* 23:996–1001.

——— (1930) *Psychopathology and Politics.* Chicago: University of Chicago Press.

——— (1932) "The Triple Appeal Principle." *American Journal of Sociology* 37:523 ff.

——— (1935a) "Verbal References and Physiological Changes During the Psychoanalytic Interview." *Psychoanalytic Review* 23:241–247.

——— (1935b) *World Politics and Personal Insecurity.* New York: McGraw Hill.

——— (1936a) "Certain Prognostic Changes During Trial (Psychoanalytic) Interviews." *Psychoanalytic Review*: 241–247.

——— (1936b) *Politics: Who Gets What, When, and How.* New York: McGraw Hill.

——— (1937) "Veranderungen an Einer Versuchsperson wahrend einer Kurzen Folge von Psychoanalytischen Interviews." *Imago* (Vienna) 23:375–380.

——— (1948) *Power and Personality.* New York: W. W. Norton.

——— (1951) "Democratic Character." In *The Political Writings of Harold Lasswell.* Glencoe, Ill.: Free Press.

——— (1954) "The Selective Effect of Personality on Political Participation." In Richard Christie and Marie Jahoda, eds., *Studies in the Scope and Method of the Authoritarian Personality.* Glencoe, Ill.: Free Press.

——— (1956) *The Decision Process: Seven Categories of Functional Analysis.* College Park: University of Maryland Press.

——— (1963) *The Future of Political Science.* New York: Atherton Press.

——— (1970) "The Present State of the Study of Politics." In Charles E. Merriam, *New Aspects of Politics.* Chicago, Ill.: University of Chicago Press.

Lasswell, Harold, and Gabriel Almond (1934) "Aggressive Behavior by Clients on Public Relief." *American Political Science Review* 28.

Lasswell, Harold D., with Richard Arens (1961) *In Defense of Public Order: The Emerging Field of Sanction Law.* New York: Columbia University Press.

Lasswell, Harold D., with R. D. Casey and B. L. Smith (1935) *Propaganda and Promotional Activities: An Annotated Bibliography.* Minneapolis: University of Minnesota Press.

Lasswell, Harold D., with Henry F. Dobyns and Paul L. Doughty (1971) *Peasants, Power, and Applied Social Change: Vicos as a Model.* Newbury Park, Calif.: Sage.

Lasswell, Harold D., with Merritt B. Fox (1979) *The Signature of Power: Buildings, Communication, and Policy.* New Brunswick, N.J.: Transaction Books.

Lasswell, Harold, and Dorothy Blumenstock Jones (1939) *World Revolutionary Propaganda: A Chicago Study.* New York: Knopf.

Lasswell, Harold D., with Abraham Kaplan (1950) *Power and Society.* New Haven: Yale University Press.

Lasswell, Harold D., with Nathan Leites (1949) *The Language of Politics: Studies in Quantitative Semantics.* New York: George W. Stewart.

Lasswell, Harold D., with Daniel Lerner, eds. (1951) *The Policy Sciences.* Stanford: Stanford University Press.

Lasswell, Harold D., with Myres S. McDougal (1960) *Studies in World Public Order.* New Haven: Yale University Press.

Lasswell, Harold D., with Robert Rubenstein (1966) *The Sharing of Power in a Psychiatric Hospital.* New Haven: Yale University Press.

Lerner, Daniel (1958) *The Passing of Traditional Society.* Glencoe, Ill.: Free Press.

Lijphart, Arend (1968) *The Politics of Accommodation.* Berkeley: University of California Press.

——— (1984) *Democracies.* New Haven: Yale University Press.

——— (1994) *Electoral Systems and Party Systems.* Oxford: Oxford University Press.

Lindblom, Charles E. (1977) *Politics and Markets.* New York: Basic Books.

Linz, Juan (1970) "An Authoritarian Regime: Spain." In E. Allardt and Stein Rokkan, eds., *Mass Politics: Studies in Political Sociology.* New York: Free Press.

Linz, Juan, and Alfred Stepan (1978) *The Breakdown of Democratic Regimes.* Baltimore: Johns Hopkins University Press.

Lipset, Seymour Martin (1959) "Some Social Requisites of Democracy." *American Political Science Review* 53 (September): 69–105.

——— (1960) *Political Man.* New York: Doubleday.

——— (1981) "Second Thoughts and Recent Findings." In *Political Man: The Social Basis of Politics.* Expanded and updated ed. Baltimore: Johns Hopkins University Press.

——— (1994) "The Social Requisites of Democracy Revisited." *American Sociological Review* 59 (February): 1–22.

Lipset, Seymour Martin, and Stein Rokkan (1967) *Party Systems and Voter Alignments.* New York: Free Press.

Lipset, Seymour Martin, and Gerald M. Schaflander (1971) *Passion in Politics.* Boston: Little, Brown.

Locke, John (1924) *Of Civil Government.* New York: E. P. Dutton.

Loewenberg, Gerhard, ed. (1979) *Comparing Legislatures.* Iowa City: University of Iowa Press.

Lowe, Adolf (1936) *The Price of Liberty: A German on Contemporary Britain.* London: Hogarth Press.

Lowi, Theodore (1969) *The End of Liberalism.* New York: Holt, Rinehart & Winston.

Machiavelli, Nicollo (1964) *The Prince.* Trans. Mark Musa. New York: St. Martin's Press.

Macridis, Roy C. (1955) *The Study of Comparative Government.* Garden City, N.Y.: Doubleday.

Maine, Henry (1963) *Ancient Law.* New York: Beacon Press.

Mannheim, Karl (1949) *Ideology and Utopia [Ideologie und Utopie].* Trans. Louis Wirth and Edward Shils. New York: Harcourt Brace.

March, James G. (1958) *Organizations.* New York: John Wiley.

——— (1965) *Handbook of Organization.* Chicago: Rand McNally.

——— (1988) *Decisions and Organizations.* New York: Blackwell.

Marks, Gary, and Larry Diamond, eds. (1992) *Reexamining Democracy.* Newbury Park, Calif.: Sage.

Marsh, Alan (1975) "The Silent Revolution, Value Priorities, and Quality of Life in Britain." *American Political Science Review* 69:21–30.

Marvick, Dwaine (1977) *Harold D. Lasswell on Political Sociology.* Chicago: University of Chicago Press.

Maslow, Abraham (1954) *Motivation and Personality.* New York: Harper.

Merriam, Charles E. (1931) *The Making of Citizens: A Comparative Study of Civic Training.* Chicago: University of Chicago Press.

——— (1934) *Civic Training in the United States.* Chicago: University of Chicago Press.

——— (1970a) "Progress in Political Research." In Charles E. Merriam, *New Aspects of Politics.* Chicago: University of Chicago Press.

——— (1970b) "The Present State of the Study of Politics." In Charles E. Merriam, *New Aspects of Politics.* Chicago: University of Chicago Press.

Merriam, Charles E., and Harold F. Gosnell (1924) *Nonvoting: Causes and Methods of Control.* Chicago: University of Chicago Press.

Michels, Robert (1949) *Political Parties: A Sociological Study of the Oligarchical Tendencies of Modern Democracies.* Glencoe, Ill.: Free Press.

Milbrath, Lester M. (1965) *Political Participation.* Chicago: Rand McNally.

Mill, John Stuart (1961) *A System of Logic.* London: Longmans.

——— (1962) *Considerations on Representative Government.* Chicago: Regnery.

——— (1965) *Principles of Political Economy.* Toronto: University of Toronto Press.

Miller, Arthur (1974) "Political Issues and Trust in Government." *American Political Science Review* 68:951–972.

Miller, Warren (1994) "An Organizational History of the Intellectual Origins of the American National Election Studies." *European Journal of Political Research* 25:247–265.

Mitchell, William (1991) "Virginia, Rochester, and Bloomington: Twenty-five Years of Public Choice and Political Science." *Public Choice* 56:101–119.

Montesqueiu (1977) *The Spirit of Laws.* Trans. David Carrithers. Berkeley: University of California Press.

Moore, Barrington (1966) *Social Origins of Dictatorship and Democracy: Lord and Peasant in the Making of the Modern World.* Boston: Beacon Press.

National Academy of Sciences (1987) *Biographical Memoirs.* Washington, D.C.: National Academy of Sciences.

Nie, Norman H., Sidney Verba, and Jae-on Kim (1974) "Political Participation and the Life Cycle." *Comparative Politics* (April): 319–340.

Nozick, Robert (1974) *Anarchy, the State, and Utopia.* New York: Basic Books.

Odegard, Peter (1928) *Pressure Politics: The Story of the Anti-Saloon League.* New York: Columbia University Press.

Olson, Mancur (1965) *The Logic of Collective Action.* Cambridge: Harvard University Press.

——— (1982) *The Rise and Decline of Nations.* New Haven: Yale University Press.

——— (1990) "Toward a Unified View of Economics and the Other Social Sciences." In Alt and Shepsle, eds., *Perspectives on Positive Political Economy.* Cambridge: Cambridge University Press.

Ordeshook, Peter (1990) "The Emerging Discipline of Political Economy." In Alt and Shepsle, eds., *Perspectives on Positive Political Economy.* Cambridge: Cambridge University Press.

Ostrogorski, Moissaye (1964) *Democracy and the Organization of Political Parties.* Ed. S. M. Lipset. New York: Doubleday.

Packenham, Robert (1992) *The Dependency Movement: Scholarship and Politics in Latin American Studies.* Cambridge: Harvard University Press.

Pareto, Vilfredo (1965) "Les Systemes Socialistes." In *Oeuvres Completes,* vol. 5. Geneva: Droz.

Parsons, Talcott (1951) *The Social System.* Cambridge: Harvard University Press.

Parsons, Talcott, and Edward Shils (1951) *Toward a General Theory of Action.* Cambridge: Harvard University Press.

Parsons, Talcott, and Neil Smelser (1956) *Economy and Society.* London: Routledge and Kegan Paul.

Pitkin, Hannah (1967) *The Concept of Representation.* Berkeley: University of California Press.

Pocock, J. G. A. (1975) *The Machiavellian Moment: Florentine Political Theory and the Atlantic Republican Tradition.* Cambridge: Cambridge University Press.

Pollock, Sir Frederick (1890) *The History of the Science of Politics.* London: Macmillan.

Popper, Karl (1972) *Objective Knowledge: An Evolutionary Approach.* Oxford: Clarendon Press.

Powell, G. Bingham (1982) *Contemporary Democracies.* Cambridge: Harvard University Press.

Przeworski, Adam, and Henry Teune (1970) *The Logic of Comparative Social Inquiry.* New York: John Wiley.

Putnam, Robert D. (1973) *The Beliefs of Politicians.* New Haven: Yale University Press.

——— (1993) *Making Democracy Work.* Princeton: Princeton University Press.

——— (1995) "Bowling Alone: America's Declining Social Capital." *Journal of Democracy* 6, no. 1 (January): 65–78.

Pye, Lucian (1962) *Politics, Personality, and Nation Building.* New Haven: Yale University Press.

———, ed. (1963) *Communication and Political Development.* Princeton: Princeton University Press.

——— (1966) *Aspects of Political Development.* Boston: Little, Brown.

——— (1985) *Asian Power and Politics.* Cambridge: Harvard University Press.

——— (1988) *The Mandarin and the Cadre.* Ann Arbor: University of Michigan Press.

Pye, Lucian, and Sidney Verba, eds. (1965) *Political Culture and Political Development.* Princeton: Princeton University Press.

Rabi, Muhammad (1967) *The Political Theory of Ibn Khaldun.* Leiden: E. J. Brill.

Rangavajan, L. N. (1987) *Kautilya: The Arthashastra: The Science of Statecraft.* New Delhi: Penguin Books.

Rawls, John (1971) *A Theory of Justice.* Cambridge: Harvard University Press.

Reich, Charles (1970) *The Greening of America.* New York: Bantam Books.

Rhys, Ernest, ed. (1934) *The Ethics of Aristotle.* London: J. M. Dent and Sons.

Ricci, David (1984) *The Tragedy of Political Science.* New Haven: Yale University Press.

Riker, William (1962) *The Theory of Coalitions.* New Haven: Yale University Press.

——— (1990) "Political Science and Rational Choice." In Alt and Shepsle, eds., *Perspectives on Positive Political Economy.* Cambridge: Cambridge University Press.

Rogow, Arnold, ed. (1969) *Politics, Personality, and Social Science in the Twentieth Century.* Chicago: University of Chicago Press.

Roscher, Wilhelm (1892) *Politik: Geschichtliche Naturlehre der Monarchie, Aristokratie, und Demokratie.*

Rose, Richard (1990) "Institutionalizing Political Science Research in Europe." *European Journal of Political Research* 18:581–603.

Roszak, Theodore (1969) *The Coming of the Counter-Culture.* Garden City, N.Y.: Doubleday.

Rutherford, Louise C. (1937) *The Influence of the American Bar Association on Public Opinion and Legislation.* Philadelphia: Foundation Press.

Sabine, George, and Thomas Thorson (1973) *A History of Political Theory.* New York: Holt, Rinehart & Winston.

Sartori, Giovanni (1976) *Parties and Party Systems.* Cambridge: Cambridge University Press.

——— (1987) *Theory of Democracy Revisited.* Chatham, N.J.: Chatham House Press.

Saxonhouse, Arlene (1993) "Texts and Canons: The Status of the Great Books in Political Science." In Ada Finifter, ed., *Political Science: The State of the Discipline.* Washington, D.C.: American Political Science Association.

Schattschneider, Elmer E. (1935) *Politics, Pressures, and the Tariff.* New York: Prentice Hall.

Schlozman, Kay Lehman, Sidney Verba, and Henry Brady (1995) "Participation Is Not a Paradox: The View from American Activists." *British Journal of Political Science* 25:1–36.

Schmitter, Phillippe, and Gerhard Lehmbruch, eds. (1979) *Trends Toward Corporate Intermediation.* Beverly Hills, Calif.: Sage.

Schmitter, Phillippe, Guillermo O'Donnell, and Lawrence Whitehead (1986) *Transitions from Authoritarian Rule.* Baltimore: Johns Hopkins University Press.

Schumpeter, Joseph A. (1947) *Capitalism, Socialism, and Democracy.* New York: Harper.

Seeley, Sir John Robert (1886) *An Introduction to Political Science.* London: Macmillan.

Seidelman, Raymond (1985) *Disenchanted Realists: Political Science and the American Crisis.* New York: State University of New York Press.

Shapiro, Martin (1993) "Public Law and Judicial Politics." In Ada Finifter, ed., *The Status of the Discipline.* Washington, D.C.: American Political Science Association.

Shils, Edward A. (1954) "Authoritarianism: Right and Left." In Richard Christie and Marie Jahoda, eds., *Studies in the Scope and Method of the Authoritarian Personality.* Glencoe, Ill.: Free Press.

——— (1960) *Political Development in the New States.* The Hague: Mouton.

———, ed. (1991) *Remembering the University of Chicago: Teachers, Scientists, and Scholars.* Chicago: University of Chicago Press.

Siegfried, Andre (1930) *Tableau des Partis en France.* Paris: Grasset.

Simon, Herbert (1950) *Public Administration.* New York: Knopf.

——— (1957) *Models of Man.* New York: Wiley.

——— (1958) *Administrative Behavior.* New York: Macmillan.

Skinner, Quentin (1978) *The Foundations of Modern Political Thought.* Vol. 1. Cambridge: Cambridge University Press.

Skocpol, Theda (1979) *States and Social Revolutions.* Cambridge: Cambridge University Press.

——— (1984) *Vision and Method in Historical Sociology.* Cambridge: Cambridge University Press.

Smelser, Neil (1976) *Comparative Methods in the Social Sciences.* Englewood Cliffs, N.J.: Prentice Hall.

Smelser, Neil, and Gabriel Almond (1974) *Public Higher Education in California.* Berkeley: University of California Press.

Smith, Thomas (1985) "Requiem or New Agenda for Third World Studies." *World Politics* 37 (July): 532–561.

Smith, Tony (1979) "The Underdevelopment of Development Literature." *World Politics* 31, no. 2.

Somit, A., and J. Tannenhaus (1967) *The Development of American Political Science.* Boston: Allyn and Bacon.

Spencer, Herbert (1965) *The Study of Sociology.* Ann Arbor: University of Michigan Press.

SSRC Committee on Comparative Politics (1971) *Report on Activities.* New York: SSRC.

SSRC Interuniversity Research Seminar on Comparative Politics (1952) "Research in Comparative Politics." *American Political Science Review* 47:641–675.

Strauss, Leo (1959) *What Is Political Philosophy?* Glencoe, Ill.: Free Press.

——— (1989) *The Rebirth of Classic Political Rationalism.* Chicago: University of Chicago Press.

Strauss, Leo, and Joseph Cropsey (1987) *A History of Political Philosophy.* Chicago: University of Chicago Press.

Sutton, Francis (1982) "Rationality, Development, and Scholarship." *Items* 36 (December): 49–57.

Thompson, Dennis (1970) *The Democratic Citizen.* Cambridge: Cambridge University Press.

Thompson, Edward (1963) *The Making of the English Working Class.* New York: Vintage Books.

Tilly, Charles, et al. (1976) *The Formation of National States in Western Europe.* Princeton: Princeton University Press.

Tingsten, Herbert (1963) *Political Behavior.* Totowa, N.J.: Bedminton Press.

Tocqueville, Alexis de (1945) *Democracy in America,* trans. Reeve, ed. Bradley. New York: Knopf.

——— (1955) *The Old Regime and the French Revolution.* Garden City, N.Y.: Doubleday.

Tonnies, Ferdinand, ed. (1957) *Community and Society.* Trans. Charles Loomis. East Lansing: Michigan State University Press.

Valles, J. M., and Kenneth Newton, eds. (1991) "Political Science in Western Europe: 1960–1990" (special issue). *European Journal of Political Research* 20:225–466.

Verba, Sidney (1959) *Small Groups and Political Behavior.* Princeton: Princeton University Press.

——— (1987) *Elites and the Idea of Equality.* Cambridge: Harvard University Press.

Verba, Sidney, Bashiruddin Ahmed, and Anil Bhatt (1971) *Caste, Race, and Politics.* Beverly Hills, Calif.: Sage.

Verba, Sidney, and Norman Nie (1972) *Participation in America.* New York: Harper and Row.

Verba, Sidney, Norman Nie, and Jae-on Kim (1977) *Participation and Political Equality: A Seven Nation Comparison.* Cambridge: Cambridge University Press.

Verba, Sidney, Kay Lehman Schlozman, and Henry E. Brady (1995) *Voice and Equality.* Cambridge: Harvard University Press.

Wahlke, John, and Heinz Eulau (1962) *The Legislative System.* New York: Wiley.

———— (1978) *The Politics of Representation.* Beverly Hills, Calif.: Sage.

Wallerstein, Immanuel (1979) *The Capitalist World Economy.* Cambridge: Cambridge University Press.

Walzer, Michael (1983) *Spheres of Justice.* New York: Basic Books.

Ward, Robert, and Dankwart Rustow, eds. (1964) *Political Development in Japan and Turkey.* Princeton: Princeton University Press.

Weber, Max (1921) "Politik als Beruf." In *Gesammelte Politische Schriften.* Munchen: Drei Masken Verlag.

———— (1922) *Wirtschaft und Gesellschaft.* Tubingen: J. C. B. Mohr.

———— (1949) *The Methodology of the Social Sciences.* Trans. Shils and Finch. Glencoe, Ill.: Free Press.

———— (1958) *From Max Weber.* Trans. Gerth and Mills. New York: Oxford University Press.

———— (1968) *Economy and Society.* Trans. Roth and Wittich. Berkeley: University of California Press.

Weiner, Myron (1962) *The Politics of Scarcity: Public Pressure and Political Response in India.* Chicago: University of Chicago Press.

White, Leonard D. (1929) *The Prestige Value of Public Employment.* Chicago: University of Chicago Press.

————, ed. (1942) *The Future of Government in the United States: Essays in Honor of Charles E. Merriam.* Chicago: University of Chicago Press.

Wildavsky, Aaron (1986) *A History of Taxation and Public Expenditure in the Western World.* New York: Simon and Schuster.

Wilson, James Q. (1993) *The Moral Sense.* New York: Free Press.

Wilson, Woodrow (1887) "The Study of Administration." *Political Science Quarterly* 2 (June).

———— (1895) *The State: Elements of Historical and Practical Politics: A Sketch of Institutional History and Administration.*

Womack, John (1968) *Zapata and the Mexican Revolution.* New York: Knopf.

Wood, Bryce (1971) *A Report on the Activities of the Committee.* New York: Social Science Research Council, Committee on Comparative Politics.

Woolsey, Theodore (1892) *Political Science: The State Theoretically and Practically Considered.* New York: Scribner.

Wright, Quincy (1942) *A Study of War.* Chicago: University of Chicago Press.

Yankelovich, Daniel (1972) *The Changing Values on Campus.* New York: Washington Square Press.

———— (1974) *The New Morality: A Profile of Youth Values in the 70s.* New York: McGraw-Hill.

# Index

234    *Index*

210, 213; and private sector,
140–141; and public services, 140,
142; and socialism, 131–132. *See also*
Civic culture; Democratization;
Participationism; Political stability
*Democracy and Its Critics* (Dahl), 138
*Democracy in America* (Tocqueville), 36
Democratization, 16, 26, 35–36, 46, 47,
87; of economic order, 138; in
Europe, 49; third wave of, 138, 200.
*See also* Political stability
Demographic change, 168–169, 204
Dependency theory, 16–17, 57, 114–118,
122–123. *See also* Developing areas
Depew, Chauncey, 7
Depth psychiatry, 78, 79
Depth psychology, 40
Despotism, 33
Deutsch, Karl, 16, 50, 97, 135
Developing areas, 15–16, 43, 60,
99–101, 102–104. *See also* Area
studies; Dependency theory
Development: and modernization, 16,
17, 36, 96, 116, 117–118
*Development of Welfare States in
Western Europe and America, The*
(Peter and Heidenheimer), 144
Diamond, Larry, 47
Dictatorships, 134
*Directory of European Political
Scientists,* 51
Distributive patterns. *See* Redistribution
Divine law, 30
Dogan, Mattei, 47
Dollard, Charles, 95
Downs, Anthony, 25, 58, 59–60
Dryzek, John, 55, 56
Dubois, Cora, 42
Duguit, Leon, 37
Dunn, Frederick S., 1
Durkheim, Emil, 36, 46, 94, 100

East Asian area studies, 113, 114, 123
Easton, David, 46, 100
Eckstein, Harry, 47, 198, 199, 200, 202,
210
Economic Man model, 59
Economic models: in rational choice
theory, 24, 58, 59, 141

Economic orders: and polity, 132–133.
*See also* Capitalism; Democracy;
Marxism
Economic security: as value, 180, 182
Economic slowdown, 190–191
*Economic Theory of Democracy, The*
(Downs), 25
Education, 69, 96, 172–174; and effect
on values, 181, 183–185, 186, 187,
188, 190, 192
Ehrmann, Henry, 9, 50, 91–92, 95, 96
Elections, 41, 43, 44, 45, 50, 58, 97,
166, 187, 203; in Europe, 49, 50;
nonvoters in, 65, 73, 76, 106; voter
turnout in, 69, 77
Elites, 5, 6–7, 46, 59–60, 69, 85, 90,
205; competition among, 40, 81, 82,
210
Ellis, Havelock, 76
*Emerging Discipline of Political
Economy, The* (Ordeshook), 59
Empiricism, 23, 35, 38, 41, 47–48, 55,
64, 65, 93; and rational choice, 60–61
Employment studies, 3–4, 5, 41, 69, 73,
82
Enlightenment, 30, 32–34
Environmental conservation, 191, 192
Equality, 34, 36
Equilibrium: analysis of, 81; of civic
culture, 200, 203, 209, 210–211
Erikson, Erik, 7, 100
Ethical neutrality, 52–53, 57, 114, 115,
116, 117, 118, 121
Ethics, 55; of absolute ends, 53, 54, 120;
of responsibility, 53, 54, 67, 120
*Ethics* (Aristotle), 28
Ethnocentrism, 150, 151, 152, 153, 156,
158, 159, 160
Eulau, Heinz, 44, 46
European area studies, 110, 113–114,
123
European Council on Political Research
(ECPR), 51
*European Journal of Political Research,
The,* 49, 51
European political science: postwar, 45,
48–50
Evidence-inference methodology, 24,
25, 32–34, 38
Evolutionism, 35

# About the Book

Reflecting an extraordinary career, *Ventures in Political Science* collects Gabriel Almond's most important work on the development of political science and democratic theory.

An absorbing introduction—providing personal and historical context—precedes Almond's masterful "History of Political Science." Equally notable are essays on capitalism and democracy, the crisis of political culture in the 1960s, and the history of area studies. Two especially evocative pieces, published here for the first time, compare the cultures of communism and fascism and discuss the background of *The Civic Culture* study.

Significant—and stimulating—this is a not-to-be-missed book for any student of political science.

**Gabriel A. Almond,** one of the most important political scientists of the twentieth century, received his Ph.D. from the University of Chicago in 1938. During his lengthy career, he has taught at Brooklyn College, Yale University, Princeton University, and most recently, Stanford University. His many publications range from *The American People and Foreign Policy* (1950) and *The Appeals of Communism* (1954) to *The Civic Culture* (1963), *Crisis, Choice, and Change* (1973), *A Discipline Divided* (1991), and seven editions of *Comparative Politics Today.*